# PRAISE FOR *IN GUNS WE TRUST*

"This groundbreaking book uncovers the often-overlooked relationship between faith, politics, and firearms, revealing how a significant faction of American society has embraced a culture that intertwines their religious beliefs with a staunch defense of gun rights. The book challenges readers to confront uncomfortable truths about complicity in the ongoing firearms crisis, illuminating the narratives that fuel this unholy trinity. With a keen journalistic eye and a commitment to uncovering the complexities of American identity, *In Guns We Trust* is an essential read for anyone seeking to understand the intricate dynamics at play in one of the most contentious issues facing the nation today. Prepare for a compelling journey that will reshape your understanding of faith, power, and the pervasive grip of gun culture in America."

—**Shannon Watts**, founder, Moms Demand Action

"Imagine losing a child to gun violence and then being betrayed by the same group that committed to praying for you. *In Guns We Trust* offers history and insight into how Christian nationalism has rendered Christians in the United States impotent in the face of injustice. With astute precision, William J. Kole offers an insider view on how white evangelical churches and communities have largely traded their commitment to Christ for guns."

—**Nelba Márquez-Greene**, licensed therapist and mother of Ana Grace, murdered at Sandy Hook

"With his captivating storytelling, journalistic curiosity, and prophetic lament, William J. Kole shines a much-needed light on how many Christians have actively participated in furthering the scourge of gun violence.

He invites us to envision a different future where everyday Christians courageously reckon with our history of complicity by actively moving toward peacemaking. I highly recommend this much-needed resource to any North American Christian wanting to grapple more deeply with the injustice of gun violence."

—**Joash Thomas**, author of *The Justice of Jesus*

"As a gun safety advocate and woman of faith, I have seen firsthand how bad religion and guns can become dangerously intertwined, with devastating consequences for our communities. Our movement has long sounded the alarm on the ways extremism, easy access to firearms, and the gun industry fuel America's gun violence crisis. *In Guns We Trust* weaves these threads together, offering a powerful look at how we got to this moment—where guns are the leading cause of death for young people—and how we can build a safer future, one where we choose to love our neighbors, not arm ourselves against them."

—**Angela Ferrell-Zabala**, executive director of Moms Demand Action

"*In Guns We Trust* is a ringing alarm clock, a wake-up call. If Jesus is totally nonviolent, as Gandhi and Dr. King insisted, then Christians are called to be nonviolent. Few Christians take seriously the last words of Jesus to the church: 'Put down the sword.' We have taken up the gun and unleashed an epidemic of gun violence instead of obeying his teachings on nonviolence. *In Guns We Trust* demands a reckoning. William J. Kole lays out our predicament. We have to 'put down our guns,' do whatever we can to ensure that no child, no person, is ever killed in the US again, and practice the nonviolence of Jesus so that, finally, we might learn the meaning of the words 'In God We Trust.'"

—**Rev. John Dear, activist**, Nobel Peace Prize nominee, and author of *The Gospel of Peace, The Nonviolent Life*, and *The Questions of Jesus*

"*In Guns We Trust* is a gripping and thought-provoking page-turner that challenges readers to confront America's deep-rooted relationship with firearms. Journalist William J. Kole masterfully weaves together startling facts—such as the reality that there are more guns than people in the United States—with profound questions about the ties between guns, white evangelicals, and politics. This book compels us to ask why, despite heart-wrenching tragedies like Sandy Hook, the country has yet to enact sweeping gun reforms. With the keen eye of a seasoned journalist, Kole presents a deeply reflective exploration that respects America's proud hunting traditions while holding up a mirror to where we stand today on one of the nation's most divisive issues. *In Guns We Trust* is essential reading for anyone seeking to understand the forces shaping our nation's gun culture and policies."

—**Ebony Reed**, coauthor of *Fifteen Cents on the Dollar: How Americans Made the Black-White Wealth Gap*

"America is in the midst of an excruciating gun crisis, with no end in sight. And evangelical Christians, perhaps more than any other voting bloc, hold the political power to influence our response. Why won't they budge? *In Guns We Trust* is William J. Kole's attempt to answer this question. And as a veteran journalist who spent decades in the evangelical church, he's the perfect man for the job. The resulting book is unforgettable. Part sermon, part history lesson, and part investigative deep-dive, *In Guns We Trust* is also a valuable reminder that our path isn't preordained. In one of the book's most moving chapters, Kole travels abroad to show us how other countries have changed course after horrific gun crimes. We can, too, he insists. Whatever your opinions about guns, you will learn something from this book. And beyond guns, the book is a glimpse into the collective psyche of one of the US's most influential social groups. This is an urgent, courageous, and important book."

—**Philip Eil**, author of *Prescription for Pain*

"*In Guns We Trust* is a vivid and essential American journey. William J. Kole leads us into a world of evangelical Christianity where the Second Amendment and the Ten Commandments are both sacred texts. With searing clarity, Kole explores how the interplay of faith and firearms is reshaping politics, culture, and the very notions of what it means to be a Christian in America."

—**Brian Murphy**, author of *The Root of Wild Madder* and *81 Days Below Zero*

# IN GUNS WE TRUST

*The Unholy Trinity of*
*White Evangelicals, Politics, and Firearms*

# IN
# GUNS
# WE
# TRUST

WILLIAM J. KOLE

Broadleaf Books
Minneapolis

IN GUNS WE TRUST
The Unholy Trinity of White Evangelicals, Politics, and Firearms

Copyright © 2025 William J. Kole. Published by Broadleaf Books. All rights reserved. Except for brief quotations in critical articles or reviews, no part of this book may be reproduced in any manner without prior written permission from the publisher. Email copyright@broadleafbooks.com or write to Permissions, Broadleaf Books, PO Box 1209, Minneapolis, MN 55440-1209.

30  29  28  27  26  25         1  2  3  4  5  6  7  8  9

Unless otherwise noted, Scripture quotations are taken from Holy Bible, New International Version®, NIV® Copyright ©1973, 1978, 1984, 2011 by Biblica, Inc.® Used by permission. All rights reserved worldwide.

Library of Congress Control Number: 2025930275 (print)

Cover design by John Calmeyer
Cover image © 2025 Getty Images; M4 Carbine/1301279441 by Gabe Ginsberg; Jesus Christ Statue/7219493 by Mart Production on Pexels

Print ISBN: 979-8-8898-3563-9
eBook ISBN: 979-8-8898-3564-6

Printed in India.

*For my grandsons, Parker and Cedar.
May our gun scourge be a distant
memory by the time you're my age.*

"You are different with a gun in your hand; the gun is different with you holding it. You are another subject because you hold the gun; the gun is another object because it has entered into a relationship with you. The gun is no longer the gun-in-the-armory or the gun-in-the-drawer or the gun-in-the-pocket, but the gun-in-your-hand, aimed at someone who is screaming."

—Bruno Latour, *Pandora's Hope*

# CONTENTS

| | | |
|---|---|---|
| | PREFACE | 1 |
| CHAPTER 1 | THE GOSPEL OF GUNS | 7 |
| CHAPTER 2 | HOW GUNS BECAME GOOD | 33 |
| CHAPTER 3 | A WELL-REGULATED MILITIA | 57 |
| CHAPTER 4 | HOME ON THE RANGE | 83 |
| CHAPTER 5 | THE FEAR FACTOR | 107 |
| CHAPTER 6 | GUNMAKERS FOR GOD | 131 |
| CHAPTER 7 | PISTOLS AND POLITICS | 157 |
| CHAPTER 8 | GUNS AND THE GLOBAL CHURCH | 183 |
| CHAPTER 9 | SWORDS INTO PLOWSHARES | 209 |
| CHAPTER 10 | NO GUNS IN HEAVEN | 233 |
| | ACKNOWLEDGMENTS | 259 |
| | NOTES | 261 |

# PREFACE

I was born an infidel and reborn an evangelical.

On February 24, 1981, I was a college junior with a tangled blond mane of Peter Frampton ringlets and a puka shell necklace, hitchhiking home from Boston University in the pouring rain, when a West African civil engineer pulled over in rush hour traffic to give me a lift. In simple terms, he shared a faith he said had changed his life, and we ended up at his church just as a midweek service was letting out.

There, I prayed with a few believers who, like me, were in their early twenties. Someone pressed a New Testament into my hands, and a radiant young woman who bore a striking resemblance to someone I'd hit on recently in a bar told me the angels were celebrating my conversion with dancing. For an unchurched agnostic who'd spent the second half of the '70s smoking weed, dropping acid, reading Thomas Pynchon, and watching *Monty Python*, evangelical Christianity offered a joy, a purity, and a camaraderie I'd always craved. I went all in.

Within a few years, I was a full-time lay missionary for the evangelical Assemblies of God denomination in Belgium, where I met my wife, a Detroiter who shared my faith and fervor. As my three-year assignment ended and I repatriated to the United States, I considered enrolling in seminary, but the ministry never seemed quite the right fit for someone who'd always felt journalism was his true calling. I was right about that, and a decade later, I was back in Europe, this time as a foreign correspondent for The Associated Press (AP).

# PREFACE

In Amsterdam, we hosted weekly Bible studies in our home, and I served as an elder overseeing a large and dynamic international charismatic church. In Vienna, I led worship at an English-language evangelical parish attended by UN diplomats and other expatriates. I joined the board of an international Christian relief and development agency, and I signed on as vocal percussionist for a Christian acapella group, once beatboxing before a crowd of ten thousand. I had become, I realized, a sort of religious unicorn: a journalist for a major news organization *and* a professing believer.

But during those decades, something tectonic was shifting beneath my feet. Most of my fellow white evangelicals, who had always leaned conservative, were tilting hard to the right politically. They were adopting intolerant stances on immigrants and LGBTQ+ people that I didn't share. Nor could I grasp their fear, which sometimes seemed to border on paranoia, that the culture beyond the church doors was conspiring to strip them of their religious freedoms and deny them their way of life.

Most troubling of all: their inexplicable fervor for firearms. Aggressively promoting the right to own and carry an instrument designed specifically to take a human life felt like a betrayal of everything Christianity promised me when I'd first believed: abundant life through a savior who calls us to love our enemies. Actively resisting lifesaving gun control measures and electing pro-gun politicians who vowed to shoot down those reforms seemed even more duplicitous.

I was New England bureau chief for AP when a gunman armed with a military-style assault rifle massacred twenty first graders and six adults at Sandy Hook Elementary School in Newtown, Connecticut. Our teams spent more than six gut-wrenching weeks intensively covering the story. Meanwhile, Americans across the political spectrum clamored for change, and our collective outrage produced a momentary glimmer of hope. Surely the slaughter of so many innocents would be a tipping point: a transcendent moment we'd all look

## PREFACE

back on as the day we permanently holstered our weapons, came together to pass commonsense gun control legislation, and reclaimed our sanity.

And it was, for a few days. My own church dimmed the sanctuary lights and convened a somber prayer meeting. We wept for Sandy Hook's children and our own, and we cried out for healing and mercy. We, like so many in the aftermath of such tragedies, sent our thoughts and prayers to the families and survivors of the tragedy.

And then we spoke of it no more.

That's how it is with "thoughts and prayers": the fleeting good intentions with which the proverbial road to hell is paved. Such words absolve us from doing anything to make sure such a horrible event never happens again. If you really give a damn, you *do* something.

♦ ♦ ♦

My exodus from evangelicalism was triggered by a revelation so personally startling, it's what roused me to launch the investigation you're about to read.

On a sweltering weeknight in 2016, I was rehearsing onstage with my Massachusetts megachurch worship band when I noticed my bass player, an earnest and affable man I'll call John, stop to loosen his guitar strap.

"Too much lasagna for supper?" I teased.

"Nah," he said. "It's just that the strap is rubbing against my 9-millimeter."

The truth took a few seconds to sink in. John had come to practice with a SIG Sauer semiautomatic handgun.

I must have looked as dumbfounded as I felt, because he quickly assured me he had a concealed carry permit. But that's not what had me so shaken. Moments earlier, we'd been singing about divine mercy and grace. Suddenly a beautiful space in my life was reduced to a

# PREFACE

jarring juxtaposition of God's peace and John's piece. What fresh hell was this?

Not long thereafter, I realized, to my horror, that John wasn't the only one showing up armed at the altar. John's wife carried a small-caliber pocket pistol in her purse, and several of the men in the congregation possessed concealed firearms. They claimed to do so under the auspices of a church "security ministry," but it looked and felt more like vigilantism to me.

I left that congregation, but the guns stayed behind. They're surely still there, spirited into the sanctuary every Sunday, cleaned and oiled and loaded and ready for Lord knows what.

I've learned the hard way not to try to commiserate about this reality with my evangelical friends. At best, they'll bristle and respond with a full-throated defense of the supposed virtues of concealed carry. And at worst, they can be downright menacing. One hard-liner in Texas told me bluntly that he's never without his gun—not even at church: "I will be armed, and you won't even know it. Chew on *that*, pal."

Today, I think of my thirty-five years in the white evangelical movement, with its bewildering mix of beauty and bigotry, as a long, strange, Moses-style detour in the desert. It wasn't all bad, of course, and I mean the beauty part. I've developed intimate friendships, and the person of Jesus will forever move me. Christ's words in the Sermon on the Mount—especially those darn beatitudes that bless all the "wrong" people, including the peacemakers—inspire me. And the mere flicker of a candle in a dimly lit chapel can stop me in my tracks.

Christianity has changed my life. Unfortunately, so has evangelicalism.

The silver lining for you in my years of affiliation with white evangelicalism is that I have a book's worth of insider insights into the marriage between evangelicals, guns, and politics. I know the vocabulary and the logic of the evangelicals who are pledging allegiance to

# PREFACE

guns. I even joined the National Rifle Association (NRA). Becoming a card-carrying member of the NRA gave me the access and street cred I needed to approach some of the cagier personalities in the gun community I interviewed for this book.

For the irreligious reader of the pages that follow, I volunteer as tribute. For the reader immersed within or adjacent to white evangelicalism, I hope to paint portraits of you or your loved ones in ways that are recognizable, compassionate, and perhaps convicting. Together we'll make the most of my misadventures as we seek to untangle why, of all the Constitution's 7,591 words, many white evangelicals believe these twenty-seven comprising the Second Amendment are holy writ:

> *A well regulated Militia, being necessary to the security of a free State, the right of the people to keep and bear Arms, shall not be infringed.*

We'll also examine what needs to be done to fix our gun problem. We'll meet dissident Christians like Shane Claiborne, Mike Martin, and Scotty Utz, who are turning AR-15 assault rifles into garden tools—almost literally beating swords into plowshares. We'll also encounter a group of wonderfully imaginative rogue nuns who are buying stock in gun companies so they can exert influence from the inside as shareholders.

As you'll see, there are practical steps we can take together to end the madness. We'll examine how Australia, New Zealand, and the United Kingdom have done just that, with lasting success. But here in the United States, it starts with winning over the hearts and minds of the 60 million white evangelicals—many of them armed—who are reshaping the nation's political landscape from the front lines of the culture wars.

What this book *isn't* about is guns owned for shooting sports. Hunting is a proud tradition in many American families, and rifle, pistol, and shotgun events test enthusiasts' mettle and skills from high school clubs to the Olympics. I've enjoyed both.

## PREFACE

My approach is not intended to be doctrinaire. Like everyone else, I'm struggling to practice what I'm preaching in these pages, starting with Jesus's all-encompassing command: *Love your neighbor.* I merely wish to hold up a mirror to America's most devout people, who mystifyingly and stubbornly cling to a belief that the answer to our gun problem is more guns, and ask a single piercing question: *Why?*

Why do people who claim to follow a man called the Prince of Peace devote themselves so religiously to ensuring military-grade weapons are easier to buy than some forms of birth control? How did a group of Christians who claim to be staunchly pro-life come to so warmly embrace guns, whose primary purpose is to kill? When will we vote for politicians who will summon the courage to enact commonsense, lifesaving gun measures—simple things like universal background checks—that surveys consistently show most Americans want?

To my many evangelical friends, who have the political clout to change the country's trajectory on gun violence, I offer an olive branch and a beatitude of my own:

*Blessed are the kingmakers, for they can save lives.*

# 1 | THE GOSPEL OF GUNS

Floodlights bathe the stage in a purple haze as I step back from the microphone and tap a foot pedal, sending a riff from my Stratocaster reverberating out across the arena. The window shades are drawn, and the house lights are down, so I can barely make out the crowd packing the floor and the balconies, but I know their eyes are closed as they murmur to their Maker.

Not mine. I'm gazing up at the hall's domed ceiling in wide-eyed wonder, reveling in the amped-up beat I can feel vibrating in my sternum—and hoping against hope for a fleeting glimpse of God.

This isn't a rock concert, although it has all the trappings of one. It's an evangelical church service. And in our secular society, these are four words you won't often hear, especially from a journalist like me: I love to worship.

I've been a musician since I was a kid, but for me, the time before the sermon known as praise and worship transcends music. In an era of singular self-absorption, where so many of us hide behind carefully curated and burnished Instagram versions of ourselves, worship offers me an opportunity to keep it real: with myself, with my fellow Christians, and, most importantly, with God. Reporters, like cops, see the worst of society, and we can be a hard-hearted and cynical lot. Through worship, a sacred practice that stretches back millennia to the ancients, I find myself connected—mysteriously and metaphysically—to the only Being in the universe who can soften and break up the scar tissue within my soul.

It's 10:00 a.m. on a Sunday, and all around me, hands are raised in surrender. Had you wandered in off the street, you'd be forgiven for thinking it was a mass response to an unseen gunman's demands. What you'd surely never suspect in a congregation like this of several hundred rapturous souls: Dozens of guns, maybe more; holstered and hidden from view but no less lethal. These are my people.

Or they were, before I realized how many of them are armed to the teeth.

◆ ◆ ◆

It's no secret that America is awash in weapons. In fact, there are far more guns than Americans themselves: 120 firearms for every 100 citizens, the Switzerland-based Small Arms Survey says.

That's 393 million firearms in total, not counting police or military weapons or untraceable homemade "ghost guns," in a nation of 330 million people. That's nearly twice as many guns per capita as the Falkland Islands, the second-ranked nation on the global rankings, with sixty-two guns for every hundred people. Every year, 3.6 million babies are born in this country, and 22 million guns are sold. That's six guns for each of those newborns.

There could be even more. Since 1899, more than 494 million guns have been manufactured for the US market alone, according to federal Bureau of Alcohol, Tobacco, Firearms and Explosives data, and more of those weapons than you might think could still be in circulation. Rifles and revolvers, which if properly maintained can easily last a century or longer, are among the most durable of all durable goods.

And all that American firepower is even more concentrated when you consider that 74 million of us are aged seventeen or younger and can't own guns, meaning even more guns are in the hands of a smaller number of adults. Little wonder that the United States is home to nearly five times more gun dealers than McDonald's restaurants. Our country is bloodied by more mass shootings than there are days in the year, according to the reckoning of some researchers—nearly *twice* as many such incidents as days, actually. Although mass shootings fell to 503 in 2024, in 2023 there were 658 such incidents, which the Gun Violence Archive defines as shootings in which at least four people, not including the shooter, were either wounded or killed. Only 2021 saw more, with an all-time high of 689 mass shootings. And because these mass casualty events are happening everywhere—in cities, in the suburbs, in rural farm towns—no one is safe.

Our gun glut is lethally consequential. Firearms are now the leading cause of accidental death among young children and teenagers, with gunfire fatalities increasing 50 percent between 2019 and 2021, eclipsing even car crashes. Firearms deaths in some states now rival those in far-flung conflict zones, reports the Commonwealth Fund, an independent research group. Gun homicides in Mississippi are nearly double those in Haiti, and they are higher in each of these three states—Alabama, Louisiana, and Mississippi—than in Mexico, a nation long bloodied by violence between rival drug cartels. Montana and the New Jersey suburbs have more gun deaths per capita than Colombia and Nicaragua, respectively.

Suicides are also rising in the United States, and having a gun within reach vastly increases the odds that an attempted suicide will result in a death; indeed, firearm suicides hit an all-time high in 2022, according to the Centers for Disease Control and Prevention. Having easy access to a gun also increases the chances that a domestic dispute will turn deadly, or that a thief will overpower you during a home invasion and wound or kill you with your own weapon. It's an inconvenient truth that the National Rifle Association wishes you'd ignore: Your home becomes more dangerous, not safer, the moment you bring a gun inside.

Even if all new guns were to stop being made or sold in America today, there are still, by some estimates, 24 million AR-15 military-style assault rifles alone in circulation, says Philip Cook, a professor emeritus of public policy at Duke University. And there's little indication that the number of firearms overall will significantly diminish. An exhaustive study by the nonpartisan Pew Research Center found that roughly three-quarters of all Americans who owned a gun in 2017 said they couldn't see themselves ever *not* owning one.

What few realize, though, is just how many weapons are owned, concealed, and carried—often even within the sanctity of a church—by those who profess to uphold life as sacred and most readily offer thoughts and prayers when it's taken: white evangelical Christians. It's not just outsiders to the faith who don't realize this; I identified as an evangelical for three and a half decades, and for years, I had no idea that gun ownership among evangelicals is more than four times higher than among some of those who adhere to other major faith traditions. Forty-one percent of white conservative Christians own a gun, the Pew analysis finds, compared to one in ten Jews and Muslims in this country and fewer than one in three people across the general population.

That four in ten white evangelicals own a gun may seem mind-blowing. But Gina Zurlo, a prominent sociologist and religious historian who codirects the Center for the Study of Global Christianity at Gordon-Conwell Theological Seminary in Massachusetts, thinks even *more* white evangelicals are gun owners than this Pew study suggests. Zurlo, coeditor of the World Christian Database, says an estimated 65 percent of white evangelicals "own and carry guns" and an unspecified number of those people even bring their guns to church.

The Reverend Rob Schenck, a dissident evangelical in Washington who spent nearly four decades on the Christian far right, now calls out the hypocrisy of evangelicals who claim they uphold the sanctity of life while carrying a gun. In a widely read op-ed for *The*

*Washington Post*—"I'm an Evangelical Preacher: You Can't Be Pro-Life and Pro-Gun"—Schenck turns the tables on his critics. "The Christian gospel should quell our fears and remind us of our Christ-like obligation to love all people, even those who intend us harm," he writes. "This generous view of the world calls us to demonstrate God's love toward others, regardless of who they are, where they come from or what religion they practice. Assuming a permanently defensive posture against others, especially when it includes a willingness to kill, is inimical to a life of faith."

In an interview, I asked Schenck if he still feels that way. He nodded three times and answered without hesitation: "Absolutely":

> I'm not an absolute pacifist in the sense that there should be no violence at any time under any circumstances. Sadly, I think there are times when violence is warranted. To me, it's just one of the great, regrettable realities about humanity. But it's the reason I argue we should delegate that act to the fewest numbers of people. We don't just open it up and say, "Everybody start shooting everybody now," which is really what the Republicans—driven in large part by the arguments of evangelicals and others—are doing. They're basically saying, "Let's just open up the streets to firefights, and may the strongest, best-equipped shooter prevail."

◆ ◆ ◆

So, what is an evangelical? Descriptions vary, but it can be helpful to define a people by the way they define themselves. Let's use a paraphrase of the National Association of Evangelicals' definition: An evangelical is someone who has had a personal "born again" conversion experience with Jesus Christ; regards the Bible as the ultimate moral authority; supports missionary work and actively shares their faith with others; and emphasizes Christ's virgin birth, sacrifice on the cross, and resurrection as the keys to redeeming humanity.

Collectively, evangelicals form a movement that cuts across nearly four dozen distinct Protestant traditions and denominations. It can even include some Roman Catholic charismatics—believers who follow the Vatican's teachings but also embrace the indwelling of the Holy Spirit and spiritual gifts such as faith healing and prophecy—as well as "Messianic" Jews who recognize Jesus as Messiah, or savior. No matter their denominational affiliations, white evangelicals tend to be (or lean) overwhelmingly Republican.

Culling from numerous firearms studies, a profile emerges. Statistically, the typical American gun owner is a cisgender, heterosexual, married white man who is politically conservative; middle-aged and middle-class; lacks confidence in the government; and lives in the rural South or West. He also considers himself individualistic and punitive, meaning he supports the death penalty for capital crimes such as murder. His guns—plural, as he usually owns more than one—are primarily for personal protection rather than for target practice or hunting.

And he is an evangelical.

Intriguingly, according to research by Wake Forest University sociologist David Yamane, he also tends to be something of a spiritual isolationist: one who rarely attends religious services despite holding theologically conservative positions. Experts say the relationship between church attendance and gun ownership can fluctuate and merits a closer look.

Among these Bible-thumping gun owners is T. S. Weaver, a seminarian, pastor, and blogger in Texas who sees no inconsistencies between his lifelong conservative Christian faith and his handgun. Weaver considers himself a deeply committed believer. In fact, having been baptized as Jesus himself was, in the Jordan River, he's arguably more serious than most. "Guns should be used in a God-glorifying and moderate way," he writes in a blog post. "Though I respect Christian pacifism, I just don't find it mandatory."

At least he's given it some thought. The same can't be said of Gretchen Smith, a native Tennessean who likes to pose, in the style of those crass calendars some auto mechanics display showing scantily clad models holding tools, with a cache of AR-15s and other military-style weaponry. Why so many guns? Smith's social media accounts contain the clues. "God! Country! Family!" reads her bio on X, cloaking herself in that most omnipresent of all Bible verses, John 3:16: *For God so loved the world he gave his only son, that whoever believes in him should not perish but have everlasting life.*

Smith and her 200,000 followers, who include thousands of like-minded evangelical extremists, engage almost exclusively in fake-news fearmongering about what they insist is the enemy within: an apocalyptic army of undocumented immigrants supposedly preparing to lay siege to the United States. The none-too-subtle takeaway: Only your guns will save you.

♦ ♦ ♦

Evangelicals aren't only fervent gun owners. In what critics denounce as an unholy alliance, they also own and operate some major gun manufacturers.

The AR-15 rifle used to slaughter twenty-one innocents at Robb Elementary School in Uvalde, Texas, in 2022 was made by a company established by an evangelical entrepreneur on a trinity of values: faith, family, and firearms. Georgia-based Daniel Defense, founded in 2000 by Marty Daniel, also manufactured the rifles used five years earlier in what is still the deadliest single mass shooting in US history: a hotel sniper's systematic mowing down of 60 concert revelers on the Las Vegas Strip.

Thirty Uvalde parents and teachers sued Daniel Defense in federal court, arguing that the gunmaker bears responsibility for the massacre of nineteen schoolchildren and two teachers. That lawsuit, and others, accuse the company of deceptive and provocative marketing aimed at selling deadly weapons to teens, in part by glorifying the AR-15 in video games.

Daniel Defense has called the suits against it legally baseless and politically motivated, and its unrepentant CEO doubled down on X, posting: "Daniel Defense stands with Americans everywhere who will not be bullied into silence or political inaction as the freedoms and protections ensured by the Second Amendment are under attack."

The gun manufacturer also shamelessly exploits evangelicals' distrust of the government. In a promotional video, the company shows its CEO telling a small boy he's teaching how to shoot that "there are two types of people in the world: good people and evil people. And just in case evil people get in charge, good people need to have the ability to fight back."

Meanwhile, Daniel and his wife, Cindy, have donated hundreds of thousands of dollars to Republican candidates, including fellow pro-gun evangelical Herschel Walker, the football star who mounted an unsuccessful attempt in 2022 to unseat Democratic US Senator Raphael Warnock in Georgia. "We are in business, we believe, to be a supporter of the gospel," Daniel tells the far-right outlet *Breitbart News*.

Daniel Defense isn't the only evangelical-owned gunmaker with a public relations problem. Indiana-based FosTecH, which touts itself as a Christian company, was recently fined for illegal lobbying after offering Republican state lawmakers AR-15 rifles at a discount. We'll look in much more depth at conservative Christians' involvement in the gun industry in chapter 6. For now, here are just two more glimpses into that world, to help us see its breadth.

Spike's Tactical, a gunmaker in Florida, markets a Christian "Crusader" assault rifle that is engraved with a cross and a Bible verse. "We named it Crusader and engraved Psalm 144:1 on the lower receiver to hoist the flag of our faith and to make a statement, reminding our customers that we are with you. The war is here. We have a duty to defend our homeland and our way of life," the company says. In case you're curious, Psalm 144:1, a verse often invoked by Christian nationalists, reads: "Praise be to the Lord my Rock, who trains my hands for war, my fingers for battle."

And arguably the most overtly Christian manufacturer of AR-15s marketed to the general public is CMMG, based in Fayette, Missouri, which credits its success to "coming to God in prayer daily, seeking Him, and asking for the wisdom to follow His direction." So fervently does it believe its military-style gunmaking pleases God that the company has posted this prayer prominently on its website:

> For CMMG, Lord God, we pray for Your wisdom in managing the enormous responsibility that comes with this business. We walk in obedience to Your path, we are in your mission, as you have a better direction. Let us not worry ourselves about things that we cannot control but take time daily to come to you in vocal and silent prayer, both alone and together. We give thanks for our customers and team members who support our employment and allow us to bless others. Keep us safe as we continue to produce quality products so that we have work for our hands and serve our neighbors. This work allows us to provide for our families and community, and the defense thereof. We know that ensuring the safety and well-being of our families is a necessity for the serenity and stability of this world. Protect our customers, and their families, and grant them peace of spirit.
>
> For all things that we do not know to prayer [*sic*] for, Lord God, we humbly leave in Your hands. Come, Lord Jesus. The grace of the Lord Jesus be with God's people. Amen.

Evangelicals also number among the nation's most prominent gun industry lobbyists in Washington. Larry Pratt, the executive director emeritus of Gun Owners of America, is an outspoken Christian conservative who has been labeled an extremist and a pivotal figure in the rise of right-wing militias by the Southern Poverty Law

Center, which monitors hate groups. Gun Owners of America, for its part, long has positioned itself as a more aggressive alternative to the National Rifle Association.

"Larry Pratt stands at the intersection of guns and Jesus, lobbying for absolutely unrestricted distribution of firearms while advocating a theocratic society based upon Old Testament civil and religious laws," the SPLC says, adding: "He believes that white Christians must arm themselves for self-protection in the inevitable social implosions and riots that are soon to come."

♦ ♦ ♦

White evangelicals are far more resistant than other Americans to even discussing, let alone implementing, the commonsense gun reforms most of us say we want—measures such as mandatory universal criminal background checks and pre-purchase waiting periods designed to keep people in a rage or with a rap sheet from rushing out impulsively to buy a firearm. The nonprofit and nonpartisan Public Religion Research Institute, whose surveys size up the most important cultural and religious dynamics shaping American society and politics, asked adherents of all the major religions if they supported gun control measures. A majority of respondents across all faith groups said they did, with a single notable exception: the nation's estimated 60 million white Protestant evangelicals.

Politically, the evangelicals among whom I used to find a home are a force to be reckoned with. Multiple surveys show 80 percent of evangelicals faithfully vote, making them far and away the most dependable electoral bloc in the nation. Their numbers and their turnout have cemented their status as influencers and kingmakers in presidential elections and congressional midterms alike. It's difficult to win the White House without the blessing of the religious right, and in red states, it's practically impossible to gain or defend a US House or Senate seat without their backing.

Evangelical influence in an increasingly pluralistic America, however, is projected to diminish over the next half-century. By 2070, if current trends continue, Christians will make up less than half of the US population—supplanted by those who identify instead as atheist, agnostic, or "nothing in particular." The "nones," as the religiously unaffiliated have become known, already comprise 28 percent of the population.

For now, though, evangelicals retain considerable political sway, and as a result, gun laws are being loosened, not tightened. More than half of the states—mostly red states that, not coincidentally, are home to the most evangelicals—now allow gun owners to conceal and carry their weapons without a permit or training. In fact, in the year after the Uvalde massacre, state legislatures enacted more laws *expanding* access to guns than constricting it.

It's a reflection of both evangelicals' symbiotic relationship with the NRA and their transactional ties to Donald Trump and the MAGA movement. Although in decline, riven and weakened by charges of fraud and corruption, the NRA remains highly influential. Many of the gun rights group's 4 million members decide whom to vote for based on a given candidate's confirmed (or even perceived) stance on gun control. The NRA doles out grades ranging from $A$ to $F$ to current members of Congress, based on how "gun-friendly" it judges them, and an unfavorable rating can cost a federal lawmaker reelection. Democrats and other gun control advocates often wear an $F$ as a badge of honor, but for the conservative Republican candidates most evangelicals favor, anything less than an $A$ is a scarlet letter.

And just as white evangelicals' fierce defense of the Second Amendment right to bear arms has made them indispensable to the NRA, it has endeared Donald Trump to them. Opposition to abortion is what first drew white evangelicals to Trump, but his perceived support for gun rights—another evangelical policy priority—is a large reason why eight out of ten white evangelicals reelected him in 2024. At an

April 2023 meeting of the NRA, Trump touted himself as "the most pro-gun, pro–Second Amendment president you've ever had in the White House." It's a message amplified by *Field Ethos*, his son Donald Trump Jr.'s glossy quarterly for hunters and other outdoors enthusiasts. The magazine published a full-page ad featuring a Thompson submachine gun—a model similar to those 1930s Tommy guns made famous by mobsters and government crimefighters like Eliot Ness—engraved with *President Trump* and *Save America 45th*.

Trump's record on gun control is more complex than he'd like his supporters to think. Early in 2018, before a gunman slaughtered seventeen people at Marjory Stoneman Douglas High School in Parkland, Florida, Trump instructed the federal Bureau of Alcohol, Tobacco and Firearms to administratively outlaw civilian possession of bump stocks—devices that help a shooter pull the trigger on a semiautomatic weapon incredibly quickly, essentially making it fire like a machine gun. That drew a rebuke from the conservative Federalist Society, which denounced it as "troubling" and a "clear policy failure."

Even US Supreme Court Justice Neil Gorsuch, one of Trump's handpicked conservative appointees, criticized the bump stocks ban as "bureaucratic pirouetting." And in the end, the high court overturned the ban in mid-2024, ignoring the fact that the Las Vegas mass shooter used the device to squeeze off more than one thousand rounds.

After Parkland, Trump met with US senators and argued forcefully for comprehensive gun control measures that the NRA had opposed for years, including expanded background checks, an assault weapons ban, and raising the minimum age for commercial gun sales from age eighteen to twenty-one. The very next day, though, after huddling privately with NRA officials, he abruptly backed down. Something similar played out after a mass shooting in El Paso, Texas, in 2018: Trump asked his advisers why he couldn't take action on banning assault rifles and then dropped it when told he'd lose.

By early 2020, Trump had noticeably changed his tune, promising the American people in his State of the Union address: "So long as I am president, I will always protect your Second Amendment rights to keep and bear arms." At the start of the COVID-19 pandemic, he designated gun shops as essential businesses, allowing them to stay open. And in the run-up to his 2024 reelection, Trump resharpened his pro-gun rhetoric, vowing to undo minor gun restrictions put in place by the Biden administration. "No one will lay a finger on your firearms," he vowed.

Like the NRA, Trump continues to appeal to evangelicals because of how he has stoked and exploited the rise of Christian nationalism—a pugnacious creed whose followers cling to the notion that the United States is a Christian nation divinely settled in the 1600s and still blessed by God. Many Christian nationalist groups invoke patriarchy and white supremacism in shades of varying intensity.

This uniquely religious brand of nationalism traces back at least to the late Reverend Jerry Falwell's Moral Majority—a movement firmly rooted in white Americans' fears over the court-ordered end of racial segregation in the US. White evangelicals greeted desegregation laws with defiance, but they also knew better than to openly associate with segregationists. So, when South Carolina's fundamentalist Bob Jones University refused until the early 1970s to admit Black people, and even then, only under federal pressure and the threat of losing its nonprofit and tax-exempt status, Falwell framed the dispute as one of religious freedom, not racism.

The opportunistic NRA did the same. Tapping into deep-seated white supremacist sentiment while capitalizing on widespread post-Vietnam and post-Watergate public distrust of government, it began co-opting religious language to identify with Christian conservatives, gain their trust, and reframe gun ownership as part of the very fabric of American identity.

Having a handgun was recast as a "God-given" right—a term increasingly used in the NRA's magazine, *American Rifleman*, along with rising references to good and evil. The late actor and staunch gun rights advocate Charlton Heston, who famously played Moses in the blockbuster Cecil B. DeMille film *The Ten Commandments*, used spiritual language and religious symbolism to further cement the link between God and the Second Amendment during his own NRA presidency from 1998 to 2003.

"The NRA has been incredibly effective in building on the Moral Majority's efforts in the culture wars by grafting gun rights onto larger cultural issues," such as white evangelicals' worries about racial tensions and their xenophobia toward immigrants, says Jessica Dawson, a researcher in behavioral science and leadership at the US Military Academy at West Point. One example: When a shooter from El Salvador opened fire inside celebrity pastor Joel Osteen's Houston megachurch early in 2024, *Fox News* and the far right falsely portrayed her as transgender and used her immigrant status to step up attacks on supposedly militant LGBTQ+ people and migrants—two other conservative Christian targets.

Guns and God form "a complex relationship that may be impossible to disentangle," Dawson concedes in a sweeping 2019 study. But it's a nexus—along with a persistent "us versus them" mentality—that continues among evangelicals today. Polls consistently reveal a sort of white evangelical inferiority complex: a fear that their influence is waning, their religious beliefs are under fire, and America is becoming a more difficult place for them to live.

They are culture warriors with their backs against the wall, running low on metaphorical (if not actual) ammunition.

◆ ◆ ◆

So what? Why should non-evangelicals care? If evangelical churches are experiencing a similar decline in adherence as other churches—and they are—and if the United States is an ever more pluralistic society, why should we care about what a subset of Christians believes about guns?

Because Americans' appetite for political violence is increasing, and otherwise law-abiding Christian conservatives—many, as we've seen, with ample firepower to back up their ire—figure prominently among them. Because if you're among the majority of people insisting on basic measures such as universal background checks, white evangelicals are determined to stand in your way and thwart new legislation. Because tens of millions of your fellow Americans firmly believe God blesses guns—so much so that he inspired the writing of their constitutional right to own and carry them.

God and guns create a combustive mix. Early in 2024, the nonpartisan Public Religion Research Institute surveyed Americans about the greatest threats to democracy, and found strong support for political violence among those who insist the United States is a Christian nation and believe the long-since-debunked "Big Lie" that the 2020 presidential election was stolen from Trump. More than three in ten white evangelicals agreed with the statement: "Because things have gotten so far off track, true American patriots may have to resort to violence in order to save our country."

The problem with theocracies, of course, is that they're always also autocracies. The mullahs who run Iran, one of Washington's sworn enemies, have taught us that. And the problem with Christian nationalists, apart from a militaristic worldview, is their refusal to acknowledge any personal responsibility for the things that are seriously wrong with America.

In their increasingly apocalyptic outlook, informed for many by a literal reading of the mysterious Bible-ending book of Revelation, they tend to excuse themselves from righting wrongs or addressing social ills. Why bother when scripture foretells Christ's return, an epic battle in which good finally vanquishes evil, and the Earth's ultimate destruction? For many evangelicals, the climate crisis, racism, poverty, and soaring gun violence all elicit a "meh" response and grumbling about wokeism. That's despite Christ's own teachings to care for the poor, the widowed, the orphaned, and the imprisoned.

*Black lives matter?* Not particularly—all lives matter. *Gay rights?* Straight out of Sodom and Gomorrah. *White privilege?* Not a thing—and stop playing the race card. *Gun problem?* More like a mental health problem.

In fact, virtually every time a gun owner goes rogue and massacres innocents, evangelicals insist the problem isn't guns; it's mental illness. After a gunman killed eight people and wounded another seven at a shopping center in Texas in 2023, Republican Governor Greg Abbott deflected calls for tightening access to weapons and called mental health problems "the root cause." Even if that were true, evangelicals have a history of opposing universal health care and spending on mental health services, and in extreme instances, they've been slow to embrace the benefits of therapy, instead encouraging followers to pray away anxiety and depression.

But it's not true: New research suggests that mental illness plays a negligible role in mass shootings. "Individuals with serious mental illness . . . have higher risks of committing lethal violence, but these absolute risks are very low and result in modest contributions to societal homicides," concludes a study published in the *American Journal of Medicine* that compared the interaction of mental illness and gun violence in Australia, Britain, and the United States. "In the US, the high rates of gun ownership and access to firearms—not mental illness—seem more plausible explanations. . . . Combatting the epidemic of US homicides and suicides from gun violence without addressing guns is tantamount to combatting the epidemic of deaths from lung cancer from smoking without addressing cigarettes."

A common evangelical tactic is to blame gun violence on the evil that's present in the world. Tighter regulation of firearms, evangelicals argue, won't do anything to address humanity's sinful condition. We heard this from US House Speaker Mike Johnson, a devout Southern Baptist who opposes universal background checks, after a gunman killed eighteen people in Lewiston, Maine, in that state's deadliest mass shooting. "The problem is the human heart," Johnson said. "It's not guns."

Religious conservatives trace the unraveling of goodness in society and widespread gun violence to the US Supreme Court's 1962 ruling that effectively outlawed prayer in public schools. Many also point to what they see as the other scourges of secularization—video games, Hollywood's glorification of violence, no-holds-barred social media, pornography, and the perceived breakdown of the traditional American family—as root causes.

"By invoking the evilness of humanity, such leaders provide a theological gloss to the 'guns don't kill people; people kill people' argument that has long overshadowed our national conversations about gun violence," says Neil J. Young, cohost of the history podcast *Past Present*. "This same paranoid fantasy undergirds much of religious conservatives' opposition to gun control," he says. "While no personal arsenal is likely to turn back the federal government's forces, many religious conservatives, especially white evangelical men, worry that any limitation on gun rights will infringe on their ability to protect their loved ones."

◆ ◆ ◆

Christ's admonition to turn the other cheek doesn't mean looking the other way. That's what white evangelicals are doing, however, when they deny the climate crisis, brush off social injustices, and ignore the obvious dangers that guns pose to society. Too many are apostles of apathy.

And yet, when roused in the name of God, the religious right is capable of trading its indifference for unrestrained fury. That nationalist Christians are among the most armed Americans, after the police and the military, is deeply troubling.

These dynamics were on full display during the January 6, 2021, insurrection at the Capitol, where religious symbols and objects were a common sight. "While Trump may have incited the riot at the Capitol that led to his second impeachment, many of his followers already had all the encouragement they needed: They believed God wanted them to do this," Peter Manseau, curator of American religion at the Smithsonian Institution, writes in an op-ed for the *Washington Post*. "Not only was this assault accompanied by Jesus flags, Bible quotes and loudspeaker sermons, it was undertaken—according to many of the attackers themselves—in Christianity's name."

Political scientists and pundits caution that the next January 6—"next" because in the current politically polarized climate, another seems inevitable—likely will involve more firearms. Gun purchases soared to an all-time high of 22.5 million at the peak of the pandemic in 2021, according to FBI data analyzed by the nonprofit gun watchdog group *The Trace*. And although sales have declined since then, gun manufacturers are adapting. They are now marketing their weapons to consumers of color who are shifting to the political right—customers who fall well outside the longtime industry standard of "old, male, and pale." The growing appeal of guns to more demographic groups is a troubling trend for anyone concerned about the sheer number of firearms in the United States. A Northeastern University study found that of the 7.5 million Americans who bought a gun for the first time between 2019 and 2021, half were women, a fifth were Black, and another fifth were Latino. And since Trump's reelection, there has been a surge of LGTBQ+ people buying guns for personal protection and applying for concealed carry permits.

The appeal of Christian nationalism crosses racial divides, to a certain extent. The nonpartisan Public Religion Research Institute's most recent American Values Atlas shows that 55 percent of Hispanic

Protestants, most of whom identify as evangelical, hold Christian supremacist beliefs. But white evangelicals still dominate that worldview at about 66 percent, making them the largest subset to do so.

In a telling, if alarming, sign of how deep conservative Christians' theocratic tendencies can run, a 2020 Pew Research Center study found that seven in ten white evangelicals—citing tension between their religious beliefs and mainstream American culture—think the Bible should have more influence on US laws than the will of the people. Even Jon Dunwell, an evangelical pastor and a state legislator in deep-red Iowa, thinks that's scary. "Talibanistic," he calls it in an interview with *The New Yorker*.

In a landmark 2018 study that took a deep dive into this mentality, sociologists Samuel L. Perry, Andrew L. Whitehead, and Landon Schnabel found that those who are most fiercely opposed to federal gun restrictions of any kind tend to be those who are most insistent that Christianity ought to "be officially promoted in the public sphere."

"Access to guns is about protecting the freedoms of white conservatives to suppress disorder," says Perry, of the University of Oklahoma. "This is why, among white Americans who believe the United States should be a Christian nation, 82 percent believe, 'The best way to stop bad guys with guns is to have good guys with guns.' The goal isn't to rid the world of gun violence. The goal is to suppress 'bad guy violence' with righteous violence—our violence. And that requires guns." Consequently, Perry says, the ritual of deflection, denial, and defiance continues: "Horrific deaths, followed by thoughts and prayers, calls to return to God, and no change."

Christian nationalists consistently cite the Second Amendment as far and away the most sacred constitutional right—more important than freedom of speech or even freedom of religion. Days after the 2018 Parkland massacre, then-NRA boss Wayne LaPierre doubled down, claiming the right to bear arms "is not bestowed by man but granted by God to all Americans as our American birthright."

"Gun ownership is a more important right than voting," asserts Matt Walsh, a darling of the Christian far right who describes himself as a theocratic fascist. "Voting is not really a human right at all but a privilege that should be reserved for those who are qualified to do it properly. It should be easier to buy a gun than vote."

◆ ◆ ◆

Bottom line: America is a virtual armory sitting atop a powder keg of Christian nationalism. And by and large, supporters of anti-gun legislation are seriously underestimating the evangelical base holding the match.

The United States has the dubious distinction of being by far the most religious and the most armed of all the wealthiest Western nations. And armed extremist militias and other fringe groups whose members at least nominally identify as evangelicals pose the biggest threat. "The growing presence of firearms in political spaces in the United States endangers public health, safety, and the functioning of democracy," researchers at the Johns Hopkins Bloomberg School of Public Health's Center for Gun Violence Solutions conclude in a new report, warning that the threat of armed insurrection is rising.

Shane Claiborne, an anti-gun evangelical street preacher in Philadelphia who turns weapons collected in amnesty buybacks into garden tools—thus almost literally beating "swords into plowshares," as Isaiah 2:4 puts it—sees a certain level of distrust in the government as healthy in a democracy. But those who circulate conspiracy theories and are girded and ready to battle the nation's own military, in the name of God and country, have moved beyond that level of distrust. "They are the 3 percent of gun owners who own half of the . . . guns in America. They are the ones who send death threats and march in the streets in full camo while holding semiautomatics," Claiborne says. "They are the folks who think it makes sense to arm four-year-olds. They are not the majority of gun owners, but they are a forceful, intimidating minority." (For more on how Claiborne and other evangelical reformers are fighting back peaceably and creatively see chapter 9.)

The proliferation of conspiracy theories among evangelicals has produced an echo chamber of fear and distrust that podcaster and gun control advocate Amy Sullivan, a Christian, wants no part of. "Too often leaders respond to gun violence by encouraging us to fear each other, to arm ourselves and see threats in every unfamiliar face," she says. "But we know that God has not given us a spirit of fear. And we cannot love our neighbors from the inside of a bunker."

In this increasingly combustive environment, in which guns, religion, and politics are inextricably intertwined, it's practically impossible to build the bipartisan support needed to enact even the simplest gun reforms, says Amanda Tyler, executive director of the Baptist Joint Committee for Religious Liberty. "It's making it really difficult to have a debate about sensible gun laws and even over measures that public polling shows most people agree on," she tells *Baptist News Global*, adding: "Christian nationalism has a hold on our ability to proceed."

To Perry, Schnabel, and Whitehead, the sociologists studying evangelicals' resistance to even the smallest gun control measures, there's a simple if worrying explanation: "For them [evangelicals], gun control is a direct attack on a God-given right, and mass shootings are the result not of easy access to firearms but instead of the moral decay of what should be a Christian nation."

◆ ◆ ◆

On one hand, Christianity is a faith steeped in bloodshed. It began with the blood, sweat, and tears of the incarnation—the birth of Jesus—and culminated in the sacrificial blood of Christ shed during his crucifixion.

Christianity's enduring emblem, the cross, symbolizes what was in ancient Rome a cruel if not unusual method of capital punishment: crucifixion. (It is gallows humor among believers, but Mike Warnke, an evangelical stand-up comic—yes, that's a thing—jokes darkly that wearing a silver crucifix on a chain is akin to adorning oneself with a tiny, bejeweled gallows, gas chamber, or electric chair.) Bloodshed in the name of Jesus intensified with the unjust torture and wholesale slaughter of Muslims during the medieval Crusades. And it arguably continues today, as ultraconservative believers block attempts at enacting even a modicum of gun restrictions to reduce the carnage that's touching so many American families.

Yet Christ ordered Peter to put away his sword, as recorded in the New Testament. He exhorted his followers, when we're assaulted, to turn the other cheek and love our enemies. It is his most challenging command—a decree that instantly made Christianity the world's most radical religion and its first adherents an existential threat to their Roman oppressors. By turning away from brute force and refusing to respond in kind, Jesus's followers exchanged humanity's usual fight-or-flight response for an active and nonviolent challenge to their subjugators. They also refused to bow to the Roman gods, and all of this made them a political threat in the emperor's eyes.

"You can't even imagine what this sounded like in first-century Jerusalem," says the Reverend Robert Spitzer, a Jesuit priest and a retired president of Gonzaga University. Or, for that matter, what such a command sounds like now, in the twenty-first century.

As Shane Claiborne writes: "We believe in a God who would rather die than kill. We believe in a God whose last words are grace and forgiveness for the people who are killing him. We believe in a God who interacts with evil without becoming evil, who exposes our violence to heal our violence, who endures death to save us from death. We are atheists to the god of war and believers in the Prince of Peace."

It may be hard to believe now, but for decades, many large evangelical denominations embraced nonviolence. The Pentecostal movement I exited, the Assemblies of God, was officially pacifist until the late 1960s, and as we'll see in chapter 2, many other denominations had pacifist roots. But today, many Assemblies of God members are unapologetically pro-gun, and at 3 million strong, they make up the nation's seventh-largest denomination.

These days, an Assemblies of God pastor can hold a "Bring Your Gun to Church Day." Fliers for an "open carry celebration" encouraged Ken Pagano's 150 congregants at New Bethel Church in Louisville, Kentucky, to wear or carry their weapons into the sanctuary and "celebrate our rights as Americans!" What could possibly go wrong? (Enough, apparently, that the church's insurance company abruptly canceled its policy.)

And in Greenwood, Arkansas, another Assemblies of God pastor who encourages the arming of his flock says he's considered putting up a sign outside his church that reads: *We don't call 911*. The implicit message, the Reverend Quinton Rowan says: "If you come in here messing with us, we're going to take care of business."

And they're getting support for their views from leading evangelical institutions. Writing in the *Liberty University Law Review*, a journal published by the nation's largest conservative Christian college founded by Jerry Falwell, evangelical lawyer and legal scholar Benjamin Boyd offers startlingly blunt advice to religious Americans: Take your guns to church.

First, Boyd addresses church leaders: "Instruct your flock to take their guns to church. The Church's leaders must reject statist usurpations into the Church's sanctuaries and create specific internal plans for armed congregational defense, which may include directives for firearms storage, tactical training, and congregational notification, a determination of who enters the sanctuary, under what terms, and in what manner, and a plan to guard its sanctuaries from the State's efforts at disarming both church members and church leadership."

Then, he addresses the people in the pews: "Take your guns to church. First, defend the right of armed self-defense in the church by developing comprehensive biblical convictions on this subject. Your life—and the life of your family members and your brothers and sisters in Christ—may depend upon it."

Conspicuously absent from his sixty-three-page screed: the words of Jesus.

"We've become weary with well-doing," Rob Schenck, the anti-abortion activist turned gun safety advocate, tells me in an interview with a sigh. "It's a struggle to be a disciple of Jesus. He asks us to do things contrary to our human nature. One of those things is to trust God and trust humanity and not give in to fear. But it's a whole lot easier not to do those things. Just get the gun, put it at your side. Now you feel like the most powerful person in the room, and you don't even have to worry about trusting God anymore. You've got your weapon."

♦ ♦ ♦

What changed in the last half-century that could have prompted evangelicals to reverse course on guns? And why? And, more urgently, can anything in heaven or down here on Earth persuade them to stop glorifying not only their weapons but their resistance to reimagining, in a restrained and sensible way, the Second Amendment?

These are questions of the highest consequence. For if we can't get evangelicals and the far-right congressional leaders they're propping up to at least discuss gun violence, any meaningful measures aimed at staunching the incessant flow of American blood appear destined to elude us.

In the chapters that follow, we'll explore why believers traded pacifism for pistols, when they came to view the Second Amendment as God-breathed, and how some evangelicals are even using shooting ranges to share their beliefs and grow their churches. We'll take a deeper dive into the culture of fear that has pervaded evangelicalism, visit a Christian-owned company that manufactures AR-15-style assault rifles, and learn how white evangelicals are defending gun rights in Congress and state legislatures. And we'll examine how evangelicals in other countries navigate the thorny ethics of gun ownership, see what dissident believers in the United States are doing to get firearms off the streets, and hear from prominent gun safety advocates and others about specific steps we can take to exit the vicious circle of our gun scourge, starting by treating it more like a public health challenge than a public safety crisis.

*Exit* is the operative word here. I long to leave the bloodshed behind. If you've read this far, you likely do, too.

But Genesis comes before Exodus, so first, let's retrace the history of "the gun gospel." How did faith in the Jesus who said "love your enemies" morph into a belief in God, guns, and politics? And more specifically, how did the Assemblies of God—the very denomination that introduced me to Jesus, and trained and commissioned me as a lay missionary—make the monumental leap from espousing pacifism to embracing concealed carry?

# 2 | HOW GUNS BECAME GOOD

In 1815, an American dreamer with wispy hair, a high forehead, and piercing blue eyes dipped a quill into an inkwell and penned a poem lamenting his young nation's losses at the end of the War of 1812. More than two centuries later, the twenty-one-year-old's pacifism still comes through his words:

> Hail sacred peace, thy gentle reign
> Is now restored to us again,
> Thy radiant smiles and cheerful voice,
> Bids every virtuous heart rejoice.
> But can thy smiles disburse the gloom
> That reigns within the warrior's tomb,
> Or can it assuage the widow's grief,
> Or to the orphan speak relief?

That poet's name drops loudly and incongruously today: Eliphalet Remington II.

Within a year, experimenting on the forge his father used to hammer out hoes, hatchets, and other farming tools in upstate New York, Remington would produce a flintlock rifle. That gun, superior to any other he'd fired in his pursuit of deer and partridge for the family's table, was the start of a firearms dynasty, one that would go on to outfit not only multiple generations of hunters but legions of soldiers in the United States and abroad.

Few are aware of Remington's pacifist leanings or the fact that his temperament was arguably more suited to his company's typewriters and sewing machines than its rifles and revolvers. He died in August 1861—just a few months into the Civil War—blissfully unaware of the terrible toll his guns would extract in that conflict, the Spanish-American War, World Wars I and II, and beyond.

Nor could he know, from his final resting place, that one particular Remington firearm would put twenty-six innocents in their own early graves in 2012: the Bushmaster .223 assault rifle, used to massacre twenty first graders and six teachers at Sandy Hook Elementary School in Newtown, Connecticut, not far from Eliphalet's birthplace in Suffield, Connecticut.

History doesn't record how Remington reconciled his Puritan faith with his profession as a purveyor of pistols. But his roots as a gunmaker with a gentle streak underscore how prevalent pacifism once was—in word, at least, if not always in deed. Today, by contrast, nonviolence as a virtue has pretty much gone the way of the buggy whip, even among the nation's most devoutly religious citizens.

Modern white evangelicals have no qualms about owning and carrying multiple handguns. Not even the Bushmaster or the equally lethal AR-15, the weapon of choice in so many mass shootings, give most born-again believers pause. That represents a significant break with long-standing Christian tradition.

And I mean *really* long-standing, as in stretching back across two millennia, all the way to the OG.

♦ ♦ ♦

In a back alley strewn with shards of broken pottery, rotting fruit, and other detritus of workaday life, menacing figures emerge from the shadows and approach a dozen men, who are huddled around a fire. There is a greeting, and a kiss, and then the scene erupts into chaos.

Amid shouting and swearing, weapons are brandished, and a scuffle ensues. Then the flash of a blade, screams, and bloodshed.

This clash was one for the ages. It went down in 33 CE, in the Garden of Gethsemane, on Israel's Mount of Olives, just outside Jerusalem. The target: Jesus of Nazareth.

Christ's betrayal at the point of a sword is arguably the closest the New Testament gets to gun violence. The first crude firearms using gunpowder to propel a projectile through a metal tube would not be invented for another thousand years, in China. But murderous violence has been around since our earliest days.

Some religious scholars point to the account in Genesis of Cain killing his brother Abel in a fit of jealousy six thousand years ago as the origin story of violence. Anthropologists, though, trace the use of deadly force to a 430-thousand-year-old skull found in a cave in northern Spain that bears the unmistakable marks of lethal—and deliberate—blunt force trauma. Experts who have examined Cranium 17, as it's known, say its owner died after a prehistoric perpetrator used a club or a rock to inflict two nearly identical blows on the victim's forehead in what they call "the earliest case of murder in the hominin fossil record." The skull was recovered from a deep shaft, and scientists theorize that the murderer likely tossed the body there, *Sopranos*-style, in an attempt to disappear the evidence. And a forensic analysis of the skeletal remains of Shanidar-3, a Neanderthal who lived about forty thousand years ago in what is now Iraq, shows he was fatally stabbed with a spear.

We haven't evolved much, have we? Cavemen: They're just like us.

Jesus was no stranger to violence, and he had plenty to say about it. For millennia, his followers have scrutinized, twisted, co-opted, and manipulated his words, recorded in the four Gospel accounts—Matthew, Mark, Luke, and John—to suit their political leanings.

At a time when white evangelicals double down on their Second Amendment right to bear arms, even as America is bloodied by mass shootings and other gun violence on an unprecedented scale, grasping something of the historical Christ's point of view seems prudent. Whether you personally care what Jesus taught about violence is beside the point, really; since evangelicals claim to follow his example, figuring out Jesus's perspective on violence is essential. And he was anything but ambivalent on the subject.

Informed by one of Judeo-Christianity's central tenets handed down from God to Moses and inscribed on a stone tablet as the sixth commandment—"Thou shalt not murder"—Jesus, with a few exceptions, took a decidedly dim view of violent struggle.

In his Gospel, Matthew quotes Christ as calling out hateful anger, which he considered to be as sinful and evil as a physical attack: "You have heard that it was said to the people long ago, 'You shall not murder, and anyone who murders will be subject to judgment.' But I tell you that anyone who is angry with a brother or sister will be subject to judgment" (Matt 5:21–22). It's a sentiment repeated in John's first letter to the early church: "Anyone who hates a brother or sister is a murderer, and you know that no murderer has eternal life residing in him" (1 John 3:15).

Then there's the biblical admonition to turn the other cheek, contained within Christ's Sermon on the Mount: "You have heard that it was said, 'Eye for eye, and tooth for tooth.' But I tell you, do not resist an evil person. If anyone slaps you on the right cheek, turn to them the other cheek also. And if anyone wants to sue you and take your shirt, hand over your coat as well. If anyone forces you to go one mile, go with them two miles" (Matt 5:38–41).

Jesus also said this: "You have heard that it was said, 'Love your neighbor and hate your enemy.' But I tell you, love your enemies and pray for those who persecute you" (Matt 5:43–44).

When he was arrested at Gethsemane and one of his disciples, Peter, drew a sword and sliced off the ear of the high priest's servant, Jesus condemned the act and healed the ear: "'Put your sword back in its place,' Jesus said to him, 'for all who draw the sword will die by the sword'" (Matt 26:52).

Skeptics, though, question why Jesus let Peter carry a sword in the first place. They also cite verses in which Christ appears to sanction weapons, such as, "Do not suppose that I have come to bring peace to the earth. I did not come to bring peace, but a sword" (Matt 10:34), and a particularly problematic quote in Luke 22:36, in which Jesus tells his inner circle, "If you don't have a sword, sell your cloak and buy one." The right-wing firearms advocacy organization Gun Owners of America frequently cites this passage, arguing that the sword in biblical times "was the finest offensive weapon available"—equivalent to a modern military assault rifle.

Yet, when you look at the overall arc of Jesus's words and actions, the takeaway is clear: Jesus Christ preached pacifism and nonviolent resistance. And pacifism was the early Christians' default way of looking at the world. Pacifism was the predominant view for the religion's first few embattled centuries—until the year 313 CE.

In a striking example of the old saying about there being no atheists in foxholes, the Roman emperor Constantine the Great had converted to Christianity the year prior, while fighting the Battle of Milvian Bridge—a military conquest that elevated him to the throne. Legend says he saw in the sky one of the early emblems of the faith, the Chi Rho (a Christogram formed by a sort of crude asterisk with a P sticking out of the top), and credited the Christian god for his subsequent victory over his rival, the emperor Maxentius.

In 313, walking the talk of his newfound faith, he issued a decree that ended the persecution of Christians and made it legal to be one. Encouraged by Constantine, believers joined the Roman army, and as the empire evolved into a Christian state, within a century its military became an all-Christian force.

Along with the Christianization of Roman civilization came the "just war" doctrine—the considerably fraught belief that sometimes military conflict, including the maiming and death of human beings, is morally or legally warranted, provided excessive force isn't used and the scope of the war is defined and limited. It's a concept that Christian thinkers would wrestle with and refine over the ensuing centuries. (It's also one that overzealous regimes twisted to suit their own ends, as evidenced by medieval Christianity's demonization, torture, and massacre of Muslims.)

A radical departure from that thinking came in the 1500s with the emergence of Anabaptism, a movement of Protestant reformers who rejected the just war tradition outright. Jesus, they reasoned, had taught his followers never to kill. An early Anabaptist confession, adopted in 1527, put it this way: "Thereby shall also fall away from us the diabolical weapons of violence—such as sword, armor, and the like, and all of their use to protect friends or against enemies—by virtue of the word of Christ: 'You shall not resist evil.'"

This sixteenth-century Christian pacifism was a pure and simple theology, one that emphasized love and unity. The Anabaptists' commitment to adult baptism, their rejection of the sword, and their refusal to swear oaths—all of which threatened the social order—cost many adherents their lives. Thousands were branded as heretics by fellow Christians, Protestants and Catholics alike, and were drowned or burned alive.

A century and a half later, the Society of Friends, more widely known as Quakers, preached pacifism in seventeenth-century England. The movement coalesced under the leadership of George Fox, whose spirituality was based on Jesus's Sermon on the Mount. That sermon contains the beatitudes, familiar to many of us as the "blessed are the [fill in the blank]" passage, in which Jesus gives a poetic rundown of who enjoys God's favor. The beatitudes are notable for their radical departure from our baser human instincts and hierarchies: *Blessed are the poor in spirit . . . blessed are the meek . . . blessed are the peacemakers . . . blessed are the persecuted.*

There's an account deeply embedded in Quaker mythology about one of the sect's best-known members in early America: William Penn, the peace-loving founder of the Pennsylvania colony. A friend said Penn recalled once using a broadsword as a teen to fight off an attacker on the streets of Paris; he had come to think of the weapon as "the means of saving his life without injuring his antagonist," but that his religious convictions eventually prompted him to stop carrying it. Although the veracity of that account is in some doubt, Quakers to this day are known for their avowed pacifism.

Alongside the Quakers were the Mennonites and the Brethren, like-minded religious groups whose members also embraced nonviolence. Collectively, these traditions, along with several others, comprise what became known as the peace churches. As the American colonies fomented war with Britain, these peace churches pressed for official recognition as conscientious objectors and were allowed to avoid military engagement. In fact, there was such respect for them that an early draft of the Bill of Rights, at James Madison's insistence, included conscientious objection during wartime as a constitutional right. It wasn't enacted, and some peace church faithful, perhaps sensing this issue would not end well for them, migrated to Canada.

In the 1800s, pacifism ran into a problem: slavery. There were, to be sure, plenty of pacifist Christians in the growing abolitionist movement, including William Lloyd Garrison, one of the most prominent abolitionists. Like many others, however, Garrison wrestled to square his strong convictions about nonviolence with the belief that only a civil war would end slavery, making it the ultimate just war. Dwight L. Moody, who founded the conservative Moody Bible Institute, also counted himself among the conflicted about when violence is justified: He refused to enlist but ministered to soldiers, Union and Confederate alike, on the battlefield. "There has never been a time in my life when I felt I could take a gun and shoot down a fellow human being," Moody said.

In a fascinating coincidence, another American gunmaker and son of Connecticut, Col. Samuel Colt, also died less than a year into the Civil War—just like his contemporary and competitor, Eliphalet Remington. The inventor of the Colt revolver that subdued the nation's Indigenous people succumbed to complications from gout. Colt died as one of the country's wealthiest citizens, having never fired a gun at another person.

The Church of the Good Shepherd, a lavishly decorated house of worship erected in Colt's memory by his widow, Elizabeth, still stands in Hartford in what is now a predominantly Latino immigrant neighborhood. It's known for its startlingly unsubtle architecture. One entrance, known as "the armorer's porch," is festooned with stone images of gun barrels and pistol handles incorporated into the crosses and other religious symbols.

◆ ◆ ◆

Acquiescing to the perceived need to defend the greater good by taking up arms in war, such as the one Abraham Lincoln presided over, laid a foundation for justifiable force in America. In the world wars that would follow, as Europe convulsed into ultranationalism in the 1900s, few American Christians rejected military service.

The great Christian writer and thinker C. S. Lewis even went as far as mocking nonviolence. Around 1940, in a talk to a group in his native England that was later published as an essay titled "Why I Am Not a Pacifist," Lewis insisted that Jesus's admonition to turn the other cheek couldn't possibly forbid intervening to protect a fellow human being. "Does anyone suppose that our Lord's hearers understood him to mean that if a homicidal maniac, attempting to murder a third party, tried to knock me out of the way, I must stand aside and let him get his victim?" he argued.

But then pacifism had a moment. In the aftermath of World War II, when Cold War tensions between the United States and the Soviet

Union soared amid fears of global nuclear annihilation, even the Vatican—which had long held a just war position—endorsed nonviolence as an equally defensible stance for Catholics, and the pope affirmed it in the church's official catechism. In 2007, an influential Vatican unity council and the Mennonite World Conference issued a joint statement affirming "Jesus' teaching and example of nonviolence as normative for Christians."

Early in the last century, most Pentecostal and many other evangelical denominations were also full-throated in their embrace of pacifist theology and ideology. Pacifism wasn't a popular position, as evidenced by the disproportionate numbers of evangelicals detained as conscientious objectors at Fort Leavenworth during World War I.

The Wesleyan Methodists, now the Wesleyan Church, preached pacifism. So did the Church of God, the Churches of Christ, and my old denomination, the Assemblies of God, today the world's largest Pentecostal faith community. In 1915, its official magazine, *The Pentecostal Evangel*, wrote that Pentecostals "are uncompromisingly opposed to war, having much the same spirit as the early Quakers, who would rather be shot themselves than that they should shed the blood of their fellow men."

And as the US entered World War I in 1917, the Assemblies of God's General Council proclaimed: "We cannot conscientiously participate in war and armed resistance which involves the actual destruction of human life, since this is contrary to our view of the clear teachings of the inspired Word of God which is the sole basis of our faith." That was the denomination's default position for fifty years, until 1967, when its official teaching began emphasizing "the authority of the individual conscience."

Paul Alexander, a professor of theology and ethics at Azusa Pacific University, argues in a 2009 book that this shift came about as the Assemblies of God increasingly associated with mainstream American culture. At the height of the Vietnam War, the denomination jumped on a growing establishment bandwagon that advocated patriotism, Republicanism, traditional American values, and hawkish support for US troops and military operations.

But there was also pushback. In 1968, after Robert F. Kennedy's fatal shooting, the Southern Baptist Convention (SBC)—today fiercely opposed to tampering with the Second Amendment—endorsed then-President Lyndon B. Johnson's plea for Congress to pass laws "to bring the insane traffic in guns to a halt." The SBC said at the time that it was throwing its support behind firearms restrictions because "under God, we want to do right."

So how and when did denominations pivot toward theologies that blessed the ownership of lethal weapons? Daniel K. Williams, a professor of history at the University of West Georgia, says evangelicals and members of more liberal mainline Protestant denominations hit a fork in the road in the late 1960s in terms of their thinking about guns. In a post on the faith blogging platform *Patheos*, he traces their divergence to strikingly different ideologies put forward by two influential religious magazines: *The Christian Century*, a liberal Protestant publication whose editorial board included Martin Luther King Jr., and the evangelical monthly *Christianity Today*.

*The Christian Century*, Williams says, had made support for the nonviolent civil rights movement its signature cause. "The magazine's devotion to nonviolent civil rights advocacy led the editors to question the US military commitment in Vietnam and to begin openly denouncing it in 1963," he writes. "By contrast, *Christianity Today* was skeptical of the nonviolent civil rights movement and fully supportive of the Vietnam War. Violence against international communism was justified, the evangelicals who wrote for *Christianity Today* believed. So was the violence used by American police. Billy Graham, *Christianity Today*, and many other white evangelicals were strong advocates of 'law and order' in the late 1960s."

That friction would become a full-blown rift. "While these differing attitudes toward violence in various contexts paved the way for a split between liberal Protestants and evangelicals over gun laws, it was not yet apparent in the late 1960s that this would become a point of significant division between the two groups," Williams writes. "In 1967, *The Christian Century* published three editorials in favor of gun control—which may have been the first time that the magazine had weighed in on the issue, since it had said nothing directly about gun legislation from 1960 to 1966, despite numerous editorials in favor of nonviolence during that period."

As a Cold War sense of fear and fatalism settled over the West, a macho, masculine, almost warrior-like view of Jesus became popular among white evangelicals. Many rejected the somewhat waifish, effeminate Christ portrayed in some Renaissance paintings in favor of a muscular Marlboro Man messiah—a tough-guy God whose image and likeness remain embedded within the evangelical ethos today. "In the 1960s and 1970s, conservative evangelicals would be drawn to a nostalgic, rugged masculinity as they looked to reestablish white patriarchal authority in its many guises," writes Kristin Kobes Du Mez, author of the bestseller *Jesus and John Wayne: How White Evangelicals Corrupted a Faith and Fractured a Nation*.

White evangelicals also scorned the liberation theology that became popular across Latin America, along with its Black and feminist iterations. Nonviolence was a central theme for liberation theologians and religious activists intent on breaking the cycle of violence in developing countries. It was a noble concept, but not for evangelicals, who felt the emphasis on lifting people out of poverty and oppression supplanted traditional efforts to preach the Christian message of salvation and elevated Marxism. Those evangelicals did not see the irony in the US government's brutal response in Latin America: a "Christian nation" dispatching its CIA to actively support the anti-communist death squads that killed tens of thousands of people simply because of their politics.

Underscoring the shift in how evangelicals were coming to view Jesus—and, by extension, themselves—is the fact that denominations like the Southern Baptists became noticeably more politically engaged in rightward politics. By the early 2000s, Kobes Du Mez notes, some evangelicals had begun raising their sons as "future warriors," partly in response to Douglas Wilson's *Future Men*—a book replete with encouragement for boys to play with toy guns so they'd be ready as men to defend their wives, their homes, and their nation.

These shifting currents in the white evangelical mainstream help to explain why former Major League Baseball star Adam LaRoche showed up at an NRA meeting in a T-shirt that proclaimed, with no irony: *Jesus loves me and my guns*. And why Rucki's, a folksy general store just over the Rhode Island state line in Connecticut and less than an hour's drive from my home, hangs a banner advertising *Beer, Bibles, Bullets, Books*, and asserts on its website: "Jesus Christ, the Marlboro Man and [nineteenth-century gunmaker] John Browning are all represented equally in our store."

When white evangelicals assert their right to own and carry weapons, they're ignoring how guns more broadly affect society—particularly vulnerable populations—says Christopher B. Hays, a Presbyterian minister and a professor at Fuller Theological Seminary. In 2021, he notes, Black Americans were 13.7 times more likely to die in a gun homicide than white Americans, and Latinos were 2.4 times as likely. "As a nation, we seem inured to the situation," Hays says, writing in *The Presbyterian Outlook*. "The minute parsing of Bible verses about swords misses the forest for the trees: Jesus was not a violent revolutionary, and his disciples continued to die for their faith. They were not famed for their martial skills, nor did they lead squads of fighters."

◆ ◆ ◆

Fast-forward to our bellicose modern era of hyper-partisanship and political polarization. These days, Christian gun ownership barely registers in a society marked by metaphorical if not literal saber rattling.

Having long ago abandoned their traditional reluctance to carry firearms for personal protection, many evangelicals now have no qualms about even bringing them to church. Some go even further, acquiring and stockpiling multiple weapons—in extreme cases, constructing elaborate underground bunkers stocked with ammunition, jugs of water, and crates of freeze-dried food—as part of what's become known as "doomsday prep." Such militant anti-government behavior used to be highly suspect and a good way to wind up on a federal watchlist. Now, in certain circles, it's not merely socially acceptable but seen as a noble and even spiritual act.

This environment has bred religious extremists like David Barton. In 2005, *Time* magazine included him among America's twenty-five "most influential" evangelicals. That turned out to be prophetic, and not in a good way: Barton is using his influence to spread the dangerous ideology that the constitutional separation of church and state is a myth. He has also partnered with the founder of Patriot Academy, a Texas-based organization that provides gun training with "constitutional education" centered on Christian supremacy.

It has also produced right-wing, gun-enthusiastic pastors like Quinton Rowan, whom we met in chapter 1—the one who's been thinking of putting up a menacing sign, *We don't call 911*, outside his Assemblies of God church in Greenwood, Arkansas, a few miles from the Oklahoma state line. Greenwood, population 9,605, is the sort of homespun Bible Belt country town that coal miners built. Its townsfolk place a premium on law and order, and its once snake-infested 1892 fieldstone jail, with thick medieval-style walls, draws the occasional tourist. So does its clock and bell tower memorializing an act of God: a devastating F4 tornado that nearly wiped the town off the map in 1968, killing fourteen and injuring 270.

The community's official motto is *Feels like home*. And Rowan clearly embraces the so-called castle doctrine—the notion that people have a justifiable right to use deadly force against an intruder—to protect Vital Church, his spiritual home.

A decade ago, Rowan was among several pastors who successfully lobbied the Arkansas state legislature to enact a law allowing gun owners to conceal a weapon in a church if they hold an "enhanced" carry license. In addition to that exception, which also covers bringing a gun into other "sensitive" venues such as a college building or a state office, Arkansas has been a permitless concealed carry state since 2019. "I would like to have a couple of guys licensed to carry and have them carrying within the church," he told the *Fort Smith Times Record* newspaper.

One hundred and fifty miles to the east, in Little Rock, the Reverend David Freeman of First United Methodist Church doesn't share Rowan's vision of church security. His congregation has banned firearms under an opt-out provision in the law. "It keeps us guarded and focused on fear and focused on 'What are the dangers out there?' rather than seeing the world through, 'What are the opportunities for love and to build community?'" he told NPR.

But Freeman is in the minority. And among the majority, gun doctrine can border on the objectively grotesque.

A 108-page self-published manifesto by evangelical hard-liner Greg Perry entitled *God & Guns* has a subtitle that reads, in part, *Kill Attackers in Christian Love*. The final chapter is titled "Sometimes You Love Your Enemies by Killing Them." Perry, an Oklahoman who contends pacifism is a sin and men who dislike guns are weak and effeminate, explains: "Do all in your physical power to kill your intended murderer in Christian love . . . Killing your attacker in Christian love is the best way to witness to others what should be done when faced with life-threatening, Satan-levels of violence." He agrees that giving children toy guns is inappropriate—but not in the way you might think, given this advice: "Get your kids real guns."

Brant Williams, who owns and operates Frontier Firearms in Tennessee, offers customers a discount if they profess their faith in Jesus in the store while browsing for a gun. Williams told reporters he started the discounts because "America is turning its back on Christians." He also promotes his own line of lapel pins that bear the message, *I am Christian and I carry*, along with dubiously cherrypicked scripture verses from Nehemiah, Luke, and Ephesians.

And Mark Rogers, a professional dog trainer in Fort Smith, Arkansas, runs the Christian Gun Owner website and Facebook page, where he posts instructional videos that teach believers how to improve their stance, aim, and accuracy while firing at human-shaped cardboard tactical targets. "Are you a Christian? Are you a Patriot? Are you a Gun Owner? Any combination of those?" he asks visitors to his home page, assuring them that if the answer is yes, they've found their tribe. Rogers also peddles a thirty-five-page guide for churches that want to form a "ministry" of armed volunteer security guards.

"Despite God's commands to trust him in times of despair, evangelicals have always been very fearful people," historian John Fea, himself an evangelical, writes in *Believe Me: The Evangelical Road to Donald Trump*. It's tempting to think of evangelicals' culture of fear as a recent phenomenon. We'll look in more depth at the nexus of fear and firearms in chapter 5. But fear has been an entrenched part of conservative Christianity for as long as I've been associated with it, and tracing the genealogy of fear in white evangelicalism may help us understand its salience today.

◆ ◆ ◆

The fear factor was never far from my mind when I first believed in the early 1980s. Initially, I thought fear was merely a harmless holdover from our church's uptight elders—those who'd barely navigated the '70s in plaid polyester with their faith and morals intact and who had emerged terrified of secular society. But as I embraced evangelicalism, I soon realized its adherents had reduced the culture all around us to a supercharged and singularly menacing term: the World.

In any other context, a "worldly" person is one to be admired. They are elegant and educated; well-read, well-groomed, well-dressed, and well-traveled. They speak multiple languages and are conversant and insightful about politics and pop culture alike. Truth be told, I'd aspired—even and perhaps especially as a Christian—to be worldly. I wanted to be Mr. Darcy, not a character in *Duck Dynasty*.

In many evangelicals' eyes, however, the World is evil and extraterrestrial; a place to be avoided at all costs. My church quickly disabused me of the notion that worldliness was a good trait and showed me the error of my ways—though it didn't take long for me to see the error in theirs. Instead of hitting the bars, we gathered weekly for Bible study, prayer, and something called "fellowship"—basically hanging out minus pot, pills, or booze. That part was more than fine: I'd already done a lifetime's worth of drinking and drugging in my youth.

Beyond that, and despite our piety, we were like any other pod of twentysomethings. There were hookups, heavy petting, and in at least one instance I became aware of, intercourse: a clear violation of purity culture, but nothing the Almighty wouldn't forgive. A few couples swiftly wed, mindful of that New Testament verse admonishing horny believers: "It is better to marry than to burn with passion" (1 Cor 7:9). In 1980s evangelicalism, "with passion" was often deliberately omitted, leaving panicked young lovers to squirm at the thought of hell itself as the eternal price of their guilty pleasure.

Twice on Sundays, we'd join our elders for fiery sermons more frequently bellowed than preached, usually by a pacing, physically imposing pastor with a silver pompadour. Our pastor was an archetypal evangelist straight out of Hollywood central casting, seemingly capable of calling down fire and brimstone at will. Charismatic in every sense of the term, he'd later serve eighteen months in federal prison for trying to bribe a consular officer with $3,000 in cash in exchange for visas to help Haitians escape their impoverished homeland. His heart, most of my friends believed, was in the right place. I wasn't so sure. There were other signs that evangelicals might not be the peaceable people of God I'd initially imagined. Some of those signs blinked yellow. Others flashed full-on red.

My new faith promised freedom, but it also preached fear: Jesus was returning soon, and woe to any of us who weren't ready. Youth groups regularly screened a cheesy 1972 film, *A Thief in the Night*, striking the same terror within our souls that Tim LaHaye and Jerry B. Jenkins's *Left Behind* books would reprise two decades later. Both invoked the biblical "rapture": the idea that Christ would suddenly whisk away believers before his triumphal second coming. "No man knows the hour or the day," the preachers warned, paraphrasing Matthew 24:36.

At church, we joyously sang songs like "I'm Gonna Be Gone," which celebrates the imminent exit of Christians, who would be taken up into heaven. But privately, many of us anguished over the possibility—to neurotic me, the *likelihood*—that we'd be caught caving to our humanity at that fateful moment. What were the odds, I wondered, that I'd be flipping off a driver, taking the Lord's name in vain or, heaven forbid, masturbating at the very nanosecond of his return? Decades later, I still fear making a misstep that I'll rue for eternity, and wind up grounded permanently to Earth by my own feet of clay.

Among the faithful were some inexplicably drawn to vile little pamphlets known as "Chick tracts." These miniature comic books by the late evangelical cartoonist Jack Chick attempted to convert readers through a caustic combination of guilt, shame, and fear, as well as loathing of anyone who didn't hew exactly to fundamentalist teaching. In Chick's world of hateful tropes, feminism was a social ill, homosexuality was demonic, and the Roman Catholic Church was the biblical Great Whore of Babylon led by Satan himself. Chick tracts nauseated me even from the start of my Christian journey, but apparently not one of my roommates, who'd left one atop the toilet in the ramshackle New England farmhouse we shared. When a dear friend—a devout Catholic—came to visit, he stormed out of the bathroom understandably indignant, and it took months for me to repair the damage.

*Fear God* has been a biblical admonition—an appeal to our better angels—for millennia. It's a recurring theme in scripture, most notably in Proverbs 9:10: "The fear of the Lord is the beginning of wisdom." Biblical scholars say *fear* in most instances is better translated as "respect" or "awe"; it's not the same as cowering in terror. But its classic meaning is a high-caliber weapon in the hands of Christian nationalists using the siege mentality of apocalypticism to draw people to their cause and bend them to their will.

The Ku Klux Klan took advantage of the same vulnerability half a century ago, as it sought to gain members and influence by tapping white evangelicals' supremacist tendencies. Fear was palpable again at the turn of the twentieth century in a virulently fearful Y2K movement, hijacked by some evangelicals, forerunners to today's Christian nationalists, who were stockpiling fuel, weapons, and canned goods while prophesying the end of civilization as we knew it.

And fear was front and center during the COVID 19 pandemic, when a few boisterous white evangelical pastors pushed back on government lockdowns, falsely characterizing them as an attempt to shut down their churches. Millions of conservative Christians refused vaccination, insisting the federal government was using it as a sinister subterfuge to inject them with microchips. Among them were some who claimed proof-of-vaccination cards were the biblical "mark of the beast"—a reference to end-times prophecy in Revelation foretelling a time when people won't be able to buy or sell goods unless they bear a mark symbolizing their devotion to evil.

I was initially relieved when a white evangelical pastor friend, a fellow New Englander who now lives in the South, texted me at the height of the pandemic to ask my advice about getting vaccinated. I shared with him my deeply held conviction that the speedy development of multiple vaccines was nothing short of a medical miracle: God's gift of mercy to humanity through science. In the end, though, I was dismayed to learn that he and his family opted not to be vaccinated—a decision that nearly cost his wife her life, when she became grievously sick with COVID-19 and had to be hospitalized.

◆ ◆ ◆

Not all fears, of course, are unfounded. Flight—like fight—is hardwired into our genetic coding to help ensure our survival. We *do* live in a violent, crime-ridden society, and not even houses of worship are immune or impervious to gunmen with murderous intent—something many evangelicals see as justification for bringing their guns everywhere they go. They point to the 2017 massacre of twenty-six worshipers at a Baptist church in Sutherland Springs, Texas—as of early 2025, the worst mass shooting at a church in US history—as ample reason to be armed at the altar. That bloodbath ended when an armed neighbor, plumber and former firearms instructor Stephen Willeford—a quasi-mythical "good guy with a gun"—used his own AR-15 to shoot the gunman.

"I responded to what God told me to do," Willeford later told an NRA gathering, to wild cheers. In his remarks, he called himself a "sheepdog"—an increasingly popular designation within evangelical circles, in which it is said there are three kinds of people: sheep, sheepdogs, and wolves.

"The Holy Spirit took care of me, watched over me. Each one of you would have done the same thing. I'm here today to tell you that Jesus Christ is my shepherd. What happened in Sutherland Springs was all him, and it's his glory," he said to a standing ovation.

Why do I describe "good guys with guns" as quasi-mythical? After all, they've helped subdue other shooters, including the woman who opened fire inside Joel Osteen's Houston church in 2024 and the man who began shooting during Sunday morning services at West Freeway Church of Christ in White Settlement, Texas, in 2019. The enduring belief that law-abiding gun owners keep lawlessness in check has been around since at least the 1970s, when bumper stickers warned us: *If guns are outlawed, only outlaws will have guns.* And it remains the number one argument in favor of unfettered civilian access to firearms.

But numerous studies have shown that although a well-trained, highly skilled, cool-headed everyman with a gun does occasionally manage to avert greater loss of life, it happens far, far less frequently than the NRA would have you think. Harvard University researchers who analyzed data from the National Crime Victimization Survey spanning 2007 to 2011 concluded that gun owners manage to successfully defend themselves in fewer than 1 percent of crimes. Another study found the percentage of people who used their gun in self-defense is similar to the number of Americans who claim they've been abducted by aliens (about 3 percent.) "Self-defense gun use is a rare event," concludes David Hemenway, lead author of the Harvard study.

Even so, the "good guy with a gun" mythology persists—so much that it's spawned a lively and lucrative cottage industry. A leader in the space is the Faith-Based Security Network, a Kansas-based group that advises churches and other religious organizations on how to protect themselves. Founder Carl Chinn—who was held hostage at gunpoint in 1996 while working at Focus on the Family, a global Colorado-based conservative Christian ministry once led by James Dobson—says more than a thousand US churches now have volunteer armed security details.

"There's a deep moral and ethical question here," the Reverend Rob Schenk, a leading anti-gun advocate, tells me in an interview. "That is: 'When is a Christian permitted to kill another human being and under what circumstances?' Any church that is going to introduce firearms into the life of that church has to address that question."

Schenck poses another deep and somewhat disturbing question: "Are we certain that it is always God's will that we survive a violent encounter?" It's something I've been thinking about a lot lately, and my pondering has led me to a question of my own: *Is there such a thing as a good death?* Because I'll be honest with you: Although I don't want to die—I even wrote a book about living to a hundred—if my end comes while I'm worshiping at church, I'll consider that a good death. Guns, for me, are hopelessly out of place within the walls of a house of worship.

Schenck, who's more of a pragmatist than I, grounds our conversation with an appeal to reason: "Even if you use your weapon, how can you be so sure you'll prevail?"

"I'm not saying it's God's will that we all be martyrs," he tells me. "We can be smart. We can be careful. But the chances are very, very high that even if you empty your entire magazine, you won't hit your target. There's a reason why it takes three police officers, each unloading their full magazines, to bring down a perpetrator—because the odds are absolutely against you. The fantasy that you raise the gun, you fire a single shot, the silver bullet takes down the perpetrator, and you are the hero is a complete fantasy."

Few evangelicals, Schenck concedes, are receptive to such arguments.

◆ ◆ ◆

In the broad scheme of things, is the answer to guns everywhere really more guns? Are we supposed to "harden" the perimeter around churches like some insist we must around America's schools—posting police officers or full-time armed guards, installing metal detectors, and running parishioners, like pupils, through active shooter drills?

None of those things has stopped school shootings. In fact, they're sharply increasing. According to the K-12 School Shooting Database, there have been more than one thousand incidents involving firearms on school property since 2018. In 2024 alone, 267 people were killed or wounded on school grounds, the database shows. That happened while 98 percent of all K–12 public schools reported regularly drilling students on lockdown procedures—simulations that can be incredibly stressful and traumatic for young children and their families.

As guns proliferate, faith leaders—though few of them evangelical—increasingly are speaking out. In a series of essays published in *God and Guns: The Bible Against American Gun Culture*, progressive Christian scholars take aim at the wobbly theology believers are using to justify arming themselves. Theologians like Christopher Hays, whom we met earlier, go straight for the jugular with questions as thorny and fraught as: *Can a Christian own a gun?* "Guns give us the power to kill instantaneously, and the New Testament does not countenance our seizure of such power—even in self-defense," he writes, adding: "Any Christianity that supports guns as a solution to social problems is not Christianity at all."

Hays continues: "Guns are like a wildfire that becomes more powerful the bigger it gets. The more people who have guns, the more dangerous our society is. The more dangerous our society is, the more people want guns. The more people believe that they need guns to solve their problems, the more problems guns cause. . . . Wielding power over life and death is not the way that God calls me to live. . . . To place my trust in guns is to deny my trust in God."

T. M. Lemos, an associate professor at Huron University and a faculty member at the University of Western Ontario's graduate school, wonders aloud about the generally phallic shape of a gun and sees something suspiciously Freudian at play involving masculinity and virility. She quotes R. W. Connell, a renowned Australian sociologist and gender theorist, who notes: "Gun organizations are conventionally masculine in cultural style . . . The gun lobby hardly has to labor the inference that politicians taking away our guns are emasculating us."

"This is not the vision that Jesus Christ fulfilled—quite the contrary," Lemos insists. "His crucifixion refutes, in the most dramatic way possible, the conception that divine favor rests with those who make prey of other human beings. It is remarkable that so many Christians seem not to see this."

In a conclusion to the collection *God and Guns* written by Hays and C. L. Crouch, a religious scholar at Radboud University Nijmegen in the Netherlands and at South Africa's University of Pretoria, the pair lowers the boom on evangelicals with guns at the ready. "Too many Christians worship the gun instead of God, and too few Christians protest," they write. "Authentic Christian identity is incompatible with an identity based on gun ownership. . . . To derive a sense of safety from the ability to kill your neighbor instantly is incompatible with the command to love your neighbor."

Jay Reuker, a friend of mine and fly-fishing partner, distills all of this into a single damning word: idolatry. Gunshots occasionally ring out near his home in a lively enclave on the south side of Providence, Rhode Island. But Reuker, a retired high school history teacher and a deeply committed Christian with a background most would consider traditionally evangelical, says it has never entered his mind to arm himself. "Can we please just call it what it is: idolatry?" he asks as we sip coffee in a friend's kitchen during a Bible study break.

The concept of idols is introduced early in the Old Testament. Delivering the Ten Commandments to Moses, God in Exodus 20:5 includes a stern warning to people not to create or worship any image or likeness of anything in the sky, on the earth, or in the water: "You shall not bow down to them or worship them; for I, the Lord your God, am a jealous God."

For pro-gun Christians, though, the Second Commandment often takes a back seat to another passage many consider sacrosanct: the Second Amendment. And there are almost as many ways to translate *that* as there are versions of scripture itself.

# 3 | A WELL-REGULATED MILITIA

At the height of the Middle Ages, in 1234 CE, Pope Gregory IX was reckoning with a hostile work environment. In this setting, marked by frequent run-ins with Holy Roman Emperor Frederick II, Pope Gregory approved a military order and put Dominican friars in charge of it.

The order's rather startling name? The Militia of Jesus Christ.

These militia members were basically Christian commandos who banded together to combat heresy. If they showed up at your door, you were done for. Theirs was a mission thick with irony, considering their pacifist namesake, Jesus.

Unlike members of other Roman Catholic religious orders such as the Knights Templar, these knights didn't take vows of chastity or poverty; nor did they live in community. Also known as the Militia Christi, the ancient order, now based in Paris, remains active to this day. The Militia of Jesus Christ currently operates on four continents—although rather than raising broadswords menacingly above their helmets, their modern members raise money for charity.

Like the Crusaders, who separated innumerable infidels' heads from their bodies, the Militia's thirteenth-century soldiers of Christ bore arms. But they were also held to strict rules of engagement regarding when and how they were permitted to use them. Weapons were to be carried only when deemed necessary, and they were to be deployed only "in defense of the Church." The rules were essential for reining in the bloodlust of a ruthless breed of knight, men historian Richard Weber describes as "a ruffianly lot; mafia types in armor."

As misguided and fatally flawed as its premise was, the Militia Christi was the epitome of a "well-regulated militia."

And eight centuries later, that concept divides us like no other.

♦ ♦ ♦

Never has the English language so riven society quite like the twenty-seven words that bestow upon Americans the right to have and carry guns:

> A well regulated Militia, being necessary to the security of a free State, the right of the people to keep and bear Arms, shall not be infringed.

The Second Amendment, easily the Constitution's single most hotly debated and misunderstood clause, has been the law of the land since its ratification on December 15, 1791. And over the past century, it has become both a major judicial battleground and ground zero in the culture wars. It has enabled militant white evangelicals—misperceiving largely nonexistent governmental threats to their way of life—to circle the wagons, arm themselves, and gird for conflict.

Ask pretty much anyone how to interpret the amendment, and the questions pop like rifle fire in rapid succession: What does "well-regulated" mean? What was the militia then, and what is it now? What kind of arms are we talking about, and for what modern purpose? What constitutes infringement?

Little wonder the Second Amendment is shrouded in such confusion. Americans have been asking themselves some of these questions even before the United States was a nation.

Gun control is nothing new. For many conservative Christians and others who embrace modern firearms culture, this bit of history is lost to the sands of time, but the United States had far tighter gun controls in its infancy—and even more restrictive laws while it was still a British colony. In fact, from the late 1600s to the end of the 1800s, there were thousands of gun regulations on the books, says Robert Spitzer, the Jesuit scholar and firearms historian we met in chapter 1. Concealed carry was against the law in nearly every state. And even during the heyday of the Wild West a century and a half ago, settlers had to turn in their guns when they entered a populated area and retrieve them when they left.

Our contemporary desire to shrink the glut of guns is noble, but we must tread carefully because, historically, gun control has its roots in racism. Those early laws were written to allow white Americans unfettered access to firearms while keeping them out of the hands of the Black and Indigenous Americans they saw as a threat to the nascent nation. Writing in the *Harvard Law Review*, UCLA law professor Adam Winkler retraces how white colonists and settlers were determined to ensure that Blacks, whether enslaved or free, remained unarmed. In 1825, a Florida law authorized white people "to enter into all Negro houses . . . [and] lawfully seize and take away all such arms, weapons, and ammunition." Winkler's takeaway: "For much of American history, gun rights did not extend to Black people and gun control was often enacted to limit access to guns by people of color."

For better or worse, the gun, it's fair to say, has become not only part of our national identity but a strand of something frighteningly powerful, frustratingly polarizing, and, for many believers, inextricably intertwined with their spiritual DNA.

The Second Amendment's history began well before the young nation's Congress ratified it in 1791 as part of the Bill of Rights. Had you asked the founders about it, they'd have invoked Queen Elizabeth I's decision in the late 1500s to institute a national militia—a fighting force that was no respecter of persons. By decree of the monarch, individuals, regardless of their wealth or social rank, were required to take part to defend the realm.

## IN GUNS WE TRUST

During the Revolutionary War era, militias consisted of groups of trained men who banded together to protect their towns and colonies, and by the time the United States had won its independence, and the Constitution was drafted, they were organized by the states. Each town was required to have at least one company of about sixty men at the ready to serve as the first line of defense in the event of an attack by British army regulars. These part-time armies—made up of farmers, blacksmiths, and other craftsmen and tradesmen—also formed a pool that colonial leaders could rely on when they needed to draft soldiers for extended service. They were required to be armed "as according to law." At the time, that meant a musket, a pound of gunpowder, at least twenty bullets, and a sword as a backup.

Barely a dozen years after the war, when the Constitution was being ratified, there was considerable handwringing about the role of armed forces in American society. The founders were deeply suspicious of maintaining a standing federal army, which they feared a tyrant could use against citizens, to keep them in line. Militias overseen by the states and made up of ordinary folk—husbands, fathers, sons, uncles, neighbors—seemed a much more palatable alternative.

But skeptics worried that militias themselves could pose an existential threat to liberty—a notion that Alexander Hamilton sought to dispel in a series of essays we now call the Federalist Papers. In one published on January 10, 1788, Hamilton wrote indignantly: "Where in the name of common-sense, are our fears to end if we may not trust our sons, our brothers, our neighbors, our fellow-citizens? What shadow of danger can there be from men who are daily mingling with the rest of their countrymen and who participate with them in the same feelings, sentiments, habits and interests?"

The message resonated among Hamilton's contemporaries precisely because of the context that, a few years later, would provide the bedrock for the Second Amendment: Gun ownership, apart from hunting game, was in service of the state—not the individual.

That the messenger was Hamilton is the ultimate irony, given he died in a gun duel with the sitting vice president, Aaron Burr, over personal and political conflicts. Everything about guns in America, it often seems, is marked by duplicity and hypocrisy.

◆ ◆ ◆

All of this begs two questions: What is a militia in our time? And what does "well-regulated" really mean?

Gun control advocates won't like this, but most constitutional scholars agree that "well-regulated" in the late eighteenth century didn't refer to a plethora of rules and restrictions, as many interpret it today, but rather to "well-trained" and "well-prepared." Militias needed to be ready to go at a moment's notice, which is why they trained regularly—an aspect of readiness (or "regulation") that was important enough for the founders to include in the amendment.

As for what constitutes a militia, the conservative Heritage Foundation think tank, a chief architect of conservatives' Project 2025 plan to exert far-right control over the federal government, answers bluntly: It is the citizenry. "Where is the militia today? Despite a common suggestion that the militia exists today only in the form of the National Guard, the modern militia exists today in the same place it did in 1791—in the body of the people trained to use firearms," it says.

Walter Clemens Jr., a professor emeritus of political science at Boston University, counters such an argument. "Surely the authors of the Constitution had in mind a militia organized by and subject to the government," he writes, "not a ragtag crowd of ruffians carrying shotguns and AK-47s around an abortion clinic or into the US Capitol."

Eliga Gould, a professor of history at the University of New Hampshire, also takes issue with broader interpretations that extend Second Amendment rights to private citizen militias. "If the founders were alive today, I believe they would be very concerned," he writes in a commentary for *The Conversation*.

Regardless of how you interpret the term, it's clear that today's militias are far from the altruistic citizen armies-in-waiting that stood ready to defend the common good in 1791. They are extremist groups including the Oath Keepers, Proud Boys, and Three Percenters. Members of these groups and other militias played lead roles in the January 6, 2021, insurrectionist attack on Washington's seat of power.

Florida televangelist Paula White, Donald Trump's spiritual adviser and a purveyor of the "Big Lie" that the 2020 presidential election was stolen, prayed over the crowd assembled for the January 6 Save America march. "Give us a holy boldness," she asked God, shouting into the same microphone the disgraced former president used to urge his supporters to "fight like hell."

"Let every adversary against democracy, against freedom, against life, against liberty, against justice, against peace, against righteousness be overturned right now in the name of Jesus," White exhorted. Her prayer was answered not by a divine hand but by a mob's rage.

A cadre of mostly white evangelicals, convinced they were in the center of God's will for standing with a president anointed by the Almighty, waved signs and flags invoking Christian nationalism, wore *God, Guns, Trump* caps, quoted scripture, and thanked the Lord for allowing America to be born again. Then they joined others in laying siege to the Capitol. By day's end, police officers were beaten, a rioter was fatally shot, and three others would die. The domed edifice—an icon of peaceable American democracy—was in shambles.

The facts of January 6 are not in doubt, regardless of the MAGA movement's revisionist insistence on calling the insurrectionists "patriots" and those serving prison sentences for vandalism and violent assault "hostages." But a question that has haunted many since is this: What if more of the rioters had guns?

Some did, despite the false narrative that they were all unarmed. They included a Trump supporter who was videotaped firing two shots into the air outside the Capitol and later commented in an Instagram post: "There's a war going on between the truths of God and the lies of this world the flesh and the devil." Among the most chilling images of that day was a photograph of a masked man, clad in black and camouflage fatigues and a tactical vest and carrying a holstered stun gun and plastic zip ties, vaulting over railings in the US Senate gallery. He was later identified as Eric Munchel. In an interview with Britain's *Sunday Times* newspaper, Munchel described the attack as "a kind of flexing of muscles" intended to show federal officials what Christian nationalist extremists could do.

In a telling comment on his way to the Capitol, witnesses say Munchel said: "Jesus saves, and so do guns." Federal agents who later searched his Nashville home found fifteen firearms, including assault rifles, a sniper rifle with a tripod, other rifles, shotguns and pistols, and hundreds of rounds of ammunition, according to a federal prosecutor's memo urging Munchel be detained pending trial. He was eventually convicted of federal felony conspiracy, obstruction, and weapons charges and sentenced to nearly five years in prison.

What many people miss about January 6 is that it wasn't a one-off. Rather, it reflected the increasing entrenchment of militia culture—stoked by Christian nationalist acrimony—in American society.

The white evangelical language and imagery of January 6 have been painstakingly documented by Christians Against Christian Nationalism, and its sixty-page report on evangelical complicity reads like a biblical lament. The group recorded statements made in support of the rioters by conservative radio host Eric Metaxas, who has promoted conspiracy theories alleging that leftist antifa demonstrators impersonated Trump supporters. Christians Against Christian Nationalism's report also included swift denunciations by believers like Bible teacher Beth Moore, who posted on Twitter (now X) that day: "I don't know the Jesus some have paraded and waved around in the middle of this treachery today. They may be acting in the name of some other Jesus but that's not Jesus of the Gospels."

Evangelical Christian nationalism runs so deep that it's even been embraced by the Speaker of the House. Republican Mike Johnson, a leader of the "Stop the Steal" movement that fraudulently declared Trump the rightful winner of the 2020 presidential election, has intimate ties to the New Apostolic Reformation, a network of politically ambitious church leaders who believe supernatural forces of good and evil are locked in a literal battle for control of the US. Democrats and progressives, they insist, are influenced by the demonic. And true Christians (always, in their view, conservative Republicans) are called by God to exercise dominion over their ideological opponents—not just in government but in education, the media, and other spheres of influence.

Some of the incendiary pro-gun Christian nationalistic rhetoric that emerged *after* January 6 is especially disturbing, because it underscores how widespread and deeply held the cause has become. Ahead of Joe Biden's inauguration on January 20, 2021, for example, Texas pastor Brandon Burden urged his congregation at Kingdom Life Church to keep their guns loaded. "I do believe in the Second Amendment," Burden said in a sermon livestreamed on Facebook. "If you do have weapons, please make sure you have them loaded." He also urged his flock to stock up on food and water, make sure their generators were fueled, and buy shortwave radios.

Pugnacious Pentecostal pastor, Christian ultranationalist, and staunch pro-gun advocate Micah Beckwith, elected in 2024 as Indiana's lieutenant governor, posted a video the day after January 6 saying God told him He sent the rioters to Washington and the outcome "was My hand at work." More recently, on the far-right Christian podcast *For the King*, Beckwith has warned Americans to wake up to the culture wars or reckon with "bullets and bombs."

Increasingly, far-right actors are garnishing their conspiracy theories with Christian symbolism and thinly veiled threats of violence as they preach replacing democracy with Christo-fascist theocracy. Witness Christian nationalist and alt-right online activist Jack Posobiec, who told the Conservative Political Action Convention that he and others are committed to overthrowing democracy completely "and replace it with this right here," holding the cross on his necklace.

Pastor Burden's admonition to prep for doomsday reminds me of some of the members of my wife's extended family in Michigan who erected chain-link fencing around land they owned in the northern part of the state, where the paramilitary Michigan Militia is active, and turned it into a family compound stockpiled with rations, gasoline, and guns in case society unraveled in the aftermath of the transition to the year 2000. Several members of the family my wife's sister married into belonged to the Assemblies of God, the same Pentecostal denomination we had joined (minus their penchant for Y2K conspiracy theories and weaponry.)

It's an *us-versus-them* mindset we've always had trouble understanding. But as Christian nationalism moves more squarely into mainstream evangelical thought, we've found ourselves confronting it with alarming frequency.

Indeed, the militia movement poses a "large and escalating threat," warns the Center for Strategic and International Studies, a bipartisan nonprofit policy research organization based in Washington, DC. Militant ideology, particularly among those with an overtly religious bent, is fueled by conspiracy theories centered on members' belief in a secretive "new world order" of leftist globalists plotting to erode or abolish the Second Amendment.

You'll hear versions of this often in white evangelical circles: "They're coming for our guns." Dare to disagree, and you may find yourself branded as a demon-possessed devotee of the occult.

The sheer ferocity of pro-gun propaganda is curious, considering that in fact, no one is coming for their guns—least of all the highest court in the land. If anything, over the past century, the reverse has largely been true.

◆ ◆ ◆

Time and again, the US Supreme Court has taken a decidedly dim view of attempts to chip away at the Second Amendment, and by extension, the right to keep and bear arms. Consider the arc of its most important gun rulings over the past century.

In 1929, in *United States v. Schwimmer*, the Supreme Court held that the amendment enshrines individuals' duties "to defend our government against all enemies whenever necessity arises is a fundamental principle of the Constitution." "The common defense was one of the purposes for which the people ordained and established the Constitution," the court wrote.

That context—of a militia to defend the nation from enemies both foreign and domestic—is a critical one, and it's something the justices addressed again in 1939 in *United States v. Miller*, a landmark challenge of the federal Firearms Act of 1938. The law required vendors to obtain a license from the Internal Revenue Service to sell guns and to maintain a record of purchases, and it prohibited convicted felons from buying firearms or ammunition. Specifically, the 1939 challenge involved a lower court ruling that a man's sawed-off shotgun violated the Second Amendment. The Supreme Court gingerly avoided wading fully into the issue, though it did say any shotgun with a barrel less than eighteen inches long was not "any part of the ordinary military equipment" protected under the amendment.

For decades thereafter, the high court was mostly quiet on gun rights. But Congress wasn't. In 1968—the same year that civil rights icon Martin Luther King Jr. and Democratic presidential hopeful Senator Robert F. Kennedy were gunned down, and five years after

President John F. Kennedy's slaying by an assassin wielding a high-powered rifle—federal lawmakers greatly expanded gun regulations. The Gun Control Act regulated imports; expanded licensing and record-keeping requirements; banned mail-order sales of firearms and ammunition; raised to eighteen the age at which one could legally buy a rifle or shotgun and to twenty-one the minimum age to buy a handgun; and prohibited convicted felons, people with mental illness, and users of illicit drugs from buying guns. Although it was a landmark legislation that imposed significant restrictions, even the NRA at the time called it "reasonable"—a far cry from its hardened stance today.

Congress then made a few missteps, at least as far as the Supreme Court is concerned. In 1995, in *United States v. Lopez*, the court ruled that lawmakers had overstepped their authority when they passed the Gun-Free School Zones Act in 1990, which had made it a federal offense to knowingly bring or fire a gun within one thousand feet of a school. The justices said punishing firearms offenses near schools was for the states, not the federal government, to decide.

The high court intervened again in 1997, ruling that the mandatory background checks in the 1994 Brady Law—named for former White House press secretary James Brady, who was seriously wounded in the 1981 assassination attempt on then-President Ronald Reagan—were unconstitutional.

It didn't touch the Violent Crime Control and Law Enforcement Act of 1994 that outlawed nineteen types of semiautomatic weapons and ammunition clips holding more than ten rounds for anyone not a police officer or active-duty member of the military. The assault weapons ban signed by then-President Bill Clinton was law until it expired in 2004, and Congress didn't reinstate it.

But the high court was far from finished. Fast-forward to 2008, when the Supreme Court in *District of Columbia v. Heller* ruled 5 to 4 in favor of an individual's right to keep handguns in the home for self-defense. It was a landmark decision that stated that the Second

Amendment definitively gives private citizens the right to possess an ordinary weapon and use it for personal protection—even when there's no connection to service in a militia.

In a strongly worded dissent, Justice John Paul Stevens challenged that logic: "When each word in the text is given full effect, the Amendment is most naturally read to secure to the people a right to use and possess arms in conjunction with service in a well-regulated militia." (In 2018, a year before his death, Stevens made a spirited case for repealing the Second Amendment altogether, denouncing it as "a relic of the 18th century.")

Critically, though, the *Heller* ruling came with an important caveat that even the court's majority embraced: Not everything goes. "Like most rights, the right secured by the Second Amendment is not unlimited," Justice Antonin Scalia wrote for the majority. "[It is] not a right to keep and carry any weapon whatsoever in any manner whatsoever and for whatever purpose."

The website for Giffords Law Center to Prevent Gun Violence, the gun control advocacy group founded by former Arizona congresswoman and gun violence survivor Gabrielle Giffords, notes: "The gun lobby has long peddled an extremist and dangerous view of the Second Amendment, one that doesn't allow for any commonsense gun safety protections. . . . The *Heller* decision was far from the blanket endorsement of unlimited gun rights that the gun lobby hoped it might be."

Two years later, in 2010, a divided Supreme Court again ruled 5 to 4 that the Second Amendment applies not only to the federal government but to local and state governments. That decision in *McDonald v. City of Chicago* overturned the city's DC-style handguns ban but invoked the *Heller* ruling's premise that there are limits to what kinds of weapons private citizens can own and how they can use them. Translation: You can own a handgun and use it for self-defense, but you may not buy a bazooka and aim it at your nosy neighbor.

The justices muddied the waters in 2016 when they vacated a ruling by Massachusetts's highest court that had upheld a state law banning the possession of stun guns because such weapons didn't exist when the Second Amendment was enacted. The Supreme Court rejected the premise "that only those weapons useful in warfare are protected."

That set the stage for one of the most consequential Second Amendment rulings in a generation: 2022's *New York State Rifle & Pistol Association, Inc. v. Bruen*. This decision found a New York law requiring applicants for a concealed carry permit to show "proper cause" for their need to be armed outside of their homes to be unconstitutional. In its 6 to 3 decision, the high court established a new test for any gun restriction that must now be shown to be consistent with the spirit, if not the letter, of previous firearms regulations. This ruling declared that the Constitution protects an individual's right to carry a handgun in public for self-defense.

That, in turn, lifted most state restrictions on carrying guns in public, making America less safe virtually overnight. That's what Justice Stephen Breyer argued in a dissenting opinion that rued "the potentially deadly consequences" of the *Bruen* decision: "Firearms in public present a number of dangers, ranging from mass shootings to road rage killings, and are responsible for many deaths and injuries in the United States."

A year later, in 2023, the Supreme Court reinstated a law intended to rein in the proliferation of so-called "ghost guns"—firearms without serial numbers that can be assembled from kits or created at home using a 3D printer. It also broke with its recent pro-gun past by ruling 8 to 1 that the government can disarm gun owners who are subject to restraining orders for domestic violence. And Congress renewed a law aimed at preventing people from sneaking plastic weapons past metal detectors and into airports, schools, concert halls, and sports arenas. Americans weary of gun violence celebrated these small victories.

But in 2024, as we saw in chapter 1, the court ruled that the first Trump administration had overstepped its authority when it banned bump stocks—devices that harness the energy from a rifle's recoil and channel it to a shooter's trigger finger, effectively turning a semiautomatic into a machine gun. As if that weren't questionable enough, *Slate* reports, Justice Clarence Thomas's majority opinion included material copied from a brief written by the Firearms Policy Coalition, an extreme-libertarian gun rights group known for its violent rhetoric.

Meanwhile, at least twenty-nine states allow their citizens to carry a concealed handgun without a permit. And examining the big picture, we find that lower-court rulings in favor of gun owners have dramatically increased since *Bruen*. In 2023, federal courts handed down a whopping 865 decisions in favor of gun rights, up sharply from 121 in 2021, according to a 2024 analysis by three law professors.

It's all part of a concerted effort to enact right-wing, permissive gun laws via the courts. "It's akin to the Christian right's abortion playbook, but for guns," concludes a deep dive undertaken by the nonprofit firearms reporting project *The Trace* and the magazine *Mother Jones*.

And a troubling pattern has emerged, the law professors say: "Trump(-appointed) judges are close to casting 50 percent of their votes in favor of gun rights, when the average for other Republicans is 28 percent."

♦ ♦ ♦

Part of what drives evangelicals' embrace of the Second Amendment is their conviction that the Constitution was inspired by God. It's an extension of their belief that God intended the United States to be a promised land for the Christians from Europe who settled here. In fact, four in five white evangelical respondents to a 2022 Pew Research Center survey said the founders intended America to be a Christian nation.

And white evangelicals who have cheered these Supreme Court rulings insist that the hazards of guns in the hands of private citizens are overblown. They include the Reverend Ronald Gleason, pastor of Grace Presbyterian Church in Yorba Linda, California, who contends "an armed society is a polite society." In a commentary for the Christian Research Institute, Gleason advances a flawed argument you'll often hear from pro-gun religious fundamentalists: "If the government of these United States ever becomes tyrannical and desires to take over every aspect and facet of your life, are you prepared to hand over peacefully the freedom and liberty that was purchased at such a great cost?"

I heard this rationale recently from Tim, a new acquaintance of mine and a devout evangelical doing postdoctoral work at Brown University. Tim is a staunch Second Amendment supporter, who says it "makes America great" and helps maintain the United States as "a beacon of hope" for the rest of the world. He's among the majority of white evangelicals who believe citizens must have unfettered access to guns, including AR-15-style assault rifles, in case they're needed to combat tyranny.

"What tyranny?" I asked him in a recent conversation over plates of seafood pasta at a crowded downtown Providence, Rhode Island restaurant, lowering my voice to avoid eavesdropping by the quiet diners at the table next to ours.

"The government's shutdown of churches during the COVID-19 pandemic," Tim replied, not bothering to lower his own voice. He was suggesting—as many revisionist evangelicals do—that state and federal officials used the global public health crisis as an excuse to persecute Christians. That logic breaks down quickly, as I gently suggested to Tim. And I wasn't just talking about restrictions on large indoor gatherings. (Those, of course, were an attempt to stop the spread of a virus that was indiscriminately killing millions worldwide. Yes, in-person worship services were included in the capacity limits for crowds, but so were sporting events, indoor concerts, and business conventions.) But the idea that the wholesale arming of Americans is an antidote to true tyranny is fundamentally flawed, considering the massive firepower the government has at its disposal. I mean, even if the government *did* decide to turn on its people, not even an AR-15 would be a match for drones, F16s, attack helicopters, submarines, tanks, and nukes.

"When we take into account the military might of the United States government, it is not clear how an armed populace would prevent such tyranny," Michael Austin, a professor of philosophy and ethics at Eastern Kentucky University, argues in a counterpoint to Pastor Gleason's defense of gun rights:

> If such tyranny did arise, the people could successfully resist only if they had a stockpile of weapons capable of matching the state's firepower. If the justification for the widespread possession of guns is to deter or deal with a possible future tyrannical state, then by the same reasoning there would also be a right to possess tanks, missiles, and weapons of mass destruction, all of which would be needed to truly deter or reverse such tyranny. But surely this is wrong because of the potential harm to innocent victims if these weapons were widely possessed, given the depravity of humanity. The best way for followers of Christ to preserve basic human rights and political freedoms is to be politically active in ways that support democratic institutions, traditions, and our fundamental human rights, rather than relying on guns to protect these important values.

Nathan Dahm, a homeschooled former evangelical missionary who is now a Republican member of Oklahoma's state Senate, authored the first anti–red flag law in the United States. Red flag laws allow law enforcement to temporarily remove weapons from people who are considered a danger to themselves or others and prevent them from buying a gun—a step Dahm insists goes too far.

His resistance underscores a sea shift of hardening attitudes toward even gun restrictions that many Americans consider to be commonsense regulations, like red flag laws. When the Gallup polling organization asked people in 1959 if they supported banning civilian handgun ownership, 60 percent said yes. By 2024, just 20 percent agreed, a statistical tie with the record low of 19 percent recorded in 2021.

A 2024 poll by The Associated Press and the NORC Center for Public Affairs Research at the University of Chicago found that 80 percent of Americans believe the right to own a gun is important to protect.

♦ ♦ ♦

Many modern evangelicals are convinced that the Constitution's framers were just like them. That's a dubious claim, at best. Although Samuel Adams and Patrick Henry were among the founders who embraced and espoused Christian teachings, John Adams, Benjamin Franklin, and Thomas Jefferson saw Jesus only as a great teacher—not as God.

Gregg Frazier, a professor of history and political studies at The Master's University, a private nondenominational Christian university and seminary in Santa Clarita, California, says Christianity meant something different to even the most devout founders than it does to twenty-first-century evangelicals. Most, he says, were "theistic rationalists," who saw merit in all religions in honoring God by promoting morality. "They did not intend to create a Christian nation," Frazier writes. "Not a single Founding Father made such a claim in any piece of private correspondence or any document. If they had, it would be blazoned above the entrances of countless Christian schools and we would all be inundated with emails repeating it."

Nicholas Rathod, a former director of state campaigns for the group Everytown for Gun Safety, argues that if the framers had intended to include references to Christian doctrine, they'd have done so explicitly. Instead, the First Amendment begins: "Congress shall make no law respecting an establishment of religion . . ."

Evangelical scholar J. Kenneth Blackwell, a former Ohio secretary of state, agrees that the Second Amendment is inextricably intertwined with First Amendment rights to freedom of religion, speech, assembly, and the press. But Blackwell has a different take on that: The Second Amendment right to bear arms, he contends, makes all those rights possible. It is, he says, "America's first freedom because it protects all the others."

Lost in these arguments is the Ninth Amendment that states: "The enumeration in the Constitution, of certain rights, shall not be construed to deny or disparage others retained by the people." It's a plea from the founders to read the entire Constitution and see all the amendments in their context, rather than cherry-picking the parts that fit our particular narratives.

♦ ♦ ♦

If the Constitution is indeed a living document—one that can and should be amended to fit the needs of *We the People*—there is increasingly a case to be made for the Second Amendment's repeal. Mort Rosenblum, a friend of mine and a fellow journalist and author, splits his time between France and the United States. He wryly notes: "The Bill of Rights, those first ten add-ons to the Constitution, did not envision a Donald Trump or semiautomatic assault rifles." The founders simply could not have envisioned the firearms technology we have today.

"Given America's epidemic of gun violence, perhaps we should test, license and tax owners of weapons and the weapons themselves,"

Boston University's Clemens suggests. He and others suggest that it should not be easier for a person to obtain a handgun than for a teenager to get a driver's license. Part of the reason why virtually every attempt to tighten restrictions on firearms goes nowhere is because of the influence on gun politics of white evangelicals, who won't yield an inch or brook serious discussion about rethinking the Second Amendment's outsized role in American life. They are ignoring the direct link between the number of people armed in a society and its incidence of gun homicides. They're sticking to their guns—despite insisting they are also pro-life.

If you're truly pro-life, you should be anti-gun, contended the late Tony Campolo, an internationally renowned scholar and pastor who, like me, stopped identifying as evangelical. Campolo had long challenged evangelicals to costly discipleship, and while he remained a fairly traditional Christian, he eschewed the label "evangelical" because of its negative association with hypocrisy on guns and other social issues. "'Pro-life' voters regularly vote for representatives who feature AR-15s in their Christmas card photos and who back legislation that would make the AR-15 the national gun of the United States," he wrote. "I believe that those who want to be truly 'pro-life' need to do more than oppose abortion. They need to make principled stances against war, the death penalty, climate change, and America's unusually easy access to guns."

Baptist commentator Earl Chappell calls this duplicity among gun-toting pro-lifers "the oxymoron of being both anti-abortion and pro-gun." And Dave Verhaagen, a psychologist, therapist, and author who grew up in the white evangelical tradition, more forcefully calls it out as hypocrisy: "Despite their insistence on being 'pro-life,' they express little willingness to advocate for changes that might reduce gun deaths."

In fact, it's no exaggeration, particularly given the meteoric rise of Christian nationalism, to characterize the white evangelical ethos about guns like this: *Tinker with the Second Amendment over our dead bodies.* Entire churches are asserting their gun rights. The evangelical His Tabernacle Family Church in Horseheads, New York, and its pastor, Reverend Micheal Spencer, filed a federal lawsuit challenging the state's new law prohibiting the carrying of firearms in "sensitive locations" including houses of worship. A federal appeals court later exempted churches from the law. (That showdown also produced a false narrative that circulated widely among evangelicals after the church's lawyers accused the state of "singling out houses of worship for total disarmament" and "hostility toward religion," even though the law also applied to government buildings, courts, health care facilities, libraries, public parks, summer camps, and numerous other sensitive venues.)

Recent rhetoric from prominent white evangelicals is unambiguous. Former Arizona television anchor Kari Lake, a far-right firebrand who lost both a governor's race and a US Senate race, went so far as to call for armed resistance to the criminal investigations that have targeted Donald Trump. "Most of us are card-carrying members of the NRA," she told a crowd, adding: "That's not a threat—that's a public service announcement. . . . Now is the time to cling to our guns and our religion."

Such extremism by evangelicals and others—and their growing willingness to engage in political violence—increases the threat of more armed insurrection and undermines the very functioning of American democracy, the Center for Gun Violence Solutions at the Johns Hopkins Bloomberg School of Public Health warns in a 2023 report.

And there's a direct link between owning a gun and the willingness to consider violence as a justified means to achieve a political end. An exhaustive study published in 2024 in the *Journal of the American Medical Association* by researchers at the University of California-Davis School of Medicine found this was especially true of recent gun purchasers and owners who often, or always, carry a gun wherever they go. They were 7 percent more likely than people who don't own a gun—a moderate but still "troubling" difference, the researchers said—to use their weapon to advance one of seventeen specific political objectives. Those included "to oppose Americans who do not share my beliefs"; "to oppose the government when it does not share my beliefs"; "to preserve the American way of life I believe in"; and "to preserve an American way of life based on Western European traditions"—all bedrock white Christian nationalist creeds.

"It is plausible based on our findings that some recent purchasers have been arming up for anticipated civil conflict," the UC-Davis research team concludes. "Our findings strongly suggest that large numbers of armed individuals who are at least potentially willing to engage in political violence are in public places across the United States every day."

The takeaway: The greater the number of guns in circulation, the more religious extremists there are who are prepared to use them to achieve their goals.

◆ ◆ ◆

As we clash incessantly over interpretations of gun rights that so many evangelicals see as God-given, the body count from mass shootings, suicides, and deadly domestic violence rises. And many people in other countries watch, bewildered, struggling to understand why the United States lets this happen.

Etienne Omnès, a French citizen, sees America's gun cult and concludes we are out of our collective minds. "The entire country is an arsenal," he writes in a contrarian response to a blog post with the provocative title "Why Christians Are Ordered to Have Guns." Unlike the US government, the French state is intentionally strong. Firearms are mainly for the army and police forces. "In France, our army is patrolling in the stations and even in the streets of the big cities. I encounter them daily, with their uniforms and their assault rifles," he says. "I'm comforted by their presence because I know they will not use it against me under any circumstances. Let the same M16 be in the hands of random people and I would not even leave my house." (More on how evangelicals in other countries approach guns can be found in chapter 8.)

Would repealing the Second Amendment, or at least enacting meaningful restrictions on military-style assault weapons, result in fewer mass shootings? Other nations' experiences suggest an emphatic *yes*. Australia, the United Kingdom, New Zealand, and Norway all took decisive action—in some instances deciding "enough is enough" after their very first mass shooting—and gun violence in all four countries has become exceedingly rare.

The most recent, determined, and, by all measures, successful attempt to implement sweeping gun reforms and avoid needless bloodshed happened in New Zealand. The catalyst was horrific. In 2019, a white supremacist massacred fifty-one worshipers at two mosques in Christchurch. Then-Prime Minister Jacinda Ardern wasted no time: Within a week, she'd announced a nationwide crackdown on semiautomatic rifles. Gun owners were given six months to sell their weapons back to the government, and a year later, the country introduced a firearms registry to track sales. New Zealand hasn't had a mass shooting since.

Australia, too, responded swiftly after a gunman armed with a semiautomatic rifle killed thirty-five people in Port Arthur in 1996. Within two weeks, federal and state legislators supported bans on semiautomatics and pump-action rifles, as well as mandatory gun buybacks. The legislature has since restricted the types of handguns that civilians can own and has toughened penalties for their misuse. The outcome? Only one mass shooting since 1996.

That same year, the United Kingdom tightened its laws and launched a buyback program after a man killed sixteen schoolchildren and an adult in the Scottish town of Dunblane. The UK hasn't experienced a mass casualty event involving a gunman since then.

Norway sprang into action after a far-right extremist slaughtered sixty-nine people at a summer youth camp in 2011 in that country's deadliest domestic attack since World War II. Its subsequent ban on semiautomatics didn't come until 2018. It was notable because Scandinavian countries, like the United States, already had gun laws and a deeply rooted firearms culture in which many people owned rifles and shotguns, primarily for hunting. Norway's gun safety record since 2018 is vastly better than that of the United States.

Even erstwhile Balkans troublemaker Serbia, where I traveled extensively as an Associated Press foreign correspondent and can attest has one of the world's most entrenched gun cultures, outlaws automatic weapons. After seventeen people, including eight children, were killed in two mass shootings in 2023, its president called for a moratorium on new permits for guns of all types and more stringent psychological screenings of gun owners. Neighboring Montenegro, meanwhile, launched a crackdown on illegal firearms after twelve people were killed in a mass shooting early in 2025.

And Canada, which banned more than 1,500 types of assault rifles and components after a gunman killed twenty-two people in Nova Scotia in 2020, has imposed a twenty-eight-day waiting period for gun purchases. Other nations that have enacted gun legislation and seen mass shootings and firearms suicides fall include Brazil and South Africa.

"To those of us who live in culturally similar nations, but where the availability of lethal weapons is limited, Americans' increasing reliance on guns even in the face of escalating horrors is unfathomable," Philip Alpers, an Australian researcher who tracks gun violence worldwide, told CNN. "As each shooting eclipses the last, as fear and ideology trump the evidence once again, it's terrifying to imagine the scale, the sheer enormity of the tipping point which might finally force

American politicians to face their collective responsibility and enact change."

Acknowledging America's ignoble status as an outlier, then-President Joe Biden rightfully asked, after a gunman slaughtered nineteen children and two teachers in Uvalde, Texas, in 2022, why mass shootings on that scale "rarely happen anywhere else in the world."

Dissident evangelicals who have been pushing for change in the United States, which has a staggering 46 percent of the world's civilian-owned guns, are understandably frustrated at the lack of will to fix what Alpers calls "America's self-inflicted problem." Shane Claiborne, a prominent evangelical social activist who helped found the nonprofit organization The Simple Way in Philadelphia and cofounded the reformist group Red Letter Christians, has worked tirelessly for gun reforms. But even he sounded exasperated after yet another mass shooting bloodied Philly's streets. "There are more regulations on fireworks in America than firearms. And there are more regulations on toy guns than real guns," he said on X. "It doesn't have to be this way."

The Center for American Progress blames apathy and the lucrative gun industry's influence-peddling: "America's gun violence epidemic is the result of an industry and culture that has made guns readily available to nearly anyone, with little interest in preventing these guns from being used to harm others."

"A disproportionate number of white evangelical Christians own guns and oppose gun violence prevention measures," it laments in a report examining the complicity of Christian nationalists in perpetuating the problem.

Individual states can take action—although as we've seen, the Supreme Court's conservative majority has undone effective restrictions in some states. Even so, there's much that can be done at the state level. Giffords Law Center to Prevent Gun Violence ranked Rhode Island, where I live, the nation's safest state with one of the lowest gun death rates, at 3.1 per 100,000. The tiny state hasn't stopped there: It recently enacted a safe storage law, the strongest in the United States, requiring all firearms to be secured in a safe or other container with a tamper-proof lock. And lawmakers have been pushing for an outright ban on assault-style weapons.

Laws aren't guarantees, however. Rhode Island's largest-ever mass shooting, which wounded nine people, three critically, happened in Providence, less than three miles from my house. The attorney general says the state is still flooded with illegal firearms. But laws are a start.

Unfortunately, getting anything done on guns—whether in the nation's capital or in its statehouses—is a challenge to rival Sisyphus's, because white evangelicals and the conservative majorities they keep electing will have none of it. As Samuel L. Perry, the University of Oklahoma sociologist we met in chapter 1, puts it: "Guns are practically an element of worship in the church of white Christian nationalism."

Perry means that metaphorically. But venture to the American South and straight into the heart of the gun culture, as I did, and you may be startled to see the prominent role that guns play at some churches—right up there with the cross, the Bible, the bread, and the wine.

# 4 | HOME ON THE RANGE

Jemison, Alabama, population 2,642, is a leafy berg tucked halfway between Birmingham and Montgomery. It's in Chilton County, home to peaches so succulent they make liars of folks in neighboring Georgia who brag about living in the Peach State.

In what is charitably called a city, winding country lanes take visitors past tidy farms with rusted iron gates and modest ranch-style clapboard houses with decorative ponds. Amid the distant drone of tractors, the thick June air is perfumed with the wholesome fragrance of freshly mowed grass mingled with the enticing scent of smokehouse barbecue.

Jemison has nineteen houses of worship, three gas stations, and two firing ranges. You'll find one of them at Rocky Mount Methodist Church. It's a small parish of three dozen or so white sixty- and seventy-somethings—most of whom come to church armed.

They include Charlotte Powell, a winsome widow with a syrupy drawl who tells me she has four firearms: a Glock handgun, two Smith & Wesson pistols, and a short-barreled shotgun she calls a "snake charmer." She also had her late husband's rifle but gave it to her son because she found it too heavy to handle.

Powell recounts how Canadian friends once told her they were afraid to visit the United States because we have so many mass shootings. In what seems to me to be a telling aside, she acknowledges she didn't respond: "Because how do you argue with that?"

## IN GUNS WE TRUST

"I've never pulled a gun, but that doesn't mean I'm not going to make sure it's with me," she says before the 10:00 a.m. Sunday service as the pianist plays "What a Friend We Have in Jesus." "We've had churches attacked. Guns are not the problem. The problem is the overall degeneration of moral fiber that makes a person think it's OK to take whatever they want in whatever circumstance."

If a shooter shows up, and if all else fails, there's Bill, thin, elderly, and ex-military, standing post in the rear of the church, his own gun at the ready. He and the pastor, the Reverend Phillip Guin, a retired Air Force chaplain who carries a Ruger handgun, conduct regular active shooter drills. "He [the pastor] tells us, 'If I'm up at the pulpit and I say get down, don't look around and see why. Just get down.' We practice that, so we're prepared for it," Powell says.

As Guin pulls on a rope in the back of the church to ring the bell in the belfry—a charmingly old-school start to the service—a woman who identifies herself only as Carla approaches me to flash a thumbs-up and say hello.

"Bet y'all wondering how many of us carry in church," Carla says, when she learns of my project.

"Do *you*?" I ask her.

"Oh, yes. Right now. Semi," she answers, patting her purse.

"How many guns do you own?" I ask.

"Only got one here," she answers.

An uncomfortable silence follows, broken by a giggle from her. "Mm-hmm. You know, I see nothing wrong with it."

You'll increasingly find packing parishioners all over the country, but Rocky Mount's shooting range and overt "gun ministry" make it unusual among churches even in the rural Deep South. This chapter explores how some congregations are doubling down on gun culture by incorporating it into the very fabric of their faith. And they're finding guns useful for outreach, too.

Why settle for fellowship over a potluck supper when you can share your faith at pistol practice?

♦ ♦ ♦

Across much of America, God and guns are inseparable, consequences be damned.

The River at Tampa Bay, an evangelical megachurch in Florida, went viral a few years ago when it posted this menacing sign in all caps at every entrance to the church, along with a warning on its Instagram account:

> WE ARE HEAVILY ARMED—ANY ATTEMPT WILL BE DEALT WITH DEADLY FORCE—YES WE ARE A CHURCH AND WE WILL PROTECT OUR PEOPLE

"At the end of the day, we may ruffle some feathers, but I would rather ruffle a couple of feathers than count bodies," associate pastor Allen Hawes says. "If you're going to come here to look to do harm, you're going to be met with force."

Remember Reverend Ken Pagano, the ordained Assemblies of God minister we met briefly in chapter 1 who organized a "Bring Your Gun to Church Day" at his Kentucky church? His insurance company abruptly canceled the parish's policy, yes, but Pagano didn't miss a beat. Within weeks, he resigned his pulpit at New Bethel Church in Louisville to focus full-time on church security and Second Amendment rights.

"People have this idea that Christians have to turn the other cheek," Pagano, an ex-Marine, tells the *Washington Times* newspaper. "That's true, but I don't think there's anything in the Old or New Testament that requires them to roll over and die if someone attacks them or their family."

Bringing a gun to church, whether via concealed carry or open carry for all to see, has become commonplace among worshipers at many white evangelical churches, who see no inconsistencies between being armed and praying for peace.

The US Concealed Carry Association (USCCA), based in West Bend, Wisconsin, even provides believers with detailed "church gun" recommendations on the most practical firearms to bring into the sanctuary. Everyday guns aren't the best choice, the organization says, suggesting higher-caliber firearms and ammunition that will deliver "precision, power and penetration."

Kevin Michalowski, a law enforcement officer in rural Wisconsin who helps train churchgoers, says he answers bluntly when asked if Christians should carry a gun at church: "Hell, yes."

"Evil has come to our churches. We have seen it," he writes on the USCCA website. "If you are not ready to stop an attack on your church, then you should be ready to take cover and hope your prayers work."

That houses of worship are soft targets—buildings with porous, if any, security—isn't in question. That has become tragically clear. The worst mass shooting at a US church on record—the November 5, 2017, slaughter of twenty-six worshipers and wounding of twenty others at First Baptist Church of Sutherland Springs, Texas—is never far from some churchgoers' minds. Republican lawmakers moved quickly to loosen state restrictions on guns in churches.

Even before that massacre, other shootings targeting churches had spawned a lucrative cottage industry of companies and consultants that provide guidance on how to recruit and arm teams of parishioners whose jobs are to keep vigil during worship services. Proactive Defense is one such company. Based in Northland, Texas, they offer Wild West–style instructions on how to improve quick-draw skills when pulling a gun from its holster.

But efforts to harden churches can backfire.

In the western Michigan community of Cascade Township, Ada Bible Church shut down its own Rocky Mount–style gun range on church property in an effort to mend fences with neighbors worried about safety concerns and irritated by gunfire. The evangelical church had used the range primarily to train its own security personnel. "If they have to resort to the shooting range and security to save themselves, I think they're going to the wrong church," resident Greg Smit, annoyed by raucous bursts of semiautomatic fire, told township officials at the time.

At Community Bible Church in Stockbridge, Georgia, dozens of men meet regularly at a local gun range for a "Bibles and Bullets" study of scripture, then don ear and eye protection for fellowship while firing their weapons of choice at paper targets. Some of the targets are conventional bullseyes. Others are life-sized human silhouettes with concentric circles marking the "kill shots"—the heart and other vital organs. Men's church events can be sparsely attended. This one is standing room only.

"People are coming for the gospel and the fellowship. The shooting is a plus," participant Michael McClendon, who brings a Bible and a Bersa 9mm, tells the *Atlanta Journal-Constitution*. "I don't see anything un-Christian about shooting."

Community Bible is among a rising number of evangelical congregations so enamored of gun culture they're weaving it into the very fabric of their faith. Many of these churches use communal target practice—including events with military-style assault rifles—as opportunities for outreach, or proselytizing.

Pastor Shannon O'Dell of Brand New Church in Farmington, Arkansas, organizes gun giveaways to entice unchurched men to attend periodic "Man Night" events. "All you gotta do is show up and you got a chance to win this 1911 .45 Colt Elite," he gushes in one promotional video, filmed at a gun shop.

The brash O'Dell, who has given away other lethal weapons, including a high-powered rifle outfitted with a thermo-optic scope, has drawn the attention of Christian Nightmares, a social media account known for its satirical look at the more eyebrow-raising aspects of evangelical Christianity. O'Dell, who uses a helicopter on Sunday mornings to shuttle between church campuses, presents an irresistible target to other dissidents in the faith community, too. "Come and receive the Lord Jesus and a pistol," blogger Dan Foster quips.

This merging of guns with the gospel isn't confined to the South; nor is it a new phenomenon. In the city of Troy in upstate New York, avowed alt-right Reverend John Koletas of Grace Baptist Church—whose slogan is: *An ol' fashioned church preaching the ol' time religion*—has raffled off AR-15s and even a flamethrower during revival meetings since 2014. "I think everyone ought to have a gun," Koletas tells a local television station. His unorthodox approach has inspired mocking tabloid headlines, including this one on the front page of the *New York Daily News*: "LET US SLAY."

In Wenatchee, Washington, Grace City Church runs Project ManCard, which trains boys in hand-to-hand combat and the tactical handling of firearms while using replica assault rifles. Instructors include former members of the US military and law enforcement. Grace City's program is an offshoot of its Stronger Man Nation movement, the slogan of which is: *When the men get stronger, everything gets better*. In a YouTube video posted on the church's website, young male participants can be heard chanting: "Kill the dragon, get the girl."

And in the rural Indiana town of Lapel, The River Church launched a "God and Guns" club that offers churchgoers who own pistols, rifles, shotguns, or automatic weapons an opportunity to socialize while practicing their shooting skills or cleaning their guns. "It's all about transforming lives, renewing hope and pursuing God," organizer Aaron Riffey says.

A truly gun-crazed congregation in the rural Pennsylvania town of Newfoundland bears mentioning as well, even though, strictly speaking, it's not evangelical. Rod of Iron Ministries is a militant sect of the Unification Church that is fiercely pro-Trump and preaches fire-and-brimstone end-times theology. Its pastor, Hyung Jin "Sean" Moon, has been regularly photographed wearing a green camouflage blazer and a crown of bullets and carries a golden AR-15.

But because gun culture is so deeply entrenched in the South, you'll find far more instances of faith mixing with firearms the deeper you go into Dixie.

Before he resigned as president of Liberty University in the aftermath of a tabloid sex scandal, Jerry Falwell Jr.—whose televangelist father founded what has become the largest private, nonprofit university in the United States—built a $3 million gun range on the Lynchburg, Virginia, campus. The younger Falwell, who himself has taken to carrying a handgun around, invoked Islamic terrorism and urged Liberty students to get their concealed carry permits so they can "end those Muslims." Addressing thousands of students in the sanctity of a daily chapel service, Falwell Jr. patted his backside ominously and alluded to "what I've got in my back pocket right now"—his own hidden handgun. His young audience roared with approval.

*The Washington Post* tells the story of pastor Isaiah Stewart, who wears a bulletproof vest beneath his robes and carries a 9mm handgun at House of Healing Outreach Church in New Orleans, a city wracked with gun violence. Stewart teaches his flock how to handle a firearm. "I know people will say, 'Why is this happening in a church?'" he told the *Post*. "But if you read the Bible, Jesus told the disciples to protect themselves. . . . And to me, as a pastor, I am to look after people."

The Fountains Fellowship Church in Crowley, Texas, recently raffled off three guns—a Beretta A300 shotgun, a Winchester XPR 300 bolt-action rifle, and a Glock 43x semiautomatic pistol—to raise money to send a child to summer camp. (The raffle sold out.) Creekside Christian Fellowship in Needville, Texas, holds an annual $100 per ticket gun raffle for its scholarship fund.

Events incorporating firearms are traditionally focused on men, but increasingly, white evangelical women are signing up. Word of Life

Fellowship in Cibolo, Texas, runs a gun safety workshop geared specifically to women and billed as "A Girl 'n A Gun." And LifePoint Church in central Tennessee has thrown open its regular shooting fellowship events at a local gun range to the Baptist congregation's women. "This ministry is not the 'boys' club,'" its Facebook page chides.

As I contemplate the ubiquity of gun-embracing, Second Amendment–affirming events at evangelical churches, there's a New Testament verse I can't seem to shake. "'I have the right to do anything,' you say—but not everything is beneficial. 'I have the right to do anything'—but not everything is constructive," Paul writes in 1 Corinthians 10:23. Another translation phrases it like this: "We are allowed to do all things, but not all things are good for us to do" (NLT).

As the late theologian Walter Wink put it: "Violence is the ethos of our times. It is the spirituality of the modern world. . . . Violence, not Christianity, is the real religion of America."

Why, I wondered, would followers of Jesus Christ, the Prince of Peace, maintain such a fervent grip on their firearms? How does a congregation get to the point where it constructs a firing range next to the sanctuary so its members can practice firing their guns on church property? What does all of this mean for the future of evangelicalism in the United States?

It's these central questions that have brought me to Jemison, Alabama, and Rocky Mount church.

♦ ♦ ♦

Pastor Phil Guin is intelligent, salt-of-the-earth folksy, and chatty, with a self-deprecating sense of humor and the soft, lilting accent of a lifelong Alabaman. We bond instantly over our shared faith, and I like him immediately. In fact, my initial thought as we become acquainted is that I couldn't dislike this man, even if I tried.

## HOME ON THE RANGE

Guin, now in his mid-sixties, made international headlines in 2015 for building a gun range in a hollow behind Rocky Mount that was choked with kudzu and infested with venomous Eastern timber rattlesnakes. His motivation was simple and sincere: He wanted to give his little congregation a place to hone their skills.

The blowback beyond Alabama was swift and loud. Rocky Mount was mixing God and guns—a combustive combination that drew unwanted media attention from as far away as Australia and Russia. Now, he allows, "we're either famous or infamous."

Guin warily turned down interview requests from *The New York Times* and Comedy Central's *The Daily Show with Trevor Noah*, who'd invited him to appear live. A producer assured the pastor of Noah's sincere interest in him and in guns, he says, but Guin passed, fearing he'd be lampooned and skewered in the name of humor. "Mama didn't raise no fool," the preacher told the producer.

Guin calls himself "Aristotelian," and like the ancient Greek philosopher, he finds that inductive analysis often leads him to the center on many issues—though not, as it turns out, on the touchy issue of faith and firearms. "We got a saying here in Alabama: There's nothing in the middle of the road but a yellow line and dead possums," he says with a laugh.

Guin has agreed to talk with me, however, and we sit on a front-row pew of the church he has pastored for more than a decade. In a wide-ranging interview, with a stained-glass window over his shoulder depicting a dove descending with an olive branch in its beak, Guin settles back to recount Rocky Mount's rocky road.

The church was trying to determine what to do with the tangled rear area of its property when a now-deceased member suggested building a gun range. Guin says he was initially taken aback by the idea. But as he gave it some thought, he realized the gully, with its steep embankment at one end, was the perfect place for a range.

There were logistics beyond landscaping the area and erecting a wooden shooting stand at one end. After consulting with the local sheriff, the church established a separate entity, the Rocky Mount Hunt and Gun Club, to operate the range, and the club has taken out liability insurance distinct from the policy covering the church itself. The club also requires users to sign a liability release, and a giant banner near the entrance to the fenced-in facility lists a rundown of seven rules:

1. The gun is always loaded. Treat every firearm like it's loaded.
2. Never point a firearm at anything you do not want to destroy or kill.
3. Keep your finger off the trigger and out of the trigger guard unless firing.
4. Always be sure of your backstop (target and what's behind it).
5. Firearms must be unloaded when entering and leaving range.
6. Alcohol or drugs absolutely prohibited on range (must be sober, too).
7. Horseplay is prohibited.

There's also an eighth rule that isn't printed anywhere. But it is implicit, and Guin's flock makes sure I know about it as they gather for worship on Sunday: No shooting on the Sabbath.

"We didn't go into this ignorantly," the pastor says. "We staffed it as I would call it in the military: properly. I did a lot of research. . . . I didn't go into this empty-headed."

Some hunters use the range to sight in, or calibrate, their rifles for deer season, though it's technically not long enough to do that properly. Local law enforcement has also used the church's range to practice. Mostly, though, it's the congregation's elderly members who practice firing all those pistols they're concealing on Sundays.

## HOME ON THE RANGE

"I've got a few, and I bring some of my stuff down here sometimes with the men, and we'll have a day of fellowship and recreational shooting," Guin says. Women and supervised children also use the range for gun safety and self-defense classes, he says. He estimates that four hundred to five hundred people have been trained here in how to properly handle a weapon.

That includes the AR-15, which has come to be associated with mass shootings. It's unnerving for me to think of church folk—really any civilian—shouldering a military-style assault rifle and peeling off some spine-rattling rounds. But Guin plays down the sinister aspects of the rifle. "It's just the way they look," he says. "I've got a Ruger 10/22 semiautomatic hunting rifle with the same capabilities. It operates exactly the same way, with the same trigger pull."

In fact, the AR-15 is a frightfully powerful rifle. In *The Bodies Keep Coming*, a book exploring the grim intersection of racism, violence, and health care, Black trauma surgeon Dr. Brian H. Williams describes the damage an AR-15 can do. "It is in a destructive class all its own, creating wounds beyond the skill of even the best trauma surgeons to repair," Williams writes. "Gunshot wounds from an AR-15 frequently leave victims unidentifiable without analyzing DNA. Imagine what would happen to your body if you laid on a grenade: That's the AR-15."

Guin grew up 120 miles away in the northwestern Alabama town of Winfield, a rural community steeped in gun culture. Guns, he says, have been part of the fabric of his life: His grandfather was a collector, and he describes his father as a firearms safety "fanatic." At age seventeen, fresh out of high school and not quite ready to enroll in his father's alma mater, the University of Alabama, he instead joined the Air Force. Three days after high school graduation, he was at basic training.

In the Air Force, Guin worked in aircraft maintenance, and it was there that he encountered a chaplain who would become a mentor and, eventually, his father-in-law. Having first felt called to ministry when he was twelve or thirteen years old, Guin now embraced that calling and completed his bachelor's degree in two and a half years while on active duty, attending lunchtime classes and night school.

He met a young woman at Ichthus, a Christian music festival at the evangelical Asbury Theological Seminary in Kentucky that he describes as "kind of a Christian Woodstock." She happened to be the daughter of his Air Force mentor, and the two wed in 1980. Over the course of their forty-five-year marriage, he and Sandy have adopted ten children, most with profound special needs—four from Korea, three from the Philippines, and one each from Brazil, New Jersey, and South Carolina. As he talks, his gun hand shaking from a recent onset of Parkinson's disease, I'm struck by the depth of his compassion.

Early in his marriage, he was a United Methodist pastor when a district superintendent suggested undiplomatically that his rapidly expanding family would be an expensive distraction for both the pastor and the denomination. This deeply hurt and offended him, and it led to a career change and a pivot back to the military. Guin subsequently served as a chaplain at Air Force bases around the country between 1990 and 2012, including a stint at Arlington National Cemetery, where he presided over more than six hundred funerals. There, he absorbed exponentially more grief than most people. "I probably have a little bit of PTSD left over from some of that," he confides. "You can't do six hundred funerals and not be affected by it just a little bit."

All these life experiences informed a lot of quiet contemplation in the winter of 2014 when, now back in ministry, he searched the Bible while considering the church's firing range and the political and spiritual ramifications. "I prayed a long time about it, thought about it, and explored the scripture," he tells me. "I was born in a rural area. I was around guns my entire life, mostly shotguns and pistols. It's a hunting culture in the South, you know, like it is in the West and the

Midwest—everywhere that's not urban. It's everywhere in rural areas, typically. Young men today are also part of the gun culture, with video games and the whole bit. So, I wrestled with the decision, but I had clarity about the idea fairly quickly."

Guin had approached his Methodist district superintendent preemptively to ask him what he thought, "and he happened to be a gun guy." That cleric in turn floated the concept with the bishop of the United Methodist Church's North Alabama Conference, and he told Guin he had a thumbs-up to proceed.

"There's a certain amount of ambivalence about this topic in scripture where you're led to fall either way," he says. "There are several instances in the Gospels where Jesus mentioned swords, and where the disciples obviously were carrying a sword. I can point them out right now in Matthew and Luke." (He's talking here about Matt 10:34: "Do not suppose that I have come to bring peace to the earth. I did not come to bring peace, but a sword"; and Matt 26:52: "Put your sword back in its place." And Luke 22:36: "If you don't have a sword, sell your cloak and buy one.")

Guin also points to the armed Roman commander whom Jesus obviously was impressed by when he said, as recorded in Matthew 8, that there was no greater faith in all of Israel. "He didn't rebuke the centurion for being a centurion. He didn't rebuke him at all. He just welcomed him and thought, 'Wow, what a guy,'" Guin recounts. "And the Israelites obviously kept swords. I mean, they were a culture that had to defend itself constantly against not only rabble-rousers but hostile enemies. Clearly in the Bible you see self-defense."

Guin says he'd also agonized over these same issues, as well as the concept of a just war, before becoming a military chaplain: "There's a certain moral ambiguity. . . . You begin to wonder if what you're doing is correct or right. I had to pray about that on several occasions. Too much blood and treasure has been spent over these past several decades," he says, on warfare.

He continues: "Some of my critics who texted me or emailed me or made comments on social media or whatever—I never addressed most of that. You can't win those arguments anyway, no matter how cogent your argument," he says. He did, however, respond thoughtfully to some who wrote him.

"One of the things I wanted to make clear from the very beginning was, 'You're *talking* about gun violence, but we're *doing* something about it.' . . . We're actually teaching people how to respectfully use their guns and safely use them and store them. At least some of the violence could be alleviated through adequate gun safety lessons."

When I ask him about the studies that demonstrate that owning a gun increases the likelihood of accidentally shooting yourself or getting shot by an intruder, Guin acknowledges that gun owners have had their own firearms wrestled away from them and used against them. Even police officers, he allows, have been overpowered on occasion and shot with their service weapons. But Guin insists such outcomes are unlikely if someone is well-trained. "With a well-armed individual who is trained thoroughly and practices regularly, it's going to be far more challenging to do that," he says.

When Rocky Mount's members voted on the gun range proposal, there wasn't a single dissenter. Guin acknowledges that building the range would be unorthodox in most church contexts, but he contends it's no different from a church pursuing unconventional ministry through a coffeehouse, a movie theater, a pickleball league, or taekwondo or yoga classes: "I see moral equivalency there."

Since then, Guin says, he has consulted with several churches in Texas and the Midwest whose leaders wanted to replicate Rocky Mount's firing range and gun ministry. Mostly the questions focus on liability and insurance issues.

"Most of the county seemed to be OK with it. I didn't get too much pushback here. I was invited to speak at a couple of events about the gun range—Lions Club, things like that—and probably had a couple of unusual questions asked during the course of that time. But they were kind of just pushing me to see how far I would go, you know? And I think they realized that I was, for the most part, measured."

Outside of Alabama, however, critics savaged both Guin and his church. Greg Fallis, a writer and photographer who has taught courses in criminology and sociology at American University in Washington, DC, and Fordham University in New York, questions why Rocky Mount didn't find a more virtuous use for its land. With so many options that are clearly consistent with the central tenets of Christianity—such as a community garden, a concert gazebo, a youth basketball court, a baseball diamond, or a soccer pitch—why would a church build a gun range?

"We're talking about a church here, a building used for religious activities, for worship," Fallis writes in a scathing blog post. "I'm not a Christian, but even I understand that there's a fundamental disjuncture between a structure dedicated to a religious figure called the 'Prince of Peace' and a goddamned gun range."

Guin, who speaks admiringly of the nineteenth-century Methodist evangelist Peter Cartwright—a circuit-riding preacher infamous for carrying a Bible in one hand and a gun in the other—shrugs off his critics. "I understood from the very beginning that there were going to be people who would not like this idea, no matter what logic our approach, because they were thoroughly anti-gun and anti-violence," he says, adding: "*I'm* anti-violence. Who in our culture is *for* gun violence except for violent offenders?"

But Guin returns to the "guns don't kill people; people kill people" argument. "The gun never shoots anybody on its own. It's always the person behind it. I think there are certain people in our society who should not have guns—I'll say that boldly. They just shouldn't. But they're going to get them one way or the other because of criminal enterprises at work that sell guns."

Isn't it unsettling, though, I ask him, to see people in church with their hands raised in worship, exposing their holstered guns?

"It probably is, although I'd say that within the South it's not uncommon," Guin says. He wouldn't be surprised, he says, if as many as 70 percent of Chilton County's residents engage in concealed carry of a firearm.

He's one of them. Guin typically carries a Ruger .380-caliber pocket pistol. Fortunately, like his parishioners, he's never needed to pull it on anyone.

"If I ever have to respond to a threat, Lord, let it be that I'm defending someone else's life or liberty or property," he says, then pauses.

He furrows his brow and clarifies: "Property is another issue. That's a debate even among legal scholars, whether defending property is acceptable or not. That's another story."

♦ ♦ ♦

The castle doctrine is the legal principle that individuals have a right to use reasonable force, including deadly force, to protect themselves and their families against an intruder in their home. It has spawned numerous "stand your ground" laws, sometimes known as "make my day" statutes, in deference to a famous quote by *Dirty Harry* actor Clint Eastwood. Such laws are objectively racist. A 2022 analysis by Duke University's Center for Firearms Law finds that homicides in which white people kill Black people are judged to be justified under "stand your ground" laws *five times* more often than homicides involving a Black shooter and a white victim.

Such laws nonetheless are on the books in well over half of the states, and Alabama's version would give Guin legal cover if he ever discharged his weapon in self-defense. Guin assures me he's thought through that worst-case scenario. If an intruder broke through the door to his home, "I would shoot them dead."

"I still believe there's a biblical mandate for me as a man, and I know this is unpopular, to take care of my family: financially, spiritually, morally, and physically," he says. "I think you would, too—maybe not with a gun, but with a baseball bat."

I pause to think about that for a moment, and he's probably right. In fact, I have a baseball bat in the house for that very purpose. My given name, William, means "resolute protector," and there's no way I'd let a home invasion go unanswered. But I also can't justify keeping a loaded gun within reach so I can dispatch an intruder into eternity, as some evangelicals I've met have no problem planning to do, at least conceptually.

"I'm getting too old to use baseball bats anymore," Guin responds. "And I'm not ready to fight anybody anymore. But I'm more than willing, if I have to, to engage them with the firearm."

A few years ago, Rocky Mount chose to disaffiliate with the United Methodist movement in which it was founded in the early 1950s, although not because of anything having to do with guns or gun policy. They disaffiliated in protest of the denomination's support of the LGBTQ+ community. Although it retains the Methodist name, the congregation remains independent. "We're not beholden to anyone except one another," he says, but adds: "It was probably the most difficult decision of my life."

Putting in the gun range comes in a close second. Guin doesn't apologize for that decision. As he searched the Bible for guidance, he realized there's no explicit counsel about weaponry, requiring believers to do their best to suss out a defendable position. "There are those interesting places in scripture where nothing is said. There are assumptions made. There are areas of cloudiness," he says.

Guin repeatedly returns to one theme during our conversation, and it's one you'll hear frequently if you spend any time with white evangelicals: Society is fraying at the seams; we've abandoned our Christian values; and it's only going to get worse.

"When I was in high school in the 1970s, people would show up in the parking lot of the school with their deer rifles on a rack on their pickup truck. People carried pocketknives with them to school. What changed from the 1970s to the present? It's not so much the number of guns that is the problem. It's what's happened to our society," he says.

"There's this darkness that seems to be out there in my culture. Some of it is video gaming, but my son is an avid video gamer, and he says it absolutely has nothing to do with video games. It has to do more with the darkness. When Christianity was the predominant religion of the United States, we had lower crime rates. We had less violent crime. We had less rape. There were a lot of things that didn't happen at that time that do happen now. You know, I can probably count on one hand the number of fistfights that I saw in my high school, and I was in a couple of them. It just was a different culture."

Guin says he blames social media and the breakdown of the family, then waves his iPhone and adds: "And these horrible instruments of the devil. I think they have changed our culture in a way that we'll never get back. Something has changed, and it's a spiritual issue more than it's a gun issue, in my humble opinion. I'm sure I would get a lot of people disagreeing with me sociologically and otherwise, but . . . The mental illness crisis is part of that darkness I see that has descended upon us."

On Sunday morning, the pastor elaborates on this in his sermon:

> Darkness and chaos seem prevalent as our cultural norms seem to be collapsing around us. Things seem to be a mess. The weird and the perverse are now celebrated and embraced by our society. Once sacred cultural norms are collapsing around us or have collapsed around us. When this present darkness surrounds you, call on the name of Jesus. . . . You know, I often wonder if our republic will stand for another fifty years. Our culture is changing

rapidly. The values that we grew up with are being sacrificed on the altar of modernism and paganism. Our Bible and the orthodoxy that it held fast for 2,000-plus years is being challenged by theologians, by pastors, by lay people, unbelievers, and even comedians. There is chaos and confusion all around us. Right is wrong and wrong is right. People are afraid right now. It's a scary world out there right now.

On guns, Guin says, he is fundamentally guided by this principle: *Don't let something happen to someone else that you would not want to happen to you.* It's sort of a corollary to the golden rule: *Do unto others as you would have them do unto you.*

The golden rule, however, is not displayed on the altar at Rocky Mount. What *is* prominent is a large banner that reads: *Blessed be the Nation Whose God is the Lord.* That's Psalm 33:12, an Old Testament verse popular among nationalist Christians, so I ask Guin if he considers himself among their ranks.

"I hate labels, but OK, yeah, I'm a patriotic Christian," he says. "I still believe that our country is one of the greatest countries that's ever been known on the face of the Earth. So, if you want to call me a Christian nationalist, I prefer not being labeled that—I'm just not into identity politics, to be honest with you."

Elaborating, he adds, "I don't know if I've ever met a Christian nationalist. I mean, I've met patriotic Christians who call themselves Christian nationalists. But if they're truly Christian, they don't really want to control people. If you're truly Christian, you're not about controlling other human beings. You don't want to do that. Now, do we want to control crime? Of course. We want to control certain aspects of our society. But that's just part of having, per Romans 13, a just government."

In Romans 13:1–5, the apostle Paul admonishes Christians to obey the government:

Let everyone be subject to the governing authorities, for there is no authority except that which God has established. The authorities that exist have been established by God. Consequently, whoever rebels against the authority is rebelling against what God has instituted, and those who do so will bring judgment on themselves. For rulers hold no terror for those who do right, but for those who do wrong. Do you want to be free from fear of the one in authority? Then do what is right and you will be commended. For the one in authority is God's servant for your good. But if you do wrong, be afraid, for rulers do not bear the sword for no reason. They are God's servants, agents of wrath to bring punishment on the wrongdoer. Therefore, it is necessary to submit to the authorities, not only because of possible punishment but also as a matter of conscience.

It's a strange passage to quote for evangelicals who argue there is an existential need to be armed and ready to resist a wayward government. But I decide not to go there with Guin. He's already explaining another widely held view among evangelical gun owners: There's a reason the founders ordered the Bill of Rights in such a way that the Second Amendment follows the First.

"Implicit to the Second Amendment is the fight against tyranny. The founders recognized that our own government can become tyrannical against its very people. They witnessed that firsthand, and they didn't want us to have to deal with that ever again," he tells me. "I think I would be very hesitant as a citizen to ever give up gun ownership because of that. I think there's a certain movement across the globe right now for control, and I'm all about freedom."

While Guin is a fierce advocate of the Second Amendment, he admits to being troubled by the sheer number of guns circulating in the United States. In fact, he suspects reality may exceed the official federal estimates by a factor of five. "I don't think they're accounting necessarily for the number of guns that have been handed down from generation to generation, because there's no way to account for that."

But he gives himself a pass when it comes to his firing range. "The gun range just happens to be sort of like [what] a gun is: a tool. It's not really the focus of our ministry here at the church," he says. "I'm not here to argue with anyone over the issue. This is just where our feet landed."

And then, concluding our interview with a humility that you'll rarely see in modern evangelicalism, he adds this: "Look, I may find out in the end that I'm judged on this by God. I may. And if I do, I'll depend on God's grace and mercy."

♦ ♦ ♦

Rocky Mount's elderly congregation seems more self-assured about the church's gun range than its pastor. "We never thought of it as being something so controversial," says Charlotte Powell, the gun-packing widow.

Sunday service has just let out, and in the pew in front of me, John Wortham—a retired former military intelligence officer and a student of history—stands and turns to shake my hand and talk about guns, God, and the Constitution.

"A lot of people will make something out of the Second Amendment that says it's either for hunting, self-protection, or against tyranny. My viewpoint is you can't separate self-protection and tyranny, so it's really only two: hunting and self-protection. Tyranny and self-protection go together," Wortham begins.

Figuring out what the founders meant, of course, is one thing. Interpreting scripture in the way God intended is quite another. "Like anything in the Bible, there's so many verses, and depending how you read them and the context, they can be averse to each other," Wortham says. "If you're going to take somebody's life, and push comes to shove and it comes right down to it, I think you need to study that issue well in advance before it happens. Even before you start thinking of scenarios and what would you do . . . You need to have it settled in your heart—if you're comfortable with doing that. For me, the last act is to pull a gun [because] you're going to fire. You're not just going to pull it out. And I think the Bible gives us freedom to protect: 'Greater love hath no man than this . . .'" (That's from John 15:13: "Greater love has no one than this: to lay down one's life for one's friends.")

"It doesn't matter if it's in a war context or if it's a shooting in the lobby of a hotel or in a restaurant," Wortham continues. "The second law of thermodynamics is that the world is failing. Anything left unattended—and by that I mean without God in their heart and leading—tends to chaos."

I ask Wortham if he's a gun owner, and he says he's a hobbyist. "You know what the definition of a hobby is, don't you? The definition of a beginner? These people on TV sometimes will say, 'Yeah, he had an arsenal. They found him with a rifle and two pistols and a thousand rounds of ammo.' In Texas, that's considered a beginner." We both chuckle.

"Do you conceal carry?" I ask him.

"Yeah. Right now."

"So, you're ready for any situation," I say.

"Well, I try to be."

"Have you ever had to pull your weapon?" I ask Wortham.

"No. But as I said, you have to have it settled, as far as I'm concerned. 'Cause otherwise there's no need to carry."

Wortham says many people mistakenly maintain that the Nazis disarmed the German population. "No, they didn't. It was the Weimar Republic that had the laws that civilians couldn't own guns. The Nazis actually relaxed it a little bit, but only if you were a party member; then you could keep a gun because you could be trusted. But it doesn't matter: The end result was the same. Without weapons, you're defenseless. You're no longer a citizen—you're a servant."

For Wortham, the modern parallel is Vladimir Putin's Russia, where ordinary citizens can't have guns and are therefore powerless to resist his policies. I find this curious, since many white evangelicals seem to echo Trump's admiration for Putin and House Republicans' resistance to providing military aid to embattled Ukraine.

Christian nationalists' affection for the AR-15 is a little like that. Actor and stand-up comic Dana Gould captures the inherent disconnect between patriotism and nationalism perfectly when he says: "The pro-AR-15 argument comes down to 'preventing state tyranny.' In other words, 'I need an AR-15 because one day I might have to mow down a bunch of US soldiers. Don't get me wrong. I support the troops. I just want to be ready to murder as many as possible if necessary.'"

But like any other subset of society, evangelicals are not a monolith. The same goes for gun owners in general.

While in Alabama, I drop in on a gun show in the Birmingham suburb of Trussville. The gentleman at the check-in desk asks me if I'm carrying. The ultimate irony of gun shows is that gun owners who conceal or open carry are asked to surrender their weapons at the door.

I'm curious to see what kinds of characters I'll find in the Deep South firearms subculture. Neo-Nazis, white supremacists, and Christian nationalists had overrun a gun show I visited in my native Massachusetts, unapologetically displaying swastikas, SS insignia, and other Nazi memorabilia. There, display tables were strewn with Oath Keepers patches. Today I expect the same, or worse, of Alabamans.

Instead, the most offensive symbol on display is a single miniature Confederate flag sticking out of a wooden box filled with used revolvers. Most of the sew-on patches being peddled in Trussville are to identify the wearer's blood type; a few are just plain whimsical, like the one that reads: *MAMA SAYS I'M SPECIAL*. These Southern firearms vendors are far more discreet than their northern brethren.

In fact, upon returning home to Rhode Island, I notice a neighbor's pickup truck is suddenly sporting a large new Christian nationalist bumper sticker: *When Tyranny Becomes Law, Rebellion Becomes Duty.*

Although support for Christian nationalism—and by extension, guns—is strongest in rural, conservative states, you'll find both wherever you find white evangelicals. And they're arming themselves largely out of fear that they're fast becoming a persecuted minority.

You and I may view it as an unfounded paranoia. Yet for millions of conservative Christians, their identity as a persecuted minority is no less palpable—and maybe more so—for our skepticism.

# 5 | THE FEAR FACTOR

Heads up, evangelicals: They're coming for you.

They're coming for your Bibles. They're coming for your guns. They're coming for your children. They're coming for your freedoms.

They're coming for your very way of life.

This is a myth, of course. White evangelicals are arguably the most privileged class in America, with influence and political clout that many truly vulnerable segments of society—think communities of color, the marginalized rural poor, and the embattled LGBTQ+ population—can only dream of.

And yet it persists, driving the narrative around the supposed need to be armed for self-protection. Or, in a darker and more extreme rationalization, for overthrowing the government.

It's a siege mentality you'll see reflected in hundreds of online forums and chat rooms as well as across mainstream social media platforms. Extremist groups, including anti-government militias, are using it as a recruiting tool. Donald Trump has repeatedly invoked it, telling NRA members, "They're coming for your guns!" He has assured rallygoers in the Midwest he'll "end the war on Christians," and has even railed against a nonexistent "war on Christmas."

I've been a Christian for more than forty years. And I just keep thinking: *What war?*

Fear begets fear. It's a vicious circle: Evangelicals are acquiring weapons to help themselves feel more secure, but no gun can ease their anxiety about their standing in American life. Rather than making society safer, guns make our world more dangerous and unpredictable—precisely what most law-and-order Christians will tell you they're trying to avoid. In the city of Atlanta alone, about two thousand guns are stolen from their owners' vehicles every year. That's double the rate of firearms theft just five years ago, and many of those weapons end up in the hands of criminal gangs.

Social scientists, meanwhile, point to rising evidence that suggests fear of crime itself may make public safety worse; and more guns in the home increases the likelihood of a suicide or a homicide. "Decades of social science research shows that people tend to overestimate their chances of becoming victims . . . and that fear of crime sometimes reflects underlying racial or ethnic prejudice," Neil Gross, a professor of sociology at Colby College, says in a *New York Times* op-ed.

Evangelicals are no exception, and they've been shown to greatly exaggerate what they perceive as threats to their faith. An insightful example: In 2022, the pollster YouGov asked them how many Americans are atheists, and white evangelicals said 33 percent. In reality, only 3 percent of Americans don't believe in God.

Among lower- and middle-class white evangelicals, fear manifests in unfounded but strongly held convictions: Their lives aren't better because of the immigrants, Muslims, and the detached political elite (read: Democrats) who are weakening the country.

Some, embracing such falsehoods, simply hunker down and work to maintain their livelihoods, raise their families, and contribute to their communities. Some adopt MAGA demagoguery or believe and spread QAnon conspiracies.

Others buy a gun.

♦ ♦ ♦

Truth is, no one is coming for anyone's Bibles or guns. That, however, hasn't stopped the politics of fear from flourishing. And surveys show it's become a key reason why evangelicals and others feel compelled to buy and carry firearms.

The Pew Research Center asked Americans if they thought life has become harder in the United States for people with strong religious faith. Seventy percent of evangelicals said yes, compared to 47 percent of respondents overall.

The Survey Center on American Life conducted a separate poll in 2023 asking people if they thought Christianity was under attack: 60 percent said yes, and 61 percent of white evangelicals said they feel like they're now as big a target of discrimination as members of racial minorities. Meanwhile, the number of evangelicals who think gays and lesbians suffer significant discrimination fell by nearly half.

"Fears that conservative Christians are facing an increasingly hostile cultural climate are being fanned by political elites," says Daniel Cox of the Survey Center on American Life. He adds: "Encouraging white evangelicals to believe their political foes are bent on their complete destruction leads to a most simplistic approach to political conflict—every issue is divided into winners and losers."

A caveat here is critical: These fears are distinct from the anxiety disorders that many Americans suffer from. As someone who's battled depression and anxiety myself, I'll be the first to say there's no shame in it. More than 19 percent of adults and one in four adolescents battle chronic functional anxiety rooted in physiological or psychiatric causes for which there are excellent treatments. If you're struggling from anxiety, don't buy the line that well-meaning but seriously mistaken evangelical pastors and believers all too often will feed you: "Try praying or reading your Bible more." Instead, seek out your primary care doctor and a licensed therapist.

Right-wing candidates, including avowed Christian nationalists, regularly rev up supporters with false narratives about stolen elections and extremist rhetoric. Centered on the supposed tyranny of the federal government, such rhetoric serves to make anarchy and armed rebellion more mainstream. And the gun industry and its influential lobby fan the flames.

In a special report—*Paranoia and Profit: Armed Extremism and the Gun Industry's Role in Fostering It*—the organization Everytown for Gun Safety highlights the insidious ways in which the firearms industry profits from fear and hate. "The industry and its lobbying apparatus have for decades warned target audiences of unhinged existential threats all around them, from supposed criminal hordes threatening their homes to tyrannical bureaucrats threatening their rights," the report says, adding: "In the face of these supposed threats, the firearms industry offers a single solution for those who feel at risk: guns, and the deadly violence they can achieve."

My neighbor across the street, Roger, trafficked in these fears. Or maybe he was victimized by them; it's hard to say. What I can tell you is that he died in possession of a formidable cache of AR-15s. A gruff retired corrections officer who lived alone with his dogs, espoused QAnon conspiracy theories, and railed loudly against the Black Lives Matter movement, Roger declared that if protesters roused by the police murder of George Floyd ever marched to our neighborhood, he'd be ready.

As we've seen, unfounded fears of a deep-state conspiracy to eradicate Christian values date back at least to the 1970s, when the late Reverend Jerry Falwell's Moral Majority and other players on the religious right stood shoulder to shoulder and boosted their profiles and followings by appealing to the latent paranoid streak that so often lurks within the human soul. More recently, evangelicals have used such fears to dehumanize, demonize, and "otherize" LGBTQ+ citizens, the Black Lives Matter movement, and other groups they accuse of contributing to the undermining of traditional values and the breakdown of the heterosexual American family.

Their latest target: restrictions on guns.

"This same paranoid fantasy undergirds much of religious conservatives' opposition to gun control," historian Neil J. Young says. "While no personal arsenal is likely to turn back the federal government's forces, many religious conservatives, especially white evangelical men, worry that any limitation on gun rights will infringe on their ability to protect their loved ones. If defending the traditional family has been a largely metaphorical concern for the religious right when it comes to abortion and gay rights, it's very much literal when it comes to guns."

Writer Alan Noble frames it more forcefully. Writing in *The Atlantic*, he contends the only way to counter and correct these misapprehensions "is for white evangelicals to engage in conversation with real people and not with the malevolent ghosts haunting their imagination."

This fear factor increasingly is preoccupying experts who study gun violence. "It all plays upon fear, which is one of the most visceral, motivating emotions we have," says Tim Carey, law and policy adviser at Johns Hopkins University's Center for Gun Violence Solutions.

"When that powerful raw emotional response is co-opted for political means, it can lead to the results we're seeing today, where people are clinging to and actively perpetuating the exact harms they're afraid of," he tells me in an interview. "The reality is that these guns are causing more harm. They're causing more death. Clinging to firearms and proliferating them in society is exacerbating the very fears that they're worried about. And it's almost like this negative feedback loop: we acquire more guns; society becomes less safe because of those guns; and because we're afraid because society is less safe, we acquire more guns. The key is to try to break the cycle and change the narrative of fear."

Carey readily acknowledges he hasn't been dialed into the singular role that white evangelicals play in the gun ecosystem. Few firearms scholars have. That needs to change, he says. "Candidly, evangelicals and the religious connotations and attachments to the gun rights movement are not something that at least I reckon with—and I think it's something that needs to be discussed," Carey says. "Otherwise, it will continue with the status quo. And that's something that's perpetuating the situations we find ourselves in."

Tragically, mass shootings have become such a routine part of that status quo that Carey doesn't see even a bloodbath as a precipitating event capable of breaking the political impasse. "Candidly, if Sandy Hook wasn't enough to inspire widespread federal action on guns, then I don't think events in themselves will be enough anymore," he says.

Even mass shootings themselves grip us with arguably outsized fear. The probability of being caught up in one is infinitesimally small—roughly the same odds as being slain by a jihadist (another irrational fear that some evangelicals share.) But it's also not nothing. Since 2014, nearly 42 million Americans—more than an eighth of the population—have lived within a mile of a mass shooting, according to a CNN analysis of gun violence and census data.

Worries of being a victim of a mass shooting far exceed the probability of that happening. That anxiety is "way out of proportion with the risk," says James Alan Fox, a renowned Northeastern University criminologist who maintains a database of mass killings. "The epidemic is fear of mass shootings, not the mass shootings themselves," he tells *Slate*.

As Cameron MacKenzie, an associate professor at Iowa State University who specializes in decision and risk assessment, puts it: "Mass shootings are very low probability but very high consequence events."

In our conversation, I ask Carey: "If there's one thing you could tell evangelicals and other strongly pro-gun Americans—if you could appeal to their better angels and their overall pro-life stance—what would you say to them?" He doesn't hesitate with his answer. "Gun violence prevention is not an absolute. It's not an ultimatum. It's not an absolute dichotomy," he says. "It's not either you have gun rights or you don't. There is in all of law a balance between freedom and security. Laws are security; liberties are freedoms. And we have to strike a balance between those two to live in a society together. We can't just have one or the other. These measures aren't designed to prevent you from owning or using a firearm. They're specifically tailored to ensure that dangerous people don't have access to firearms. There's a balance here, and it's to protect human life."

As we've seen, there's a preponderance of evidence that US states with the weakest gun laws have the highest rates of firearm mortality. "We have a wealth of information showing that more guns make people less safe," Carey says. In particular, he calls out "stand your ground" laws that give citizens legal cover to fire on intruders rather than take the more sensible action: retreat. "They increase firearm homicides in states as opposed to decreasing them. They're encouraging people to escalate and engage in situations that may otherwise have ended with people just walking away," he says.

The gun lobby, Carey agrees, is skillfully capitalizing on our deepest fears. "They're very effective in using stories to scare people: the story of the home intruder, the story of the subway at night in New York City," he says.

◆ ◆ ◆

What if we're afraid of the wrong things? Anthony L. Fisher, senior opinion editor for the *Daily Beast*, suggests as much: "Patriotic culture warriors are terrified of drag queens, 'illegals,' and extremely rare vaccine injuries. But tens of thousands of annual gun deaths—meh." The carnage, he writes, "doesn't move the right's culture war outrage needle. Not one bit."

From Matthew Teutsch, director of the Lillian E. Smith Center at Piedmont College, comes a warning: Among evangelicals with a persecution complex, the politics of fear risks becoming the violence of fear. "Fear is a powerful weapon," he says.

Right-wing evangelicals who traffic in such fears propagate an "inherently abusive, authoritarian kind of Christianity" that keeps America from properly addressing gun violence, contends Chrissy Stroop, a prominent *ex*vangelical writer, speaker, and advocate. "Reactionary Christians allowed themselves to be driven by fear of change, fear of modernization, fear of any knowledge that challenged their understanding of their faith," she writes for the website Religion Dispatches. "But what, deep down, are they really afraid of? While they would contend that to give up their views on such matters as prayer in school and the so-called traditional family would lead to a destructive nihilism, it's their inability to trust their own moral compass that leads them into a violent and ultimately nihilistic politics."

Evidence abounds that the debate over guns has become a zero-sum proposition: You're either for imposing a complete ban on civilian firearms ownership, as other countries have done, or you support free and unfettered access to weapons where everything goes, including AR-15s and high-capacity magazines. There's no in-between.

Lost in this polarized environment are the commonsense gun restrictions we keep talking about, such as universal mandatory background checks and a ban on military-style assault rifles. Despite broad public support, they languish amid a cultural deadlock that views compromise as capitulation.

Over the past few decades among evangelicals and fundamentalists, "a mood of fear emerged—the belief that catastrophe was just around the corner, a sense that those who didn't share their views were out to destroy their country, their values, their children," says Jim Eckman, a pastor and theologian in Nebraska.

"For many evangelicals, politics became a contest between the Children of Light and the Children of Darkness. They raged against their opponents, whom they saw less as fellow citizens than as their enemies," says Eckman, who hosts a radio program titled *Issues in Perspective*.

This us-versus-them dynamic lends a sense of urgency to the rise of Christian nationalism—especially when it's paired, as we've seen, with an unprecedented glut of guns.

Wrongly justifying the need to use those guns on each other isn't a big leap, Curtis Chang and Nancy French argue in their 2024 book, *The After Party: Toward Better Christian Politics*. "The connection between relational division and political violence makes intuitive sense when you ponder the basic question: 'How do you get to the point where one group of citizens can contemplate physically harming another group of citizens?'" they write.

"This happens only if those two groups are socially separated into an *us* and a *them*. Once *them* no longer appear in the social lives of *us*, it becomes easier to dehumanize them. Add in the fear, often stoked by political leaders, that 'they are out to get us,' and the situation grows more volatile."

Feeding such fears has become the mark of the ascendent New Apostolic Reformation (NAR) movement we've touched on in previous chapters. Its adherents are combining the usual fears of secular humanism with worries about a coming global economic meltdown in their appeal to white evangelicals to join their ranks—all under the guise of a potent "prophetic" approach claiming to impart a revelation from God to his modern followers. They frequently invoke the need to engage in spiritual warfare, but with fiery rhetoric that blurs the line between prayer and actual warfare. David R. Brockman, a scholar in the religion and public policy program at Rice University's Baker Institute and an instructor at Texas Christian University, calls the NAR "Christian nationalism on steroids."

"The danger lies in their claims that their side has divine authority while their opponents are the tools of literal demons," Brockman writes in an expose for *Texas Observer* magazine. "Many of us who are not NAR adherents—Christian and non-Christian alike—may find in today's politics something 'demonic,' if only in a metaphorical sense. But we find it in very different places than do these prophets: in some politicians' vigorous embrace of autocracy; in the vilification of migrants; in the relentless efforts to take away hard-won rights from women, the LGBTQ+ community, and people of color; in the shameless use of public office for self-enrichment; and in the exploitation of religion for political gain. Of course, there is nothing supernatural about those evils. They're just the latest examples in a long, sad history of human iniquity."

Clearly there *are* things to worry about—crime and poverty, for starters—and fear isn't inherently bad. It's a primal instinct we've evolved to save ourselves from clear and present dangers. But fear can make us foggy—not a good state when we're making an important decision such as whether to buy a gun.

Zachary Sikora, a clinical psychologist at Northwestern University's Feinberg School of Medicine, is an expert in the science of fear, and he says that as the brain's amygdala senses fear and kicks in, the cerebral cortex—the part of the brain responsible for reasoning and judgment—becomes impaired. When that happens, it's difficult to make good decisions or think clearly: a likely explanation for why gun purchases spike after mass shootings.

In that context, white evangelicals lack a healthy fear of truly existential threats, such as human-caused climate change. Many either deny it exists outright or shrug it off, reasoning it doesn't matter when biblical prophecy promises a new heaven and a new Earth (and, in so doing, both shirking the scriptural admonition to be good stewards of the planet and alienating themselves from the rest of society).

Meanwhile, Christian nationalism stokes unreasonable fears of violence, and the National Rifle Association and other like-minded gun rights groups exploit them, too. Gun sales beyond the purchase of firearms for sport are largely driven by these fears and have contributed to America's massive glut of guns.

"Siege mentality, whether threats are real, perceived, or a combination thereof, has a way of cutting people off from alternative viewpoints and messaging that might contradict their worldview," Leslie Cohen writes in *The Cairo Review of Global Affairs*.

And it's nothing new. Cohen quotes Thomas Lecaque, a professor of history at Grand View University in Des Moines, Iowa, a private liberal arts college affiliated with the Evangelical Lutheran Church in America, who observes: "People have been panicking about the collapse of Christianity since the nation's founding."

The evangelist Billy Graham was beloved by many evangelicals, but Graham helped weaponize fear among fundamentalist believers. It began in the 1950s, long before he'd go on to become "America's pastor," when he railed against the threat posed by godless communism. The National Prayer Breakfast in Washington, DC, was born of Graham's charismatic fearmongering, and it, too, has been regularly hijacked by evangelical leaders with an agenda at the Capitol.

Before Graham, evangelicals "used to be the dissenters, the contrarians, the non-establishment, the counterculture," says the Reverend Rob Schenck, the longtime national antiabortion activist we met in chapter 1 who now advocates for restrictions on America's firearms free-for-all. "Until the Billy Graham era," he says in our interview.

"I have great affection for Billy Graham, God rest his soul," says Schenck. "But if you look at what Graham did, he mainstreamed evangelicalism. He took it from a minority that existed on the margins of society and very much identified with the underclass—certainly the working class—and took it into the middle and upper middle classes and even arguably above that as a mainline religious institution," Schenck says.

Franklin Graham, who inherited his father's ministry and mantle as president of the Billy Graham Evangelistic Association, has come out repeatedly and forcefully against any gun restrictions. He's even prayed publicly for gun rights to continue unimpeded. And he posts regularly about gun access on social media, including this head-scratcher on Facebook: "I've been asked to pray at the opening session of the NRA Annual Meeting and for their prayer breakfast. There's been an ad circulating asking me to call on the NRA to support universal background checks. I want you to know that God has already done a universal background check on every one of us. He created you and knows everything about you. Nothing is hidden from His eyes." (Maybe nothing is hidden from God, but there's plenty that we mere mortals can't see—for instance, whether that customer who just walked out of the local gun shop with a newly purchased semiautomatic has a criminal record.)

More recently, the evangelical movement is being remade in the image of the Christian nationalist: someone who sees America's diversity as a threat, not a strength, and wants the country declared a Christian nation, an age-old impulse of many believers that has had disastrous consequences. That, Schenck notes, was arguably the most grievous error of the Roman empire.

"Once you do that, then you need an army. If Christian nationalists see the Christian nation as needing to protect itself against aliens and strangers and foreigners and invaders, then we need a Christian army. And an army needs to be armed," he says, warning: "The next thing we might see are Christian militias."

Indeed, fear of the deep state has supplanted the Graham-era fear of foreign communism. It's a bottomless well that the Christian right returns to regularly to stoke religious insecurities, framing it as an epic battle pitting evil against good.

Stowe Boyd, a thinker and an expert in what he terms the anthropology of the future, frames it this way: "The evangelicals and other white identity demographics fear the 'collapse of society, as they know it,' the white majoritarian world order."

In my own lifetime, fear and faith have been inseparable—at least within the evangelical movement, where "hellfire and brimstone" preaching persists.

Fear of pop culture and cultural touchstones such as video games remains rampant. My son, Nicholas, is one of the industry's most sought-after video game character designers, and I marvel at his ability to create virtual worlds of stunning beauty. He's a devout Christian, and I believe his gifts are God-given.

My grandsons, too, play video games—not gory games like *Manhunt* and *Mortal Kombat* but action-adventure experiences like *Minecraft* and *The Legend of Zelda*. Those games have helped the boys develop quick reflexes, creative and strategic thinking, and a deft touch on the joystick—all skills sure to be in high demand in the job market of our AI-driven future. Yet many evangelicals see evil lurking in all video games, and they demonize the entire industry.

When I began my faith journey as a college student in the early 1980s, Bill Gothard and his Institute in Basic Youth Conflicts were prominent. Gothard, an authoritarian minister, taught that even singles like us in our mid-twenties were to continue to submit to our parents. Unfurling what he called the "umbrella of authority," Gothard's sketchy seminar—later rebranded the Institute in Basic Life Principles—leveraged believers' innate shame, guilt, and regret—and our fears of hell—to keep us in line. Dating was forbidden; instead, we were supposed to confine ourselves to strictly chaperoned "courtship," sanctioned by our fathers. Men were to dominate, and women were to submit, dress modestly, homeschool their children, and be dutiful and reverent to their husbands—patriarchal doctrine that critics contend helped mask sexual abuse within the ministry and domestic violence in followers' homes. Off-limits were TV, movies, pop music, blue jeans, sleeveless blouses, and even Cabbage Patch dolls, which Gothard said were possessed by Satan.

My first Christian girlfriend attended one of Gothard's workshops, and it tied her in spiritual knots. My wife did, too, years before we met and says she benefited from his instructions to write down the names of everyone she'd ever wronged, then go back to each one to offer a soul-cleansing apology. But a 2023 Amazon Prime docuseries, *Shiny Happy People*, exposes the more cultish aspects of the group that I'd always suspected existed, based on what I'd heard from friends who got involved in it in the early 1980s.

Gothard's teachings "in a nutshell are based on fear and superstition and leave you in a place where you feel like, 'I don't know what God expects of me,'" Jinger Duggar Vuolo, a former Gothard disciple and member of the Duggar family featured in the TLC reality show *19 Kids and Counting*, tells *People* magazine. "The fear kept me crippled with anxiety. I was terrified of the outside world."

In her book, *The Exvangelicals: Loving, Living, and Leaving the White Evangelical Church*, fellow journalist and recovering evangelical Sarah McCammon describes being traumatized as a girl by the gospel of fear: fear of disappointing God; of violating purity culture in a moment of weakness; of being left behind in the rapture, the prelude to Christ's sudden second coming; of going to hell.

"What if, despite the prayers and the promises in the Bible and the reassurances of my parents and pastors, I wasn't *really saved*? And even if I was saved, and it was all true, then what?" McCammon recalls. "There was still so much to fear."

So many Christians have suffered this fear, whether inflicted intentionally or unknowingly, there's even an official psychological diagnosis: "rapture anxiety." Sufferers deal with PTSD, perfectionism, hypervigilance, and difficulty in experiencing pleasure, sexual or otherwise. Meanwhile, the study of religious trauma, sometimes called "church hurt," is an emerging discipline: The Global Center for Religious Research conservatively estimates that a third of all US adults have experienced it at one point during their lifetimes.

♦ ♦ ♦

Fear is the antithesis of faith.

At the Massachusetts megachurch where I used to serve as a worship leader, we often sang a stirring hymn by Stuart Townsend called "In Christ Alone." The song's lyrics describe the way we need not fear death, because Jesus has authority over our futures. Nothing, the lyrics declare, "can ever pluck me from his hand."

Then some of my fellow parishioners walked out of the service just as they entered: with holstered guns pressing on their chests.

"The most frequently cited command in all of scripture, Old Testament and New Testament, is: 'Fear not,'" Tim Alberta, author of *The Kingdom, the Power, and the Glory*, tells PBS's *Firing Line*. "Christians are taught time and time and time again that fear is not only unhealthy but that it's abiblical—that fear is the antithesis of faith."

Sarah Ford, writing on the *Medium* blogging platform, calls the movies and books and lectures and rhetoric that manufacture and intensify white evangelicals' anxiety "fear porn"—and rightfully questions its compatibility with true Christianity. "I find many fundamentalist Christians share this worldview, this dark and dismal view of human nature, and I wonder how they can hold up Jesus as their hero: a man who came to heal and teach people who didn't deserve it," she says.

*New York Times* columnist David French, like me a Christian who used to be fully ensconced in the world of white evangelicalism, sees fear everywhere in the conservative Christian experience. "Talk to engaged evangelicals, and fear is all too often a dominant theme of their political life," he writes in an op-ed for *Time*. French ticks off a number of white evangelical beliefs: "The church is under siege from a hostile culture. Religious institutions are under legal attack from progressives. The left wants nuns to facilitate access to abortifacients and contraceptives, it wants Christian adoption agencies to compromise their conscience or close, and it even casts into doubt the tax exemptions of religious education institutions if they adhere to traditional Christian sexual ethics."

Challenging such ideology, French goes on: "The evangelical church is called to be a source of light in a darkening world. It is not given the luxury of fear-based decision-making. Indeed, of all the groups in American life who believe they have the least to fear from American politics, Christians should top the list. The faithful should reject fear."

Instead, many of us indulge it. And for too many, it ends with a swipe of a credit card at a gun shop or at the firearms counter at Walmart.

"Fear drives gun ideology. But the entire Bible echoes with the refrain: *Do not be afraid*," says Christopher Hays, the theologian we met in chapter 2.

Fear is intertwined with the gun sales that surged during the COVID-19 pandemic and 2020's nationwide racial reckoning as Americans girded for lawlessness, and that have spiked after every mass shooting. The NRA didn't waste any time capitalizing on our fears of the unknown. Less than two weeks into the pandemic, it released a video urging us all to arm ourselves. In the clip, NRA member Carletta Whiting cradles an AR-15 and tells the camera: "You might be stockpiling up on food right now to get through this current crisis. But if you aren't preparing to defend your property when everything goes wrong, you're really just stockpiling for somebody else."

That fearmongering drew a stinging rebuke from Everytown for Gun Safety: "More guns don't mean more safety. If more guns made Americans safe, then we'd be the safest nation in the world—but America's homicide rate is 25 times that of other high-income countries."

## THE FEAR FACTOR

Effective fundraising by the NRA and other gun rights organizations runs on fear and loathing, Schenck says, speaking from experience in raising millions to overturn *Roe v. Wade*.

"Platforms are built on fear and anger," he tells me:

> I've literally had fundraising consultants say to me, "We need more fear and anger. The more fear you give us, the more money we will raise for you. The madder your people are, the bigger the donation they'll send to you." Everything was cast in these dark and menacing terms. You keep in mind this imaginary prospective donor on a rural route in Kansas. Maybe she's a widow and she lives alone in her house and her nearest neighbor is three miles away. One fundraiser told me, "If you make her afraid to walk from her front door out to her mailbox, you have succeeded." They're all employing this same philosophy: the dark side of human psychology. It's just an enormous contributor to this crisis, because now people who never thought of owning a gun need a weapon by their bedside and in their kitchen drawer. Certainly in their car; maybe on their person. Take it to church.

Fear of home invasions, "of terrorists attacking churches and maniacal protesters in the streets," has contributed to our collective trepidation, Schenck acknowledges. But he counters with a challenge:

> Where do we put our faith? Who is our ultimate protector? I talk to evangelical clergy a lot, and many of them travel quite a bit, including to dangerous parts of the world. And I ask them: "Did you ever need your weapon to defend yourself?" I lived in New York City in the 1980s, and I was doing ministry work in Hell's Kitchen and in Harlem during some of its worst times. I was out at night by myself and I was never attacked. I never felt I needed a weapon. I ask them, "What makes you think you need a weapon?"

It's the fear creeping into America's pulpits that worries Schenck the most. An itinerant preacher for thirty-five years, Schenck recalls how a pastor from Sarasota, Florida, approached him at an event in Pennsylvania. The two got to talking, and when the conversation turned to guns, the pastor leaned toward Schenck and said in a hushed conspiratorial tone: "Let me show you something." Schenck recounts what happened next: "And he pushes back his sport coat to reveal a 9mm Glock and tells me: 'I always have this on me. I never go into the pulpit without it.'"

On another occasion, Schenck was preparing to talk about the questionable ethics of Christianity and firearms to a large evangelical congregation in Utah when the pastor there, in an apparent last-minute change of heart, took him aside and suggested he change his sermon. "Don't bring up guns in my pulpit," the preacher warned. When Schenck expressed surprise and asked why not, the pastor said, unsmilingly: "I've got fifty armed people in front of you in the seats. If they don't like what you're saying, I can't promise what they may or may not do." And he was quite serious, Schenck says.

♦ ♦ ♦

The gun owner's psyche can be fascinating.

Anthropologist Morwari Zafar of Georgetown University's Center for Security Studies took a deep dive into the hopes and fears of militias and gun rights activists while a research fellow at the University of Oxford's Rothermere American Institute. As an Afghan American, Zafar approached the issue clear-eyed, convinced that there's nothing that makes the United States immune to homegrown extremism on a large scale. What she found: "an almost pathological preoccupation with fear and survival."

"Many [militia] members' unwavering support for the Second Amendment was driven not by an ideological support for guns, but primarily by a desire for belonging and shared purpose in a world they perceived as profoundly endangered," Zafar writes in *Sapiens* magazine.

Both sides in America's gun debate are influenced by "a shared culture of fear," says Joseph M. Pierre, a professor of psychiatry and biobehavioral sciences at UCLA's David Geffen School of Medicine. "One side believes that guns are a menace to public safety, while the other believes that they are an essential tool of self-preservation," Pierre concludes in a study published by Nature Portfolio:

> One side cannot fathom why more gun control legislation has not been passed in the wake of a disturbing rise in mass shootings in the US and eyes Australia's 1996 sweeping gun reform and New Zealand's more recent restrictions with envy. The other, backed by the Constitutional right to bear arms and the powerful lobby of the National Rifle Association, fears the slippery slope of legislative change and refuses to yield an inch while threatening, "I'll give you my gun when you pry it from my cold, dead hands." With the nation at an impasse, meaningful federal gun legislation aimed at reducing firearm violence remains elusive.

Another study by researchers at Florida State University and the University of Arizona finds evidence to suggest that people who own guns are less afraid in general than those who don't, but they are just as afraid as non-gun owners of being victimized by a random or mass shooting. That seems "to directly contradict common rhetoric put forward by the NRA suggesting that the 'good guy with a gun' is able to bravely counter such threats," the study concludes.

The industry's own research bears that out: 88 percent of Americans are anxious about gun violence, and as a result, nearly half of all gun owners report carrying their own weapons more frequently, according to a survey commissioned by Evolv Technology, a leader in weapons detection systems.

But a pistol isn't a panacea. Ironically, owning a gun raises an individual's anxiety levels, the Association for Psychological Science says. It cites research by social psychologist Nick Buttrick of the University of Wisconsin-Madison showing gun owners tend to be more edgy and hypervigilant.

The independent and nonpartisan Center for American Progress also questions the premise that the answer to the gun crisis is more guns, and that people of goodwill who are armed can and will counteract gun owners with malicious intent. Nine times more people report being victimized by a gun than protected by one, it says, adding: "More guns in America means more gun victimizations, not safer communities or vigilante heroics."

Undeterred, the NRA and other gun rights advocacy organizations advance that false narrative to undermine sensible restrictions and drive weapons sales—an insidious tactic the center contends is "based on gun rights propaganda, evoking images of a society devoid of rule of law and under constant threat of attack from an unidentified but ever-present enemy."

In fairness to people who buy guns for self-protection, they have every right to do so. There's an old joke that goes: *Just because you're paranoid doesn't mean they're not out to get you.* But the good folks of Rocky Mount Church in Alabama will tell you they aren't paranoid. They're merely bringing their weapons to Sunday service out of an abundance of caution, nothing more.

And even amid the fog of fear and firearms, you'll occasionally find gun owners who display remarkable compassion for those who don't share their passion for weaponry. In a compelling first-person account for *The Guardian*, outdoors enthusiast and long-distance dogsledder Blair Braverman describes living with her transgender husband, Quince Mountain, in the north woods of Wisconsin and feeling vulnerable and alone after she was harassed online. What made her feel more secure? A few gun-owning neighbors who came over and taught her how to shoot. "I am extremely liberal, and very much in favor of strict gun control. And yet, when I was scared and my neighbors helped me in the best way they knew how—by showing up, distracting me, encouraging me to explore a limit of my own power—I was moved beyond speech," she writes.

Fear also manifests in the pulpit, where pastors who harbor misgivings about guns are hesitant to speak out, lest they offend the elders or congregants.

Joash Thomas, a former Republican political operative who now works as an international human rights activist, calls gun violence an injustice that persists precisely because it isn't seen as one. He lays part of the blame at the feet of US church leaders and says they have a choice: "complicity or courage." "The widespread prevalence of the injustice of gun violence in America is an indictment of the US church's failure to bring the power of the gospel to bear against this injustice. And it's an indictment of the failure of US church leaders to adequately disciple their people in understanding how the gospel of Christ compels us to lay down our lives and rights for the sake of our neighbors' wellbeing," Thomas says.

In the aftermath of the first of two attempts on Trump's life in 2024, his pro-gun supporters deflected an inconvenient truth: He was very nearly killed by an AR-15. Many of us believe that that military-style rifle has no business being in American homes, yet it was easily and legally acquired by the would-be assassin's father. It's a particularly lethal weapon that Second Amendment defenders nonetheless refuse to restrict.

Rather than address the absurdity of unfettered access to weapons of war, less than forty-eight hours after he escaped assassination at an outdoor rally in Pennsylvania, Trump announced his pick for vice president: JD Vance of Ohio. The Republicans' political platform barely mentions guns beyond a passing reference to the Second Amendment, but the *Hillbilly Elegy* author's US Senate bio tells you everything you need to know about his own faith in firearms: Vance's grandmother, who raised him, "owned 19 handguns and nurtured a deep Christian faith in herself and her family."

Mamaw's guns, incidentally, were all loaded, the candidate bragged at the 2024 Republican National Convention: "They were stashed all over her house. Under her bed, in her closet. In the silverware drawer. No matter where she was, she was within arms' length of whatever she needed to protect her family. That's who we fight for. That's the American spirit."

A similar zeitgeist is evident in Vance's hometown of Middletown, Ohio. Publicly inciting violence, its Republican state senator, George Lang, told cheering rallygoers that a civil war may be needed "to save the country."

Patti Davis, daughter of the late Ronald Reagan—a hero to many white evangelicals—describes in heart-wrenching terms the visceral terror that followed the fortieth president's own close call with an assassin in 1981. Four and a half decades later, it is a terror that still stalks her.

"In the decades since that day, I have lived with a fear of guns, especially concealed guns. Now that fear has expanded to assassins in tactical gear with AR-15-style rifles storming grocery stores, schools, churches, theaters—anyplace, really—and mowing down scores of people in minutes," Davis writes in a guest essay for *The New York Times*. "It is no comfort that my fear is shared by so many Americans. In fact, that adds another dimension. We are, increasingly, a country gripped by fear: It weakens us, gnaws at our confidence, makes us more vulnerable than resolute."

Elaborating, she says:

> Years ago, someone quoted to me a statement they attributed— probably apocryphally—to the Romanian dictator Nicolae Ceausescu. The quote was, "You can do whatever you want if you keep the people frightened enough." There are people in

America who know this and are counting on it. And to have a country in which everyone is scared of who might be legally carrying a gun as they walk through their daily lives means we have a weakened country in which anything is possible. Fear is a breeding ground for autocracy, and history shows us that every democracy that has crumbled did so in an atmosphere of fear. . . . Democracy thrives when citizens feel emboldened by their country, when they feel confident in their freedoms and in a government that exists to make their lives safer, not more at risk. Democracy dies in the dark waters of fear, and that's where we are—swimming for our lives, wondering why a strident minority wants us to drown.

Fortunately, some in the white evangelical community are challenging this deadly status quo.

"The reality is that most of America's gun culture is driven by Christians," says Scott Baker, a Bible teacher and theologian in Tennessee. "Christians in America are going to have to voluntarily divest themselves of weapons of war if we're going to muster the political will to reform our systems and markets that profit from the fear and death they sell. We must see that the fear that drives us to purchase these weapons is far more than a mere stumbling block about which Jesus warned us. We cannot continue to load our guns as we ask, *And who is my neighbor?*"

John Pavlovitz, a Wisconsin pastor, says he's tired of the hypocrisy of evangelicals defending their stockpiling of multiple military-style weapons. "A toxic religion of fear has been so ingrained in the minds of the faithful, they can no longer recognize the disconnect between middle finger-flying, gun-wielding bravado and the compassionate healer Christ they claim to be devoted to," he says. "Millions of people of faith, morality, and conscience simply cannot comprehend how the cause of guns became to so many of our families, friends, and neighbors the solitary hill they will gladly die on."

◆ ◆ ◆

Social justice activist Ed Gaskin is inspiringly multispiritual.

A Black scholar who's active in white evangelical circles, Gaskin attends a Jewish temple and a Presbyterian church in my home state of Massachusetts. He holds a divinity degree from Gordon-Conwell Theological Seminary, which has trained thousands of evangelical pastors and missionaries since the late 1960s, and he has examined the faith and firearms question from every angle. And he has questions.

"The Bible prohibits human sacrifices, yet our country continues to sacrifice human life to the gun idol," Gaskin says in a blog post. Second Amendment absolutism, he reasons, simply leads to more gun carnage. "Are evangelical Christians the problem? White evangelicals seem to have made America's gun culture integral to their faith, unlike Christians in the rest of the world," he adds. "Christians should rethink their unconditional love for unrestricted gun ownership."

There's something else we may want to rethink: the astonishing number of American gun companies that are run by white evangelicals.

There are at least a dozen such companies, maybe more. And for these firearms manufacturers, lethal weapons like the AR-15 and tactical accessories—some even stamped with crosses and verses of scripture—aren't just a business.

They see their work as a way to honor God.

# 6 | GUNMAKERS FOR GOD

Marty Daniel's company makes AR-15-style military-grade assault rifles and sells them to civilians—all for the glory of God.

Some might see a Christian firearms company as an oxymoron, but the born-again executives calling the shots at several leading manufacturers insist there's no disconnect between their gunmaking and their faith.

As you might imagine, that quickly gets complicated for white evangelical gunmakers like Daniel, who's now retired from Daniel Defense, the firearms empire he founded in 2000 in Black Creek, Georgia. Apart from overall ethics concerns, his guns have been used to commit acts of unspeakable evil. Daniel Defense made the rifles that shooters used both in the 2022 slaughter of nineteen children and two adults at Robb Elementary School in Uvalde, Texas, *and* the 2017 bloodbath at the Route 91 Harvest music festival in Las Vegas—the nation's worst mass shooting ever, with sixty concertgoers mowed down and more than 850 others wounded.

Daniel, who sums up his firm's values in three words—faith, family, and firearms—glibly deflects the flak the gunmaker has taken, insisting Americans' Second Amendment rights come directly from the Almighty. His company's social media posts have been astonishingly brash, and its co-opting of Christianity objectively grotesque. On a recent Easter, Daniel Defense posted a photo of an assault rifle atop an open Bible and draped with a crucifix below the message: "He is risen!" In a separate post on X that's since been deleted, it tweeted a photo of a small boy cradling an AR-15 in his lap beneath a verse from the Book of Proverbs: "Train up a child in the way he should go, and when he is old, he will not depart from it" (Prov 22:6).

Daniel Defense, the largest of at least a dozen manufacturers of AR-15s and tactical gear that are run by evangelicals, did not respond to multiple requests for an interview for this book. Nor did most of the others.

But one was willing to talk. One rainy week in August, I decided to visit the company to meet with its owners. Are they complicit in the gun violence that's staining American society? Or are they simply Christians with a commendable work ethic who are deeply committed to their faith, their employees, their community, and their craft? You be the judge.

Here is their story.

◆ ◆ ◆

FosTecH was born in a small town.

Yes, *that* one—Seymour, Indiana, a compact and conservative community best known as the hometown of rocker John Mellencamp, who immortalized it in his eponymous 1985 megahit "Small Town." It's nestled in the rural southern part of the state; a heartland where most cars sport optional license plates with the slogan *In God We Trust*. On the interstate, I pass one with Romans 10:13—*Everyone who calls on the name of the Lord will be saved*—hand-scrawled across its back window in that thick white paint auto dealers use to list prices on used cars. I nod to the driver, a thirtysomething man with a crewcut and neck tattoos. He stares back blankly.

Pancake flat, Seymour is a quintessentially Midwestern place, where folks are polite but mind their own business. A sign as you approach downtown captures the wholesome vibe: *Welcome to Seymour—The Only Good Litter is a Litter of Pups*. In an industrial zone on a dead-end street, next door to Victory Missionary Baptist Church, stands FosTecH. At 64 thousand square feet, the sprawling plant in a renovated former lumberyard is exponentially larger than the company's humble beginnings in 2011 in the basement of founder Judd Foster, who died a decade later from complications of COVID-19. Today, it's jointly run by the founder's brother, Todd, and cousins and siblings Mark, Paul, and David. They form a literal band of brothers: sons and nephews of Brig. Gen. Duane Foster, a decorated Air Force fighter pilot, with a shared passion for firearms and a common Christian faith. Like Daniel Defense, FosTecH describes itself in a company history written for the NRA as committed to *faith, family, and firearms*, but its alliteration includes a fourth core value: *freedom*.

The first thing you notice when you walk inside FosTecH is its elaborate security. Digital thumbprint readers restrict access to parts of the factory; a strict ban on ammunition anywhere in the milling and assembly areas is enforced; guns that briefly chambered rounds for test firing bear cautionary orange flags; and its twenty-five employees have all been subjected to exhaustive background checks. If you're a convicted felon, God might give you a second chance, but you can't work here.

FosTecH is best known for its Origin 12 shotgun that has a circular drum magazine loosely reminiscent of mobster Al Capone's legendary Tommy gun and is capable of unleashing thirty rounds in eight seconds. It also makes lightweight alloy AR-15-style rifles and something it calls the Echo Trigger that lets a shooter fire two bullets in rapid succession: once when the trigger is pulled and again when it's released.

Its guns pack considerable power and deadly precision. When I ask David if they've ever been used in a crime, he answers with a terse "yes." He declines to elaborate, citing pending litigation. But he and Mark Foster, the company's chief engineer, make it clear how they feel about any nefarious use of their firearms.

They and Paul each worked for more than two decades as full-time firefighters, and they've seen more than their share of horror, heartbreak, and human remains. Paul, the county's elected part-time coroner, still does.

"I'm 100 percent against gun violence," David tells me, as automated machinery hisses and clangs on the plant floor. "Every time I hear [about] it, it makes me sick to my stomach."

And Mark, an easygoing man with a down-to-earth demeanor, chimes in with what he insists is a Christian perspective. In a broken and violence-plagued world, "we are allowed to defend ourselves," he says, and husbands and fathers have a biblical duty to defend their wives and children. "Not only do I feel it in the Word—I know it in my heart," he says, briefly tearing up.

FosTecH, Mark says, has put together a tactical backpack he's trying to get into the hands of school resource officers, so they'll be ready at a moment's notice to swiftly subdue a would-be mass shooter. It contains a light rifle and shield the officers can keep with them at all times, "because we know that if it takes you three minutes, two minutes, to go to your car and come back, it's too late."

This strategy is what's known as "hardening" schools, which can also involve arming teachers. Researchers, questioning the effectiveness of such approaches, say they can decrease students' sense of safety and emotional well-being.

Today's gun market is soft and at a six-year low, Mark says—a challenging dynamic complicated by ammunition that's in short supply and selling for double or triple its usual price. To compensate for lower gun sales, FosTecH has been machining diesel fuel system components alongside its rifle barrels, stocks, and triggers. But the company is on solid financial footing because of its conservative growth and because a potentially lucrative new market has opened: a recent sale of Origin 12s to Singapore's national police.

If the Origin 12 turns out to be FosTecH's salvation, it will be ironic, considering the fate that befell its short-lived SBV, or short-barreled version of the powerful gun. In 2019, the US Bureau of Alcohol, Tobacco, Firearms and Explosives (ATF) declared the SBV a Title II weapon, making unregistered possession a violation of the National Firearms Act. Title II weapons, also known as NFA firearms, include machine guns, short-barreled rifles and shotguns, silencers, destructive devices such as grenade launchers, and specialty James Bond-type gadgetry like cane guns and pen guns.

The design of the SBV's folding stock came under the scrutiny of the ATF, which ordered FosTecH to recall the weapons and crush them—ultimately costing it $1 million, not counting millions more in lost sales of its most popular item. Clearly embittered by the ruling, which the Fosters contend singled them out, the company appealed directly to the ATF's deputy director. In the end, it complied rather than needlessly antagonize the feds and, as David puts it, "poke the bear."

The brothers and cousin seem open to conversation, and more curious about what I think than I had expected. So, I ask David, "Is the answer to too many guns really more guns?"

David's response seems rimmed with resignation. "At this point, there's more guns than there are people, so having two guns per person or three guns per person doesn't really make that big of a difference. This country is inundated and flooded with firearms," David answers. "It's a different place, America. We have a gun culture. Good luck getting rid of it. It's not going anywhere. We're not putting that genie back in the bottle."

He pauses, then adds quietly: "*I* would not want to be the police officer that's told to go confiscate everybody's firearms, especially in localities like this all over this country."

◆ ◆ ◆

# IN GUNS WE TRUST

Randy Gilbert, FosTecH's shipping manager, is typing serial numbers into a database. Burly, bearded, and affable, the former youth minister sees the gun business as his second calling. Gilbert, like me a native New Englander, says he's never struggled with the ethics of working for a company whose guns are used for more than just hunting or shooting sports.

"The people in the church I ministered in and in my circles don't necessarily see it as an issue either," he tells me. "I never ran into people who had that kind of conflict. In conservative states, especially when you get outside the major metropolitan areas, like in this town, you're going to be in the minority if you're someone who has a problem [with guns]," he says.

Gilbert recounts, though, that a group of older teens he was pastoring once did approach him with some questions. They were questioning gun ownership and leaning toward pacifism:

> For me, it was always about trying to point them to God and how to sort out who God is. We went over the verses where Jesus would say, "Turn the other cheek," and a lot of what I would consider the theology of a pacifist. And I was like, "Hey, I get it, and those are accurate and they're true." But there's also a verse that says God does not change. The God of the Old Testament is still the God of the New Testament. And when you see the God of the Old Testament, and when you see the God of Revelation, he's a warrior. There's no doubt about it. So for me, it's not an either/or—it's a both/and. For me, I'm able to take all I know about who God is, and I can still be part of a gun manufacturer and a peacemaker. For me, it's about taking all of who God is, not just the bits and pieces I want to. Does he want me to be a peacemaker? Yes. Does he want me to turn the other cheek? Yes. Does he want me not to defend myself? Oh, wait a minute.

Gilbert and his bosses do not deny that our country has a gun violence problem. It's just that they blame it on the erosion of the traditional American family, the abuse of psychotropic drugs, the obsession with social media, and the resultant mental health crisis—not the number of firearms in circulation. Mark describes it as "our family degradation: not having a mom and dad at home raising kids, and the extended family connections that help all that work."

"God had a design and a plan," he says. "And that design and plan creates healthy kids, healthy next generations. You break that design and plan—I'm not going to tell you that there aren't good single moms and good single dads who haven't overcome the trials and tribulations—but the success rate is much lower than if we have those in place."

David wonders aloud: "Why are we spending so much time trying to get rid of guns when it's time to work on healthy families? Maybe that might do something at the root level."

Gilbert again: "I was in youth ministry for sixteen years. I could see the deterioration of the family just in those sixteen years and the difference it made in the way they think, the way that they act, their behavior, all that kind of stuff."

I push back: "Surely, though, the sheer preponderance of firearms is to blame for the gun bloodshed staining America." Then I ask Gilbert: "Do people pack at your church?"

"Yeah, sure," he responds matter-of-factly. "For me, it's more of a protection thing." The way to end gun violence, he argues, isn't to reduce the number of weapons circulating in society; it's to enact stronger penalties for those who misuse or abuse firearms.

David interjects his own thoughts. The United States, he notes, has hundreds of millions of guns in circulation. "They're never going to be gone," he says. "When we enact more gun laws, all we do is take the guns away from the folks who may possibly be there to stop that violence."

Then he adds this surprising footnote: "If we could go back in time to a day where we could say guns never existed, I could probably be on board with that." His sentence hangs in the air for a moment, and I wonder if he knows what he just said. I wonder whether his words represent a rip of self-doubt in the cloth of his vocation, or simply a thread he manages to tuck in around the edges.

But that's not the world we live in, David notes. Many criminals have guns. "The only way you have a chance at all is if you have something that matches that force," he insists. "You can't rely on the police. It would be amazing if you could. But by the time the police get involved, it's over. I don't know if that's a Christian perspective. It's more of a moral ethic for me personally."

"Oh, it's a Christian perspective," Mark assures him. "God's Word is clear on that. We're not allowed to have vengeance, but we are allowed to defend ourselves, and we are allowed to be a part of a state that defends itself. There's no doubt in my mind on that subject. And I think a high percentage of people who carry who are believers have that same conviction."

When I mention that white evangelicals own significantly more guns than any other subset of the US population, none of them seems surprised. "It's a good group to have them," David says.

Mark lives half an hour away in Columbus, Indiana, which is Mike Pence's hometown. He recounts how the then–vice president once visited his home church with a Secret Service detail. Ahead of the Sunday morning worship service, the agent in charge asked how many parishioners would be carrying a weapon that morning. The pastor's response: at least fifty.

"The Secret Service guy's face went white, and then he said, 'This will be the safest place [Pence] is all day,'" Mark says.

Our conversation quickly shifts to the meaning of the Second Amendment and the role of private weapons in countering tyranny. "We are willing to be in front and to lay down our lives if required, just like our cops and our military," Mark says animatedly. "In the United States, we are not subjects—we are citizens. We don't relegate our own defense to the government, whether it's local, state, or federal. It ultimately comes down to a partnership. It's a joint responsibility of that defense. We have it, and we want them to help *us* with it, but we have to help *them* with it—and if we don't take on that responsibility, it's not going to happen."

Recently, Mark says, he was asked to make a presentation at the men's prayer breakfast at his church. The ministry's organizer invited him to bring some of his "toys" along to show the group. But Mark was less interested in bringing along guns his company manufactured than in bringing a message: Evil exists.

"I'm not going to tell every single one of you that you've been called to pick up and bear an arm," he says he told the men at the breakfast. "But every single one of you has been called to confront evil. How you do it will differ." Mark recalls that the group "talked about the body of Christ and how not all of us are called to do the same thing, but some of us have had that feeling, that calling, upon our lives to be that point of protection."

David jumps in, again with a generous response that catches me off-guard. (If you're getting the impression that these evangelical executives are measured, restrained, and respectful, you'd be right. I came away from my three-hour visit disarmed by their humility, integrity, and air of quiet competence.) Christians who have staked out an anti-gun stance, David says, are also trying to fight evil in their own way. "It's just a difference in *how*," he says. He laments the lack of communication and understanding between believers who are pro-gun and those who are anti-gun.

Right about now, I'm remembering how Daniel Defense and half a dozen other Christian gun companies blew off my requests for interviews, so I'm a little skeptical about what Gilbert, the former youth minister, says next: Those in the firearms industry, he claims, are more receptive to talking about the gun violence crisis than many people realize. "The [typical] firearms manufacturer is against gun violence. But you got people who [believe] if you make guns, you're for gun violence. No," Gilbert says. "Some people are very close-minded. They believe that the only way to get rid of gun violence is to get rid of every gun in the United States, and that's just not gonna happen."

But in fact, I point out, some countries—notably Australia and New Zealand—*have* rid themselves of the scourge of routine gun violence. After devastating mass shootings, those countries have charted a different course than we have by keeping firearms out of the hands of civilians, I say.

"Yeah, but we have a thing that's called the Constitution," David says.

As we wander the factory floor, our conversation veers back toward the threat of government tyranny, and I pose a question to the group. Assuming for a moment that there's a constitutional imperative for Americans to arm themselves to keep the government in check, how is an Origin 12 shotgun or even an AR-15 any match for the federal government's firepower: F16s, tanks, nuclear warheads, drones?

FosTecH's executives have heard this argument before, and they don't miss a beat. The National Guard, which is controlled by the states, has all that hardware (minus the nukes) and more, they say. And the notion of the federal government ever unleashing its full force and fury on its own citizenry, they counter, is improbable.

David offers a scenario that is at once bleak and hopeful: "Right now if the president ordered the military to strike the population, there would be some who would say yes. And I'd say there would be a faction of the military that breaks off and says no." The sheer number of Americans who have rifles and shotguns for hunting, he adds, creates the world's largest de facto standing army—a deterrent to any regime contemplating a backlash against the populace.

## GUNMAKERS FOR GOD

What do they make of the independent, loosely organized militias that have sprouted up around the country, I ask the FosTecH managers. Groups like the Oath Keepers and Three Percenters, or the Michigan Militia in my wife's home state? There's an automatic disincentive to joining such a group, David says: You'll end up on a federal watchlist and be considered a domestic terrorist.

Beyond that, though, he's clearly not a fan of homegrown militias. "I'm not going to spend my weekends playing soldier in the woods. I'm just not going to do that," he says. "I train enough to protect my family. That's OK. But I don't prepare for fighting the government. That's not in my wheelhouse. If it gets to that point, I'm not going to stress about it—I'm just going to go somewhere else."

This whole conversation, conducted over the grating din of machinery that's stamping out metal rifle components, is taking us into a disturbing and foreboding direction, we agree. But this is where the conversation invariably leads when you wade into the pros and cons of America's gun culture.

Someone mentions that Americans simply aren't as comfortable as we once were. Our long-standing sense of security has eroded, and our trust in our institutions has taken a hit. That, in turn, has driven record gun sales in recent years, and it's now driving part of the movement to restrict all those guns—especially the AR-15-style firearms that many consider assault weapons.

David has a sarcastic nickname for these types of rifles: "scary guns." In reality, he says, they're no more lethal than semiautomatic handguns, which are used in far more homicides and other crimes nationwide. As I did with Pastor Guin in Alabama, I press back: Although he's right about that, there are plenty of reasons to be frightened of AR-15s, which have become the guns of choice in school shootings and other mass-casualty events. But advocates for gun restrictions, David argues, need to define precisely what an assault weapon is. Anything less, he says, does a disservice to the vast majority of responsible gun owners.

"Are you willing to give up your Ruger 10/22 [semiautomatic rifle]? Your handgun? Your semiautomatic shotgun that you shoot clay birds with?" he asks rhetorically. "Tell me what you're getting rid of." The AR-15, he insists, is a target "just because of how it looks."

In practice, he says, its versatility as a gun that can be used for hunting, competitive shooting, *and* self-defense is why it's the most popular firearm in America. That versatility helps explain why there are more AR-15s than F-150 pickup trucks.

"Is that how we're going to ban things? That makes no logical sense," he says. "There's no common sense. It's all emotion. There's no data and facts around what they're doing. It's just emotion that doesn't work."

Paul, who also runs an excavation business with David, bears a striking resemblance to ex-NFL quarterback Brett Favre and speaks with the folksy diction of George W. Bush, urges opponents to consider the utilitarian aspects of a gun:

> Guns are a lot of different things, but a lot of people don't view guns as a tool. I do. Just like a defibrillator was when I was a fireman—put in the right hands, it's a lifesaving tool. That doesn't get looked at a lot of times with firearms. People are like, "You carry a gun. You're paranoid, aren't you?" I'm not paranoid. It's a tool for me to take care of whoever I'm with, and my family, and then myself. It gives me goosebumps saying that. I used sledgehammers that open doors. We used extrication tools that take people out of cars; bag valve masks to save people. They're all tools—and to me, a firearm is included. Defibrillators are in the back of all the cop cars. They're in the grocery stores. They're in all the churches. How many of those actually get used? There's been one in my church for a decade and it's

never been used, but it's there if you need it. It's better to have it and not need it than need it and not have it.

The cousins offer an example: A young man from Seymour was visiting a mall in another town in Indiana with his girlfriend when a gunman opened fire in the food court, killing three people and wounding two others. The young man drew his own weapon and took out the shooter fifteen seconds into his rampage, averting an even worse bloodbath.

Todd Foster, FosTecH's sales and marketing director, readily acknowledges the role that fear plays in gun sales. White Americans armed themselves in record numbers during the pandemic and the George Floyd protests and after the 2020 election. But with those tensions in the past and FBI data showing sharp drops in violent crime in a number of large cities—in Philadelphia alone, shootings were down 43 percent in 2024—the gun sales bubble has burst.

"Fear has always sold guns," Todd tells me. Five years ago, people feared they wouldn't be able to buy the kind of gun they wanted. "Now it's fear that the government is going to come and take it from me. They don't want to buy something that they're going to have to give away. That's a mindset shift. Fear has done a 180."

Not that I should have any reason to fear on this day, Todd adds coyly. By this point in the conversation, we are having lunch at a Mexican restaurant around the corner from the factory. "In fact, I would say you should feel pretty safe sitting here right now, just in case you were wondering," he says, leaning forward conspiratorially—a clear allusion to the unseen handguns he and the others are carrying.

Since mid-2022, Indiana has been among the rising number of states that allow permitless carry. Also known as "constitutional carry," its success as a deterrent is highly questionable, and I think about telling the executives about this. The online gun violence reporting initiative *The Trace* examined gun fatalities in states where permitless carry was made law, and most saw a surge in fatal shootings excluding suicides.

Still, I understand the visceral way that guns make some of us *feel* safer, even if the data suggests otherwise. And as we talk, I'm having an epiphany: Some of the very things that most bitterly divide us from each other—a visceral need to feel secure, to be in control, to not be afraid—are also what unite us. Maybe, just maybe, the beginning of an answer to our dilemma around guns lies in a deeper exploration of what we've got in common.

It's an unspoken thought, yet David seems to have read my mind. And to my surprise, he readily agrees. He asks me what alternative points of view I've been hearing and reading in my research: What are others saying and thinking about God and guns? He cocks his head to the side and says, with genuine curiosity, "You know: things that might be a nuance to us, that we need to learn from to better understand them?"

I wasn't expecting this.

♦ ♦ ♦

Despite the Indiana company's assertions of softening sales, by all indications, their industry is thriving. The lucrative gun business remains a largely unregulated $9-billion-a-year industry. And white evangelical fingerprints like FosTecH's are all over it.

Manufacturers and retailers of guns, ammunition, and accessories employ more than 384,000 Americans, according to the National Shooting Sports Foundation (NSSF), a leading firearms industry trade association. They're not hurting for customers: 4.3 million people became new gun owners in 2023 alone, and since November 2020, there have been more than 22.3 million first-time firearms purchasers—"a population the size of Florida," the NSSF boasts.

Figures from the ATF, which tracks weapons sales, reflect the industry's relative strength. In a single month in 2023, Americans bought nearly 1.2 million firearms, including about 710,000 handguns and 480,000 long guns. And in 2021 alone, the ATF says 22.5 million guns hit the US market—the most ever so far in a single year.

Evangelicals have carved out an influential industry niche with a faithful following. Most fly the Christian flag, either literally or figuratively, and invoke Bible verses to describe their corporate philosophy and their guns.

FosTecH's approach is more subtle and subdued; it describes itself on its website as "a family-owned Christian company" where "Christian attitude and love for family still hold true today." But even FosTecH, for all its earnestness, has run afoul of the law.

In 2023, the company was fined $4,500 and ordered to register with the state of Indiana as a lobbyist after it offered custom-made AR-15s to Republican state lawmakers at half-price and failed to disclose treating five GOP House members to a dinner where it spent about $1,000. That's instructive, because it shows how evangelical gun company executives feather the nests of Republican lawmakers (in this case, modestly).

Collectively, the gun industry funnels millions of dollars in campaign donations to GOP candidates. The NRA alone spent more than $30 million helping Trump get elected in 2016 and reelected in 2024, and the industry routinely spends $10 million a year on lobbying efforts. Gun opponents spend heavily, too, of course. The political accountability organization Open Secrets says groups like Everytown for Gun Safety gave more than $10 million to Democratic candidates in the 2024 election cycle.

All that lobbying is eye-opening, but the gun companies' marketing in the name of Jesus is jaw-dropping. Some Christian gun manufacturers have overtly biblical names, such as Michigan-based Psalm Products, "combining faith and firepower" to sell "Christian tactical gear" and other items, many imprinted with scriptures like John 3:16. Its mission statement reads, in part, "We believe that this is not our company, it is owned, operated and directed by our CEO 'Jesus Christ.'" The testimonials on the website include one signed simply "Bernie": "I think it's great that I can share my faith and my love for shooting by dressing out my AR-15s with charging handles, trigger guards and dust covers with Bible verses. They work great, they start some great conversations and often open the door for me to share my faith in Jesus Christ with others!"

Tennessee-based Righteous Arms, a Christian-owned retailer, sells ammunition, holsters, and optics. Buffalo Cartridge in Findlay, Ohio, supplies mostly bullets, shells and cartridges under the motto *God, Guns, Country*. "We believe in God and Jesus Christ, and we believe in our sacred right and responsibility to protect human life," the company says on its website.

Cornerstone Arms in Black Forest, Colorado, says its name conveys two convictions: "First and foremost is the fact that our faith in Jesus Christ is the cornerstone of our business, our family and our lives. The second reason for our name is the fact that we believe that the Second Amendment to our Constitution is the cornerstone of the freedom we enjoy as American citizens."

Cornerstone says it donates 10 percent of its profits to Christian ministries in the community and around the country. "We believe that if we always operate our business in a completely forthright and honest manner that honors our relationship with Jesus Christ that we will prosper," it says on its own website.

Another overtly Christian player in the firearms market is Trijicon, a Wixom, Michigan–based company that makes rifle scopes, including tactical night-vision and infrared optics. Its five core values include morality, about which it says this on its home page: "We believe that America is great when its people are good. This goodness has been based on biblical standards throughout our history and we will strive to follow those morals."

Trijicon was the subject of a 2010 ABC *Nightline* investigation into its practice of inscribing shorthand New Testament references on high-powered rifle sights that it manufactures for the US military. Among the Bible book and chapter references etched onto the rifles is "2COR4:6," or 2 Corinthians 4:6, which reads: "For God, who said, 'Let light shine out of darkness,' made his light shine in our hearts to give us the light of the knowledge of God's glory displayed in the face of Christ." Another references John 8:12, inscribed on the gun sights as "JN8:12," which says: "When Jesus spoke again to the people, he said, 'I am the light of the world. Whoever follows me will never walk in darkness, but will have the light of life.'" The Army and the Marine Corps, which at the time had a $660 million multiyear contract with Trijicon to provide rifle sights for troops deployed to Afghanistan and Iraq, said they were unaware of the scripture references. Military rules forbid proselytizing in the two countries.

A Trijicon executive acknowledged the citations, which referenced verses from Matthew, John, 2 Corinthians, and Revelation, telling *Nightline* that company founder Glyn Brindon began the practice. Brindon, an evangelical, died in a plane crash in 2003.

The Military Religious Freedom Foundation, an advocacy group devoted to preserving church-state separation in the military, said the verses not only violated the Constitution and federal law but allowed "the Mujahedeen, the Taliban, al Qaeda and . . . jihadists to claim they're being shot by Jesus rifles."

There's also Spike's Tactical, the Florida AR-15 maker we met briefly in chapter 1 that stamps a scripture verse and the cross of the Knights Templar, a religious order that fought in the medieval Crusades, into the steel of its "Crusader" rifles. Spike's rationale: Having the Bible verse there means Islamic terrorists won't be able to use their rifles. (This of course is ridiculous; like smearing bacon fat all over a gun to repel Muslims the way you'd use garlic to keep mythical vampires at bay.)

The Council on American-Islamic Relations denounced the practice as "a shameful marketing ploy intended to profit from the promotion of hatred, division, and violence." And the Reverend

John Fischer of First United Methodist Church in Apopka, the small city northwest of Orlando where Spike's is based, told a local TV station that a rifle is "perhaps the least desirable" place to put a Bible verse.

Evangelicals in the firearms space have co-opted Christianity for years—but it hasn't always ended well. Three employees of Rapture Guns and Knives, a weapons retailer in North Lakeland, Florida, were among those indicted in the January 6, 2021, insurrection at the US Capitol, including store owner Benjamin Pollock's own brother and sister, charged with assaulting law enforcement officers at the scene. Pollock opened the shop in 2012 under the slogan, *Walking by faith with steel in our hands*, and its website promises to serve "all your gun and knife needs 'til Jesus comes."

"I'm a Christian and I'm proud of it, and I run a gun shop. Some people think you can't do that, but I believe you can," Pollock told a journalist. A strong Trump supporter, he repeats a refrain you'll hear among many white evangelicals in general, but especially from those in the gun industry who've pledged allegiance to Trump: "Our country is being taken away from us. And if we don't do something about it, it'll be gone."

Amplifying the voices of these white evangelicals—who critics contend are merchants not only of death but of fear—are "gunfluencers": influencers who flood TikTok, YouTube, and other platforms with viral pro-gun videos. Many of these influencers espouse hardline fundamentalist values and Christian nationalist messages tinged with misogyny and homophobia.

T.REX ARMS, a Christian company based in Tennessee, "specializes in providing conventional and unconventional equipment for preserving human life." That's code for holsters, night-vision goggles, body armor, rifle optics and mounts, lasers, ammunition clips, and other tactical firearms accessories. But it's best known for clips of another kind: hyped-up videos of founder Lucas Botkin clad in camouflage while firing bursts from semiautomatic weapons, all posted with heavy metal soundtracks for its 1.5 million YouTube followers.

Videos like these are such a popular subgenre, it even has a name now: GunTube. And a deservedly bad rap: Much of its violent content, the Tech Transparency Project says, is targeted at underage kids and teens.

"We're a Christian company with traditional American values. Don't like us? Good," Botkin says smugly in a selfie video on Instagram, where he's got another half-million devotees. T.REX describes itself as a "Sixth Commandment, Second Amendment" company. (By now, you're intimately familiar with the Second Amendment. A refresher on the Sixth Commandment, in case you need one, like I did: *Thou shalt not murder.*)

*Mother Jones* recently published an illuminating expose on T.REX, describing how Botkin and his brothers sit weekly "in a dimly lit studio to discuss America in decay, and how like-minded, God-oriented people can save it. They often reference the end times and urge their viewers to seize control before things get worse." The magazine quotes Jon Lewis, an extremism researcher at George Washington University, as saying the gun company's political content touches on "every single one of the narratives that we've seen emerge out of the right-wing space."

"It's laying it out there that tyranny is coming," he says, "and needs to be resisted using arms."

◆ ◆ ◆

Even if Christian gunmakers have few qualms about their work, it's hard to imagine they don't feel at least a bit conflicted about the way profits soar at particular times.

Gun sales spike after every mass shooting, and profits skyrocket whenever Second Amendment advocates sense an incoming presidential administration might attempt to tighten access—even though, as we've seen, doing so in a deadlocked Congress has proven virtually impossible.

There was a rush to stockpile firearms before Barack Obama and Joe Biden took office, and shares in gunmakers Smith & Wesson and Sturm, Ruger & Co. rose sharply in the immediate aftermath of the first of the two Trump assassination attempts in 2024. It's a troubling phenomenon reminiscent of an old Amy Grant lyric from 1988's *What About the Love*: "If you tell me where there's famine / I can make you guarantees."

A friend of mine tells me about a thirtysomething evangelical he knows who worked for Smith & Wesson in Springfield, Massachusetts, before the gunmaker moved its headquarters from comparatively firearms-hostile New England to decidedly gun-friendly Tennessee. My friend's acquaintance is a skilled machinist with a deeply ingrained work ethic and pride in his work. Yet he is haunted by regret after every mass shooting—even those that don't involve one of the company's weapons—because gun sales spike and he's paid a bonus. "Profiting from gun bloodshed enriches him, and that's something he privately struggles to reconcile with his faith," my friend tells me.

By the way, it's not at all unusual for gun manufacturers like Smith & Wesson to take evasive action, given America's patchwork of laws and the uneven reception firearms companies get depending on whether they're in a red state or a blue state.

In the relatively few instances in which US states *do* manage to tighten regulations on the manufacture of weapons, gunmakers simply pull up stakes and move to a state perceived as less meddlesome and more friendly to the Second Amendment. When Smith & Wesson moved to Tennessee, *Duck Dynasty* star Si Robertson presided over the ribbon cutting.

Evangelical rifle maker Adam Weatherby did something similar with Weatherby Inc., a third-generation family arms manufacturer.

Long based in California, it is now headquartered in Wyoming. "There are more guns per capita in Wyoming than in any other state and its government and people are committed to upholding the Second Amendment," Weatherby tells the *Liberty Journal* at his alma mater, evangelical Liberty University.

In practice, the firearms industry remains one of America's least-regulated sectors. "The gun industry is a primary player in the public health epidemic of gun violence yet receives very little attention in the national debate over how to address the problem," warns the Center for American Progress, an independent and nonpartisan public policy research and advocacy organization. "The industry that produces and sells deadly weapons to civilian consumers has operated for decades with minimal oversight from the federal government and almost no accountability in the US legal system."

There's been no significant change to federal laws governing commerce in firearms in more than two decades. Meanwhile, the law is lagging badly behind rapid advances in gun technology. These developments have made it possible for consumers to sidestep the institutionalized gun industry entirely and assemble homemade—yet no less lethal—untraceable "ghost guns" from parts made with 3D printers. The shooter charged in the December 2024 murder of UnitedHealthcare CEO Brian Thompson in Manhattan allegedly used a ghost gun and a 3D-printed silencer. In a report released early in 2025, the ATF says the number of ghost guns recovered in crimes soared nearly 1,600 percent in recent years, and they're increasingly being fitted with small, easily concealable devices that can turn them into illegal machine guns in seconds.

That hasn't stopped Gun Owners of America, a hardline alternative to the NRA, from mounting a brash "Defund the ATF" campaign. Its buzz phrase is *Registration leads to confiscation*, even though there's zero evidence to suggest the ATF or any other federal agency is plotting to disarm the general population.

Christian business owners often stress the importance of integrity and moral action in their work. Theoretically, at least, Christian involvement in any industry ideally results in more ethical business practices, the exercise of personal responsibility, and calls from within for reform. Not so with guns, whose evangelical insiders seem content to make a profit while offering little more than thoughts and prayers when their products are used to take innocent lives. (Or, for that matter, with evangelicals on the retail periphery like the operators of Hobby Lobby. The Christian-owned company won't sell Hanukkah items in its stores, but it gleefully peddles Christmas ornaments and wreaths fashioned from spent shotgun shells.)

Pope Francis surely had these dynamics in mind when he publicly rebuked gunmakers like Daniel Defense. Weapons manufacturers who call themselves Christians, the pontiff said, are duplicitous "merchants of death": "It makes me think of . . . people, managers, businessmen who call themselves Christian and they manufacture weapons," he said. "That leads to a bit of distrust, doesn't it? Duplicity is the currency of today . . . they say one thing and do another."

That's the supply side of the equation. There's also the demand side, including firearms enthusiasts who pack gun shows like the one I recently spent a Saturday afternoon visiting in my native Massachusetts.

◆ ◆ ◆

On a wintry Saturday morning early in March, on a day I'd set aside to boil the sap I'd been collecting from the towering sugar maple in our backyard, I exchange the lighthearted adventure of making homemade syrup for an experience that's far less sweet: making the two-hour drive to a gun show on Boston's North Shore. My GPS leads me to an isolated industrial park, and I circle for ten minutes, trying to find a parking spot in the jammed lot surrounding a Shriner's conference center.

I squeeze past two men who are exiting with their new purchases swathed in four-foot-long camouflage fabric rifle cases, and step inside. At the entrance, more than a dozen unloaded handguns are lined up in tagged Ziplock bags on a table, looking for all the world like the impounded firearms from a crime scene that you'd find in a police evidence locker. These are not for sale. They are attendees' weapons, which they'll be able to pick up on their way out.

One vendor has a ratty mount of a rabbit on the glass case where his handguns are displayed with a handwritten sign: "Also good for four-legged animals." It's clear, however, that the two-legged variety is on most visitors' minds.

Surveying the expansive hall, I view more fit-fat white males with goatees and MAGA caps than I've ever seen under one roof. I'm also surprised by the number of women, although it quickly becomes clear that they are being actively catered to and pitched at. The aggressive marketing of small, slender handguns to women, a small but growing customer base, is the latest big thing in the industry. I overhear one seller of small-caliber pocket pistols chatting up a pair of young women: "These are great when it warms up—you can carry in a T-shirt and shorts, and no one will ever know." Another showcases colorful pistols done up in chartreuse, Day-Glo orange and green, and Barbie pink.

As we've seen, the gun industry has also come under fire for marketing firearms to young people. The Uvalde shooter bought his AR-15 just twenty-three minutes after midnight on the day he turned eighteen, the minimum age in Texas. "Why?" asks Josh Koskoff, an attorney representing the families of the Uvalde victims. "Because, well before he was old enough to purchase it, he was targeted and cultivated online by Instagram, Activision and Daniel Defense. This three-headed monster knowingly exposed him to the weapon, conditioned him to see it as a tool to solve his problems and trained him to use it."

Republicans and Christian conservatives sometimes falsely accuse the LGBTQ+ community of "child grooming." If you're looking for an example of the actual grooming of children, some firearms critics contend, take a closer look at how the gun industry trains them to worship weapons from an early age.

At the Massachusetts gun show, a subcompact semiautomatic 9mm pistol catches my eye; one with the chunky lines of a toy gun, but deceptively lethal, nonetheless. It's a Sig Sauer P365, and it's one of America's most popular handguns precisely because it's small enough to easily conceal, can hold up to a dozen rounds, and retails new for as little as $500.

The P365, it turns out, is just as sought-after outside the United States as within. That poses a fresh set of ethical dilemmas to consider. With so many Americans now armed with multiple weapons, big gunmakers like New Hampshire–based Sig Sauer—aided by the federal government—have begun exporting tens of millions of rapid-fire firearms worldwide, fueling gun violence around the globe. A Bloomberg report says many of these exported guns eventually end up in the hands of narcotics traffickers and other criminal syndicates or are intercepted and used by the authorities in corrupt foreign governments notorious for human rights abuses.

♦ ♦ ♦

Meanwhile, so many evangelicals are bringing their guns to church, there's even a trendy new way to conceal them.

Ohio-based Garrison Grip, which markets firearms paraphernalia, sells a $55 leather gun case designed to mimic those zip-up protective Bible sheaths, complete with *HOLY BIBLE* stamped in gold leaf on the front. Once you open it and use the Velcro straps to secure your handgun and ammunition magazine, though, there's no space for an actual Bible.

The Reverend Rob Schenck, the gun restrictions advocate we've met in previous chapters, uses one of these cases for a little show-and-tell at his speaking engagements. His audiences shake their heads and laugh uncomfortably. Because honestly: What else can you do?

But for Schenck, it's serious business. "Reverence for the Second Amendment risks violating the Second Commandment: Thou shalt not make for thyself a graven image," he tells me. "By trusting in our Glock 9mm, we actually betray our confidence in our true savior, who told his disciples to put down their swords."

Somehow that message isn't getting through to the people in the pews, much less to our elected representatives. As we'll see in the next chapter, advocates of reasonable gun restrictions are getting pistol-whipped, metaphorically speaking, in the halls of power.

And white evangelicals intent on preserving their gun rights at any cost are cheering the inaction.

# 7 | PISTOLS AND POLITICS

America's gun is the AR-15, and Lauren Boebert is its prophet.

The Colorado Republican, a prominent member of the far-right congressional Freedom Caucus, has cosponsored legislation to make the military-style assault rifle—the same weapon used in one of the 2024 attempts to assassinate Donald Trump—the national gun of the United States.

"Is this a joke?" an incredulous constituent asked in a letter to *The Denver Post*. Evidently not to like-minded Republicans in Congress, who've been wearing AR-15 pins on their lapels in mockery of efforts to pass gun safety laws.

Boebert is known for posing in skinny jeans and a black leather jacket while clutching an AR-15 and displaying a T-shirt that called the lethal semiautomatic a "cordless hole puncher." Her highly provocative social media posts reliably generate thousands of likes and shares from white evangelicals.

She had even conservative Christians looking through a rifle scope darkly, though, at comments she made to a family conference organized by the evangelical Charis Christian Church in Colorado Springs in 2022. Boebert's viral remarks there underscored her tone deafness on a weapon that has been used in numerous mass shootings.

"They like to say, 'Jesus didn't need an AR-15. How many AR-15s do you think Jesus would have had?' Well, he didn't have enough to keep his government from killing him," Boebert told the crowd.

Thankfully, the reaction was swift. "The Colorado congresswoman is a Christian who seems to know nothing about basic Christianity," retorted Matt Lewis, senior columnist for *The Daily Beast*. "By botching the events after Jesus was betrayed, Boebert betrays a worldview that has become ubiquitous during the Trump era: the hunger for a political savior." He adds: "Today a lot of evangelicals are making the same mistake."

Setting aside her bungled (some would say blasphemous) interpretation of scripture—the New Testament teaches that Christ willingly sacrificed his life for the sins of humanity and made no attempt to resist—Boebert's snark, and her weaponization of religion, reflect the ferocity and absurdity with which pro-gun lawmakers defend the Second Amendment. Her allies include Rep. Thomas Massie, a Kentucky Republican, who—like Boebert—has sent Christmas cards featuring a family photo in which everyone, kids included, is brandishing an assault rifle.

The rhetoric goes beyond publicity stunts, though. Boebert and several like-minded fellow Republicans have introduced the Shall Not Be Infringed Act, a bill that would "unapologetically" repeal every recently passed congressional gun control measure.

Not that there's much left to repeal. The seemingly Teflon untouchability of gun freedoms hasn't happened by accident. It's part of a deliberate strategy—one in which evangelicals and their surrogates have played a pivotal role. In this chapter, we'll examine the evangelical Christian playbook for rebuffing any attempt to tighten firearms restrictions.

The consequences of that playbook are murderous. As an enraged bystander to a mass shooting once said: In a country where guns are worshiped and politicians encourage violence, no shooter truly acts alone.

♦ ♦ ♦

Gavin Newsom has a lot to say about gun control, and depending on your politics and religious sensibilities, it's a perspective you'll either cheer or jeer. Evangelicals, suffice it to say, are neither receptive nor amused.

The California governor, a Democrat sometimes mentioned as a future presidential candidate, is proposing a Twenty-Eighth Amendment to the Constitution to help end the gun violence crisis. Newsom envisions enshrining into federal law a few widely supported gun safety measures—raising the minimum age to twenty-one; requiring universal background checks; and banning the civilian purchase of assault weapons—while leaving the rest of the Second Amendment intact.

"If Congress and the courts will not take action to help make our communities safer from gun violence, then we—the people—must do it ourselves," Newsom's political action committee says in ads promoting the proposal.

The American people, Newsom insists, are sick of Congress's inaction. But many on the right who revile him seem sick of his approach—specifically, keeping AR-15s out of ordinary citizens' hands, which they insist is wholly incompatible with the amendment's *shall not be infringed* clause. "What part of 'shall not be infringed' do you not understand? It's not that hard," Anthony Stefanicic, a seventy-five-year-old retiree, widower, and ardent Trump supporter in Roselle, Illinois, posted indignantly on X. His reaction is one of the few from pro-gun advocates that are printable.

Newsom's call for a constitutional convention to take up a new amendment hasn't gone anywhere, partly because of fellow Democrats' concerns that it could trigger a "runaway convention" hijacked by Republicans who support gun rights and might use it to advance their cause.

Unsurprisingly, the effort has also been denounced by the ultra-conservative Heritage Foundation, the Trump-allied architects of the

Project 2025 plan to implement a far-right agenda in every branch of government and aspect of American society. "The Second Amendment doesn't need amending, and peaceable citizens don't need more barriers to the exercise of their natural right of self-defense," says Amy Swearer, a senior legal fellow in the Heritage Foundation's Edwin Meese III Center for Legal and Judicial Studies.

Evangelicals' political playbook on guns is simple and effective: Reject any attempt to restrict firearms, no matter how small, by engaging directly in the gun rights debate and by electing like-minded politicians.

As MoveOn.org, a national organization working for a progressive and inclusive future, puts it: Republicans in Congress are standing in the way of *all* gun safety bills—and even blocking *research* by government agencies on gun violence. That happened late in 2023, when House Republicans voted to prohibit the Centers for Disease Control and Prevention from funding "any firearm injury and mortality prevention research."

Conservatives seek to loosen gun laws precisely at a time when gun violence is rampant in the United States. Polling in 2024 shows about nine in ten Democrats want stricter firearms laws, compared with about three in ten Republicans—and white evangelicals tend to be overwhelmingly Republican or libertarian. "Evangelicals are not some kind of 'reluctant Republicans.' They are thoroughly Republican and tend to align with those politics and positions," says Dave Verhaagen, a Nashville psychologist who has studied white evangelical thought.

"Evangelicalism has become a political monoculture," especially where guns are concerned, adds Ryan Burge, a political scientist and statistician, in an illuminating interview with Interfaith Radio. And the movement's influence on gun politics is enormous, he says, if only because white evangelical Republicans account for 13 percent of the American electorate.

"Gun ownership and Republican identity have become inseparable. The most passionate Republican voters see guns as a central part of who they are," writes essayist Noah Berlatsky. "Gun rights have also taken on a near-religious importance, as have Republican responses to gun control initiatives."

This quasi-religious fervor for firearms helps to explain why evangelical friends have confronted me on numerous occasions, expressing incredulity at my suggestion that believers shouldn't carry weapons. Some, when they've realized I'm a progressive—in white evangelical faith communities, believers like me are the ultimate misfits—have even openly questioned my commitment to Christ and my very salvation. "You can't be a Christian and a Democrat," I've often been told.

That has always stung on multiple levels. For starters, I'd personally never presume to judge the state of a fellow pilgrim's soul, particularly based on their politics but really on anything else about them. Isn't that God's job alone?

Beyond that, there's a persuasive argument that the policies Democrats pursue hew closer to the basic tenets of Christianity—caring for the widow and the orphan—than the lack of compassion you'll often find in Republicans' obsession with tax breaks that favor corporations, including the lucrative gun industry, and their opposition to anything that smacks of a social safety net for society's most vulnerable citizens. Mostly, though, the notion that the GOP, or Grand Old Party, is really "God's Own Party" is objectionable because it's such an arrogant and exclusionist view. What of Black Christians, whose faith culture can involve spending three or four hours in church on Sunday, worshipping in joyous abandon? Most of them are Democrats. The sheer contempt of conservative white Christianity is one of many reasons why, after thirty-five years as an evangelical, I can no longer identify as one.

In an elaborately constructed echo chamber of their own making, pro-gun evangelicals—and the Christian nationalist policymakers they keep electing—repeat spiritual and political narratives that are virtually indistinguishable. Both center on what historian Neil J. Young writes, in an op-ed for *The Week*, is "the long-held view among many religious conservatives that the Supreme Court's outlawing of school prayer in the 1960s, rather than the weakening of gun laws and the proliferation of firearms in more recent decades, is the root cause of this rampant violence."

"Echo chamber" isn't hyperbole, either. The nonpartisan Public Religion Research Institute surveyed a large swath of Americans to map out their core friendship networks, and it found that half of all gun owners say most or all their friends also own guns. Unsurprisingly, they're also the least likely to support stricter gun control measures.

At the same time, many are deeply suspicious of government, harboring hardline views that stray well outside mainstream thought. As we've seen, for these militant believers, some of whom participated in the Capitol insurrection, guns are more of an insurance policy against what they see as "deep state" overreach.

In the run-up to the 2022 midterm elections, conservative extremists laced gun rights into their Christian nationalist and anti-government narrative at "Stop the Steal" rallies and the "ReAwaken America" tour, headlined by former Trump administration national security adviser Michael Flynn. Amy Cooter, a senior research fellow at Middlebury College's Center on Terrorism, Extremism, and Counterterrorism, tells the gun violence journalism initiative *The Trace* that most of the far-right groups agitating in this way at gatherings and in their newsletters and social media posts prioritize Second Amendment rights "and will continue to do so, especially as things seem increasingly urgent to them."

"There's distrust in the system and a sense of unfairness that will all feed into each other and make a perfect storm of factors headed into the next election cycles," she says.

From among these extremists, a militantly theocratic evangelical pastor in battleground Wisconsin has emerged, spewing a particularly damning brand of pro-gun, antiabortion propaganda. The Reverend Matthew Trewhella of Mercy Seat Christian Church in Milwaukee has called for churches to form armed militias and self-published a book in which he encourages men to "redden their swords." He has been invited to speak to Republican party meetings around the United States and has been praised for his commitment to fighting government overreach. Gun Owners of America credits Trewhella for boosting the number of counties that have declared themselves "Second Amendment sanctuaries" where guns are welcomed and even encouraged.

In pro-gun Indiana, politicians have been trying to out-MAGA one another. State Republicans passed over a Trump-endorsed candidate for lieutenant governor and instead nominated Micah Beckwith, a Pentecostal pastor, podcaster, and self-described Christian nationalist who boasts of getting the NRA's highest possible ranking. As we saw in chapter 3, Beckwith, elected to the post in 2024, caused a stir the day after the January 6, 2021, Capitol insurrection by claiming that God told him: "Micah, I sent those riots to Washington."

Most, but not all, of the evangelicals espousing such extreme political views are white. Mark Robinson, the bombastic lieutenant governor of North Carolina and the Republican nominee for governor, embodies Black bigotry on the Christian right. In a speech delivered in mid-2024 from the pulpit of Lake Church in the town of White Lake, the self-described MAGA Republican—standing on the altar in front of a large silver cross—said people with "evil intent" needed to be put to death. Robinson didn't explicitly say who needed to be killed, but the context of his remarks made clear he was referencing those on the political left. "Kill them! Some liberal somewhere is going to say that sounds awful. Too bad. Get mad at me if you want to," he told the mostly white congregation that applauded. "Some folks need killing! It's time for somebody to say it. It's not a matter of vengeance. It's not a matter of being mean or spiteful. It's a matter of necessity." Fortunately, voters rejected his vitriol, and he was roundly defeated at the polls in 2024.

Robinson, a fervent gun rights supporter, also mounted a fiery defense of gun ownership at a national NRA meeting held in Houston just three days after the school massacre in Uvalde, Texas. He has been praised publicly as "a trophy of God's grace" and hailed for his "courage, righteousness and justice" by Tony Perkins, president of the influential Family Research Council in Washington and himself an ardent supporter of the Second Amendment.

Trump's first spoken words after a would-be assassin's bullet pierced his ear at that 2024 rally in Pennsylvania were: "Fight! Fight! Fight!" shouted as he raised a clenched fist. Those words spoke volumes, says Tim Carey, one of the nation's foremost authorities on gun violence, whom we met in chapter 5. "It's a far cry from the recommended practice, which is universal denouncing of violence," Carey, law and policy adviser for the Center for Gun Violence Solutions at Johns Hopkins University, tells me in an interview. "We need to condemn violence to show there's no tolerance of it; there's no place for it."

Trump "almost revels in it," he adds. "Trump and those in his orbit are some of the most ardent advocates of violence. He's almost continuously spreading rhetoric about violence against political opponents, against people you don't agree with, against people you're afraid of—and then somehow seems surprised when it impacts him."

How tragically ironic that America's gun violence crisis is such a clear and present danger that even our political leaders are taking steps to shield themselves from bullets. In 2024, Anthony D'Esposito, a Republican congressman and former police officer from New York, introduced legislation inspired by the Trump assassination attempt in

Pennsylvania—and a startling spike in threats against lawmakers—that would require most US House staffers to undergo active shooter training.

Christian nationalism isn't just being brandished in Washington. Even in state legislatures across liberal New England, MAGA influence is being brought to bear on gun laws. In deep-blue Rhode Island, where I live, four in five of the state's Republican senators have been displaying small white flags with a pine tree in the center on their desks. These "Appeal to Heaven" flags are a Civil War–era banner that has been co-opted by Christian nationalists and adherents of the white nationalist New Apostolic Reformation movement. Democrats who introduced and eventually won passage of a bill requiring the safe storage of guns in the home had to overcome ferocious resistance from these GOP legislators. It passed only after faith leaders converged on the Statehouse to clamor for it.

Normalizing guns in religious life results in meaningless legislative diversions instead of practical actions when gun violence erupts, sociologist Andrew Whitehead says. He notes that after the 2018 Parkland school shooting that killed seventeen students and staff, lawmakers in Florida—rather than tightening easy access to guns—passed a bill requiring the motto *In God We Trust* to be posted prominently at public schools as a supposed deterrent. Neighboring Alabama and Louisiana since have done something similar with the Ten Commandments, raising concerns about church-state separation.

"For many Americans, the gun control debate is not merely about a secular public safety issue but is instead deeply entwined with what are perceived as the God-given rights of the American public and a purported breakdown of the moral fabric of American society," writes Whitehead, the lead author of a landmark 2018 study examining the nexus of Christian nationalism and gun laws.

Indeed, largely white pro-gun evangelicals are powering the burgeoning Christian nationalism movement: a menacing and rapidly expanding platform many right-wing believers see as their political salvation.

They're increasingly shaping their support of the Second Amendment around the idea that the right to bear arms is part of God's covenant with America. They're fielding and supporting like-minded, pro-gun candidates who will help them maintain operational control of the Republican party and gain influence across local, state, and national government.

And they're standing resolutely behind Trump, overlooking his flaws and even embracing his pugnacious persona out of what amounts to pure political expedience: He's amplifying and normalizing evangelical voices in a public square that has long spurned them.

There's a reason why those *God, Guns & Trump* T-shirts were among the bestselling merch at his rallies that culminated in his 2024 reelection, again with 80 percent support from white evangelicals. When it comes to guns, Christian nationalists don't just wrap themselves in the flag; they cloak themselves in piety while touting their Second Amendment rights.

♦ ♦ ♦

The end result: negligible progress in even commonsense, no-brainer gun reforms, such as mandatory background checks no matter where you buy your firearm.

Under Joe Biden, the federal government did what it could in the face of conservative opposition. While in the White House, Biden established the Office of Gun Violence Prevention and put Kamala Harris in charge of it. Harris promptly set up the Extreme Risk Protection Order Resource Center, an office funded by a Justice Department grant to help states remove guns from people considered dangerous. Trump has been dismantling and defunding all those efforts.

Harris, incidentally, is an example of how Republicans aren't the only ones who are pro-gun. During her unsuccessful 2024 campaign for the White House, the former California prosecutor and district attorney disclosed that she owns a Glock handgun for personal protection—and wouldn't hesitate to use it. "If somebody breaks in my house, they're getting shot," Harris, a Democrat, told Oprah Winfrey in a televised appearance. The former vice president, however, has long supported red-flag laws and universal background checks.

US Surgeon General Vivek Murthy, meanwhile, declared gun violence a public health crisis—a step that office has only taken a handful of times, to address clear and present dangers such as smoking, loneliness, and the deadly influence that social media can have on children. While he held the job, Murthy called for increased funding for research and risk-reduction strategies, such as community violence intervention programs and education on secure firearm storage. He also recommended tightened regulations, including safe storage laws, universal background checks, and assault weapon bans. Most if not all of that seems destined to go nowhere during Trump's second term.

Not that it's any easier at the state level; that's where you'll find the real battle over guns.

In states where elected officials have mustered the courage and political will to enact sensible gun restrictions, fewer people die by gun violence, according to Everytown for Gun Safety, a national nonprofit. Everytown ranks states according to the strength of their gun laws, and topping the leaderboard are California, New York, Illinois, Connecticut, Massachusetts, Hawaii, New Jersey, and Maryland.

New Jersey epitomizes the kinds of crackdowns courageous states have taken. It not only banned guns in designated "sensitive places" such as libraries, museums, and nursing homes, but made it illegal for gun owners to carry their firearms onto private property without the landowner's or homeowner's explicit consent.

So does Connecticut, which the Giffords Law Center says has the nation's third-strongest gun policies after California and New Jersey and the fifth-lowest rate of gun violence deaths. The state has tightened restrictions on guns since 2012, when a shooter armed with an AR-15 killed twenty children and six adults at Sandy Hook Elementary School in Newtown.

Those states that Everytown says are making good progress are Washington, Oregon, Colorado, Delaware, Rhode Island, Minnesota, Virginia, New Mexico, Pennsylvania, Vermont, Nevada, and Michigan.

On the other end of the gun control perspective are states missing key laws—Wisconsin, Florida, North Carolina, Nebraska, Maine, and Louisiana—and those with systems deemed weak: West Virginia, South Carolina, Tennessee, Indiana, Iowa, Texas, Ohio, Alabama, Utah, and North Dakota.

Dead last and labeled "national failures" by Everytown: Kansas, Missouri, New Hampshire, Kentucky, Alaska, Arizona, Oklahoma, Wyoming, South Dakota, Georgia, Montana, Idaho, Mississippi, and Arkansas.

"If every state in the country had the gun death rates of our national leaders, we could save 298,000 lives in the next decade," the organization contends. States with strong laws in place like my home state, Massachusetts—which enacted sweeping gun reforms in 2024—have two and a half times less gun violence than the rates in states like New Hampshire—just over the border—that have failed to put basic protections into place.

Yet it's been an uphill battle even on commonsense restrictions. In Colorado, Democratic Governor Jared Polis signed into law a ban on "ghost guns"—unserialized and untraceable firearms that can be assembled from kits or parts purchased online—only to have gun owners and conservative groups file a lawsuit in federal court seeking to block it. Opponents contend it violates the Second Amendment and doesn't mesh well historically with American gun regulations.

Hawaii, which has some of the nation's strictest firearms laws, decided it didn't want guns on its world-famous beaches, so it banned them there. Opponents promptly sued to block that "sensitive places" law, declaring it unconstitutional, and a federal judge agreed.

After Washington state saw its highest number of mass shootings in more than a decade, state lawmakers took action, banning guns in public places such as libraries, parks, transit stations, and zoos. They also outlawed the sale of AR-15s and similar semiautomatic weapons, and sales of those types of lethal weapons plummeted 70 percent, judging from a corresponding decline in background checks conducted by law enforcement authorities. But those gains could be short-lived if legal challenges prevail.

One of the most startling gun legislation showdowns played out in one of the most gun-permissive states: Tennessee. Three days after a shooter killed six people, including three nine-year-olds, in 2023 at the Covenant School—a private Christian elementary school in Nashville—a trio of Democratic state lawmakers, tired of mass shootings, used a megaphone to interrupt a legislative session. Two of the lawmakers, both Black, were expelled from the General Assembly, where Republicans hold a supermajority. The third, a white ally, survived by a single vote.

Women with ties to the school who became known as the Covenant Moms subsequently launched a campaign to enact some modest gun control measures in Tennessee, one of the reddest and most pro-firearm states in the United States. As lifelong conservatives, they figured they'd have state lawmakers' ears. Instead, they got a hostile reception. They're still agitating for change. But the Assembly has been passing bills that *expand* access to guns rather than restricting it, including a new law that lets teachers conceal-carry guns at school.

"The 'seek justice, love mercy, walk humbly with your God' verse has just stuck with me. No matter how frustrated I get, just keep walking towards change in a positive way," one of the moms, Sarah Shoop Neumann, tells *The Tennessean* newspaper. (More on the Covenant Moms in chapter 10.)

Tennessee epitomizes how Bible Belt states where evangelicals have outsized influence are going in the wrong direction on guns. Republican lawmakers there have been considering lowering the minimum age to get a concealed carry permit from twenty-one to eighteen and expanding open carry to include long guns like the AR-15. In case you're wondering, Tennessee pays a steep price for its permissiveness: Its gun death rate is nearly 21 per 100,000 people, well over the national average of 14.4 deaths per 100,000.

South Carolina, too, is making gun ownership easier and more conspicuous. Any adult who can legally own a gun can carry it openly pretty much anywhere except schools and courthouses. Twenty-nine states, including nearly the entire Deep South, now allow open carry of a gun without a permit. It's not without a cost: An analysis by the left-leaning Center for American Progress finds that the cities with the highest firearm homicide rates are all clustered in the South, generally in red states with less restrictive gun laws.

Carey, the Johns Hopkins gun violence expert, says he's focused primarily on state-level efforts for precisely these reasons. "Congress is out of step with the will of the nation. There are judges in the federal circuits who speak of the Second Amendment with this almost holy religious-like reverence," he tells me. "It's dangerous because we're deifying a highly ideological view of the founders. When you look at the Second Amendment historically in every reasonable context, it has to do with a militia that no longer exists or is relevant in modern-day society. But that aspect has been lost, and the needle likely won't move back until there's a seismic shift on the Supreme Court."

He pauses to gather his thoughts, then adds this: "I do believe change is possible—otherwise I wouldn't be doing this work."

Cities have also waded into the gun control fray, though they've seen their authority to do so severely curtailed. Even before the American colonies declared independence from Britain in 1776, local governments freely imposed restrictions on when and where firearms could be used. Some took a tougher, more self-determinative approach than the colonies in which they were situated.

That's far less common today: At least forty-three states, pressured by the powerful gun lobby, have enacted so-called preemption laws that prevent cities and towns from doing anything tougher on guns than the state itself does, setting up long and costly legal battles.

In Pennsylvania, which has had a preemption law on the books since 1974, the city of Philadelphia wound up having to defend itself before the state Supreme Court after it outlawed the manufacture of homemade guns—a local regulation intended to reduce rampant gun homicides, mass shootings, and firearm suicides. Gun Owners of America predictably jumped in, asserting the restriction violates Pennsylvanians' constitutional rights.

In Hartford, Connecticut, shootings have fallen since Mayor Arunan Arulampalam opened a local violence prevention office designed to act as a clearinghouse between the city, the public, and nonprofit groups working to fight gun crimes and break the cycle of gun violence. Reverend Dexter Burke, senior pastor of the evangelical Walk in the Light Church of God, which helped start armed citizen patrols in the city, is unconvinced. "Fighting crime needs more than that," he says.

In Indiana, the city of Gary—frustrated at the firearms industry for its inaction in preventing illegal gun sales—spent decades suing to force gun manufacturers to hand over years of production and sales records. A judge finally ruled in the city's favor, but then-Republican Governor Eric Holcomb signed a law retroactively banning cities from bringing such lawsuits against gunmakers, contending the companies aren't responsible for illegal sales.

Indiana has been particularly hostile to gun control. Even though guns are the leading cause of death for children and teens in the United States, the state legislature's Republican supermajority blocked a safe storage bill from advancing. It didn't even get a hearing.

For Republicans, overreach on gun rights can become a classic case of being careful what they wish for.

Who can forget South Dakota's GOP governor, evangelical Kristi Noem? She was widely considered among Trump's top picks as a running mate in 2024—and seen as a rising star in presidential politics—until she revealed in a memoir that she'd used one of her guns to shoot a puppy who'd eaten some of her neighbor's chickens. What started as political theater ended as a theater of the absurd, shocking and angering even some of Noem's Republican supporters and sending her approval ratings crashing. (Only briefly; Trump later picked her to be Secretary of Homeland Security.)

In Colorado, Republican state representative Don Wilson triggered safety concerns and criticism when he left his handgun unattended in a state Capitol bathroom.

After GOP lawmakers in the US House demanded investigations into Hunter Biden, the president's son eventually was charged, tried, and convicted of three felony counts related to his 2018 purchase of a revolver after falsely claiming he was not illegally using or addicted to drugs on a mandatory gun-purchase form.

For Republicans and evangelicals, though, the younger Biden's conviction has become a double-edged sword: Hunter Biden was ensnared by the very gun application forms they've been trying to do away with for all firearms owners. His prosecution made for some very strange bedfellows indeed. Gun rights activists, who couldn't be more ideologically opposed, wound up rushing to Biden's defense and decrying the charges against him as bogus. Some, before his father pardoned him, even used the hashtag #FreeHunterBiden.

◆ ◆ ◆

With the opposition to commonsense gun reform so painfully pugnacious, gun control advocates are taking a page from that playbook and adopting decidedly unconventional tactics to break through all the gun rights rah-rah.

In Parkland, Florida, where a gunman slaughtered seventeen people and wounded another seventeen at Marjory Stoneman Douglas High School on Valentine's Day 2018, the family of a teen who was slain in that shooting is using AI to recreate the voices of gun violence victims to phone federal lawmakers and plead for action. Speaking as though from the grave, Parkland victim Joaquin Oliver calls members of Congress demanding to know why they've done nothing to stop school shootings: "I'm back today because my parents used AI to recreate my voice to call you. Other victims like me will be calling too, again and again, to demand action. How many calls will it take for you to care? How many dead voices will you hear before you finally listen?"

Another former Parkland student, Anthony Borges—the massacre's most severely wounded survivor, who was shot five times in the back and legs—has acquired the legal rights to shooter Nikolas Cruz's name. That means Cruz cannot give any interviews, or profit from, or cooperate with, any book, movie, or TV project, without Borges's permission.

These are encouraging examples of dissent. Unfortunately, they haven't altered the trajectory of meaningful gun reform, which continues to be met with overwhelming resistance. That's true even with attempts to introduce universal background checks and a federal ban on assault weapons—restrictions that numerous polls show the vast majority of Americans support.

Republicans' rejections of the assault weapons ban are especially fraught. Originally sponsored by the late Sen. Dianne Feinstein, a California Democrat, proposed legislation known as the Assault Weapons Ban of 2021 wouldn't just outlaw semiautomatic rifles with pistol grips, forward grips, and folding or telescoping stocks but also those fitted *with grenade launchers*. Senate Republicans shot it down as an attack on American liberty.

It's the same dubious logic that more than two dozen Republican state attorneys general applied in suing the Biden administration in federal court in Texas to block a new rule requiring gun dealers to be licensed and conduct background checks on people looking to buy a weapon at a gun show or online. The rule was the government's attempt to close what's become known as the "gun show loophole," and the Justice Department says it would affect tens of thousands of gun sales a year.

Not so fast, Texas's attorney general said, declaring the government "out of control."

It's no accident that the states banded together to sue in Texas, one of the most heavily armed states in the nation. The Lone Star State has become a case study of how the far right cultivates a no-holds-barred, anything-goes gun culture and champions it as a God-given right.

State government, dominated for decades by a GOP influenced by ultraconservative religious groups and profit-minded gun manufacturers, has turned the question of gun ownership into a referendum on freedom and faith.

Other states are using Texas as a template, starting with the basics: recruiting and electing pro-gun Republican candidates for legislative office. That strategy works: a Harvard Business School study found that Republican-dominated state legislatures are 115 percent more likely to loosen gun laws.

Most Texans have always been vigorously pro-gun, but they coalesced around expanding access to firearms like never before after a gunman killed twenty-three people and wounded another twenty-seven at Luby's Cafeteria in Killeen, Texas, in 1991—still one of the worst mass shootings in US history. Obstacles to obtaining and carrying firearms were systematically removed, transforming Texas into the most gun-friendly state in America. It has since declared itself a "Second Amendment sanctuary state."

## PISTOLS AND POLITICS

When American Rounds, an ammunition company, put bullet-dispensing vending machines in grocery stores in four states as part of a trial run, Texas was an obvious choice. (The other states were Alabama, Colorado, and Oklahoma.) American Rounds says its computerized machines use an identification scanner and facial recognition software to verify the purchaser's age, but Everytown for Gun Safety contends selling handgun rounds and rifle shells where people buy milk for their kids will simply lead to more shootings "in a country [already] awash in guns and ammo."

Texas's fiercely protective Second Amendment stance long has been led by GOP Lt. Gov. Dan Patrick, an evangelical with an A+ rating from the NRA who denounces what he calls "the crazed gun control crowd." For some Texans, though, not even Patrick's fervency is enough. When he threw his support behind background checks for gun sales between strangers, a firestorm ensued, and the lieutenant governor backed off.

Texas's experience underscores the central role that Christian conservatives often play in not only defending but expanding gun rights. "In Texas, like other red states, the NRA slid sideways into the newfound alliance between evangelical Christians and the Republican Party, aligning gun rights with the religious right. Gun ownership became a symbolic weapon in fighting the culture wars," *The Texas Tribune* writes in a special report: "A gun and a prayer: How the far right took control of Texas' response to mass shootings."

The Texas takeover has included at least one Republican megadonor, evangelical oil magnate Tim Dunn, who reportedly once told former Texas GOP House speaker Joe Straus, who is Jewish, that only Christians should hold leadership positions. Dunn, a billionaire and a conservative lay pastor at Midland Baptist Church, has donated liberally to elect Trump and expand Christian influence in public affairs. He denies being a Christian nationalist, but *Texas Monthly* magazine has dubbed him "the billionaire bully who wants to turn Texas into a Christian theocracy."

Dunn also backs the political ambitions of Kyle Rittenhouse, the vigilante who was charged but later acquitted of killing two protesters and injuring another after he traveled from Illinois to Black Lives Matter demonstrations in Wisconsin with an AR-15-style rifle. After a Christian crowdfunding site raised half a million dollars to help Rittenhouse mount a legal defense, he moved to Texas, where he and fellow far-right agitators promptly launched a nonprofit dedicated to promoting gun rights.

Rittenhouse has appeared at events hosted by then–Republican Congressman Matt Gaetz, an avowed Christian nationalist whom Trump initially nominated as attorney general before Gaetz withdrew. In a clear sign of how the GOP is veering ever more sharply to the right on guns, Rittenhouse enjoyed celebrity status at the 2024 Republican National Convention. "We want to promote the types of virtues that exist in Kyle Rittenhouse," vice presidential nominee JD Vance, elected with Trump months later, told the crowd.

Meanwhile, mass shootings haven't stopped in Texas. In fact, six of the deadliest gun massacres in modern US history have unfolded there. Despite the continuing bloodshed, however, the state's evangelical legislators merely double down on unfettered access to firearms.

After two mass shootings erupted in a single month, Republican state representative Matt Schaefer blamed "godless depraved hearts," then posted on X: "'Do something' is the statement we keep hearing.... Let me tell you what I am NOT going to do. I am NOT going to use the evil acts of a handful of people to diminish the God-given rights of my fellow Texans. Period. I say NO to 'red flag' pre-crime laws. NO to universal background checks. NO to bans on AR-15s, or high-capacity magazines. NO to mandatory gun buybacks."

He followed that up with this: "What can we do? YES to praying for victims. YES to praying for protection. YES to praying that God would transform the hearts of people with evil intent. YES to fathers not leaving their wives and children. YES to discipline in the homes. . . . YES to your God-given, constitutionally protected rights. YES to God, and NO to more government intrusions."

◆ ◆ ◆

This seemingly unstoppable Christian nationalist momentum in state and federal politics creates a firewall that makes it that much more unlikely the Second Amendment will ever be repealed.

Just proposing an amendment would require a two-thirds vote of both the US House and the US Senate—a virtual impossibility in today's deadlocked Congress—or by two-thirds of the states, meaning thirty-four, even less likely amid the fierce divide between red states and blue states. That would merely be the beginning: The amendment would have to be ratified by either three-fourths of the state legislatures—thirty-eight in total—or three-fourths of the states at constitutional conventions called to approve it. But calling a constitutional convention in today's highly polarized political environment would be risky. A convention intended to achieve gun reform easily could be hijacked by far-right extremists and used to roll back protections for members of the LGBTQ+ community or other embattled minorities.

Rousing sufficient anti-gun sentiment seems inconceivable in a country where guns are so commonplace, its citizens even forget they're carrying them. In a jarring reminder of how many Americans conceal-carry, TSA agents reported intercepting more than 1,500 guns at airport security checks in a single quarter. Most of those gun owners said it had *slipped their minds* that they had their weapons on them. And in 2024, eight Americans were arrested in rapid succession in Turks and Caicos for illegally carrying ammunition into the country while vacationing there.

The detainees included Bryan Hagerich, an evangelical Christian who lives in rural Somerset County in southwestern Pennsylvania. The British territory enacted stricter gun laws in 2022 as a response to increased gun violence and weapons trafficking. Hagerich's lawyer says he didn't realize the ammunition was in the luggage he'd packed for vacation with his wife and two young children. He faced a minimum sentence of twelve years' imprisonment but ultimately received a suspended sentence of a year. He was allowed to return to the United States after paying a $6,700 fine.

There are ample signs, as well, that Americans accustomed to daily gun violence have become numb to it—a phenomenon that could make it more difficult to rally support for a bold new approach. "Things that we used to sort of consider memorable, life-altering, shocking events that you might think about and talk about for months or years to come now are happening with seeming frequency that makes it so that we sort of think, 'That's just the one that happened this week,'" Steve Dettelbach, the head of the ATF, tells The Associated Press. "If we come to sort of accept that, that's a huge hurdle in addressing the problem."

But hope springs eternal. And numbness hasn't stopped prominent politicians and thinkers from regularly calling for repeal.

Long before the late Supreme Court Justice John Paul Stevens called for an end to the Second Amendment in 2018, a year before his death, former Chief Justice Warren Burger—a conservative appointed by President Richard Nixon—made his feelings clear in 1991: "If I were writing the Bill of Rights now, there wouldn't be any such thing as the Second Amendment." Burger denounced the amendment as "one of the greatest pieces of fraud—I repeat the word 'fraud'—on the American people by special interest groups that I have ever seen in my lifetime."

Walter Shapiro, however, sees a path: Not an easy one, or a short one, but a way forward, nonetheless. Writing in *The New Republic*, Shapiro notes that a recent YouGov poll shows 60 percent of Americans, including 33 percent of Republicans, believe the only way to end the relentless carnage of multiple mass shootings is a "drastic change in the laws." That, he argues, gives progressives cover to play the long game and launch what no doubt would take decades to accomplish: an outright repeal of the Second Amendment.

"In the early 1990s, gay marriage was a quixotic dream. Not only is it now the law of the land, but gay marriage is accepted by 70 percent of Americans," Shapiro writes. Other analysts agree: Big blue states like California and New York could get things started, and eventually other states would join in, building the momentum.

The key, says Paul Veliyathil, a devout Christian who holds joint citizenship in the United States and his native India, is to stop saying the words of the Second Amendment are written in stone and can't be changed. "As long as we are living, nothing should be written in stone. Stone-writing belongs in graveyards," he says.

For all of Tennessee's resistance to gun control, one of its favorite and most influential evangelical sons acknowledges it's time to do something: maybe not repeal the Second Amendment but enact a ban on military-style assault rifles and high-capacity magazines. Republican Bill Frist, a heart and lung transplant surgeon, businessperson, and longtime US senator and former Senate majority leader, has been on a quest for commonsense policy responses since the Covenant School shooting bloodied his hometown of Nashville.

"I am a gun owner and a hunter. I have always and will continue to strongly support Second Amendment rights. I had a 12-year Senate career where I consistently backed responsible gun ownership," Frist writes in an essay for *Forbes*. "But times are different today—misuse of guns has grown much worse, substantially worse—with markedly more death and tragedy in our neighborhoods, than even a decade ago. This demands a fresh look, free of past biases and partisan tones which have ruled so much of our earlier discussions and debate. . . . All nations have criminals and the mentally ill, but only we have an epidemic of mass shootings, and we are failing our children. Now is the time to address the massive new public health threat to kids."

♦ ♦ ♦

Persuading evangelicals to rethink their position on guns will be key, if sensible restrictions on firearms ever have a chance of passing.

That's been an uphill battle for years. As the Presbyterian cleric Timothy Keller argued during Trump's first term in the Oval Office, after evangelicals voting in large numbers propelled him there: "*Evangelical* used to denote people who claimed the high moral ground; now, in popular usage, the word is nearly synonymous with *hypocrite*."

The implosion of the embattled National Rifle Association, whose influence has greatly diminished in the aftermath of corruption scandals focusing on lavish spending by its disgraced former chief, Wayne LaPierre, looked like it might finally loosen the gun lobby's iron grip on state and federal politics. Instead, other gun rights groups with ideologies far more ultraconservative than the NRA have rushed to fill the void. They include Gun Owners of America, the National Association for Gun Rights, and the Second Amendment Foundation, all of which style themselves as more radical alternatives to the NRA, as well as smaller state-focused organizations with openly extremist views. One of those, the far-right Virginia Citizens Defense League, has members who dress in paramilitary outfits and brandish AR-15s and tactical gear at rallies outside the Virginia State Capitol.

Gun rights provocateurs are thriving as Christian nationalism spreads. After the Surgeon General declared gun violence a public health crisis, Gun Owners of America savaged the move. "This is how Republics die and tyrannies are born," it said in a statement.

It's a forbidding landscape, but even deep in the heart of Texas, gun control activists are springing up from faith communities and working for change. The Reverend Deanna Hollas, who grew up in the Texas panhandle, is the Presbyterian Church USA's first ordained minister of gun violence prevention. "We have underestimated the greed and political power of the gun industry, whose profits soar with every school shooting," she says. "The more guns we have, the more gun violence we have. This continuous, self-sustaining loop only benefits the gun industry by promoting gun sales and also the politicians who cater to gun extremists for votes."

America's greatest hope to break that endless loop lies not within its borders but well beyond, in the inspiring examples of a handful of nations that have found ways to restrict firearms and end the violent cycle of mayhem and death. As we'll see in the next chapter, evangelicals and others in these countries take a *very* different approach to guns.

It's a distinctly alternative playbook that can teach us something—if we have, as Jesus admonished, eyes to see and ears to hear.

# 8 | GUNS AND THE GLOBAL CHURCH

A row of children's acoustic guitars is lined up neatly in a second-floor window. On the playground below, there's a half-eaten clementine orange near a climbing wall, and someone has chalked a hopscotch template in the shape of a grinning dragon.

This is a place pulsing with life, yet it's also a monument to a massacre.

Nearly three decades ago, the unthinkable happened at Dunblane Primary School in the quaint central Scotland town of Dunblane. On March 13, 1996, a gunman cut the phone lines leading to the school and entered the gymnasium, armed with four handguns and 743 rounds of ammunition. By the time his killing spree was done, a teacher and sixteen of her young students lay dead. Fifteen others were wounded in what remains the deadliest mass shooting in UK history.

Not far away, in a corner of Dunblane's cemetery, I walk haltingly in the drizzle through a memorial garden, where thirteen of the children and the teacher who died trying to shield them were laid to rest. The headstones are heartbreaking. Upon many are chiseled the words, *Our wee man* or *Our wee lass*. One stone is carved in the shape of a stuffed panda: a little girl's favorite plush toy. Another, for one of the slain little boys, is decorated with a plastic action hero figure and bears an inscription in gold on black marble:

When I was One I had just begun.
When I was Two I was nearly new.
When I was Three I was hardly me.
When I was Four I was not much more.
When I was Five I was just alive.
But now I am Six, I'm as clever as clever
So I think I'll be six now for ever and ever.

By now I am wrecked. As the gravity of what happened hits home, I fight back tears. At the next child's headstone I pass—*In loving memory of our golden boy / May he run, skip, giggle, and play forever*—I sob openly. It's a Friday in late summer, and yet the chill dampness of the day mirrors the grief that cloaks Dunblane every day of the year.

Memorials like this—gardens and sculptures and cemeteries and trees and collections of stuffed animals, in memory of the victims of school shootings—can be found across America. The list is agonizingly long: San Bernardino, California; El Paso, Texas; Newtown, Connecticut; Aurora, Colorado; Orlando, Florida; Charleston, South Carolina; Littleton, Colorado; Virginia Beach, Virginia; Coral Springs, Florida; Las Vegas, Nevada; Parkland, Florida. More are in the works in Buffalo, New York, and Uvalde, Texas. Yet in all of Britain, there's only one. This one.

In the days after the Dunblane school shooting, Parliament, spurred on by parents of the slain children and a scandalized public, swiftly outlawed the private ownership of most handguns and semi-automatic weapons. There hasn't been a mass shooting at a school in the U.K. since.

"I went home to an empty house," says Mick North, a widower who was raising his five-year-old daughter, Sophie, by himself when he lost her on Dunblane's day of infamy. She'd be in her mid-thirties by now, and he'd likely have been helping her celebrate a graduate degree, walking her down the aisle, or welcoming his first grandchild.

Instead, his grief, and her death, gave birth to the Gun Control Network, a coalition that channeled anguish into action.

Rampant gun violence is a uniquely American scourge—something that becomes abundantly clear the moment you leave the country. Yet as I sit across from Sophie's father in a pub and lean across the polished oak table to hear his story over the banter of barkeeps trading gossip and dissing one another over their soccer club allegiances, I'm at once seized with hope and anger. *If Scotland and the rest of the UK could do it,* I ask myself, *why can't we? If a country can actually prevent the killing of its children, why can't we?*

The lessons we can learn from nations like the UK, Australia, and New Zealand, which restricted access to guns after unspeakable tragedies, primarily involve mustering national courage and resolve. There's an elusive X factor, though, and it is rooted in how those countries' evangelicals navigate the gun question.

Outside the United States, even in places wracked by far greater levels of personal crime and violence, the default religious response is reasonable, peaceable, and scriptural. Namely: Conservative Christians in these countries would not resort to weaponry for self-protection even if they could. Most of them simply cannot imagine owning a gun.

♦ ♦ ♦

Evangelicals make up more than a third of the world's estimated two billion Christians. In Latin America, they soon may rival the number of Catholics. In Guatemala and Honduras, they're projected to dominate by 2030, and Brazil—a nation with more Catholics than anywhere else in the world—is on the cusp of becoming minority Catholic, as tens of millions defect to evangelicalism's more exuberant style of worship.

For Latin American evangelicals, many of whom have been traumatized by decades of gun violence between governments and insurgent groups, the idea of personally owning firearms is almost unfathomable. Why? Because evangelicals in most of these countries see guns as utterly incompatible with biblical Christianity.

In Colombia, civilians have the right to own and carry guns with a license—in theory. But in practice, the nation's gun laws are highly restrictive, and successive presidential administrations have significantly limited the issuance of carry permits. More to the point, Colombian evangelicals have a difficult time reconciling firearms with faith.

German Zárate is a new acquaintance of mine, a Christian, and a sociologist in Colombia. His homeland has suffered from more than six decades of violence and remains bloodied by ongoing clashes between the National Liberation Army and dissidents of the former Revolutionary Armed Forces of Colombia, best known as the FARC. Despite high crime rates, Zárate won't own or carry a gun because he considers it incongruous with Christ's teachings.

"If we have faith in Jesus, we have to be like he was when he said: Forgive them because they don't know what they are doing," Zárate tells me. He's in good company. Across much of Latin America, evangelicals wouldn't dream of sharing their US counterparts' embrace of gun culture.

Like Colombia, Honduras is rife with deadly gun violence, unleashed by drug cartels and criminal gangs. In a first-person essay for the Jesuit magazine *America*, former Catholic missionary Patrick Gothman details the brutality that Hondurans endure. "Paradise and hell are next-door neighbors, and you can hear the gunshots at night from both places," he writes.

In a bitter stroke of irony—*injustice* is probably a better term—thousands of the guns that are used to take Honduran lives originate in the United States. Figures from the ATF show that more than fifty thousand firearms were smuggled over the US border into Honduras, as well as Mexico, Guatemala, and El Salvador, between 2015 and

2022. So many American firearms are flowing illegally into the region that a California-based group called Stop US Arms to Mexico describes it as an "iron river of weapons."

Mexico's government, meanwhile, filed a $10 billion lawsuit against US gunmakers Smith & Wesson, Colt, Glock, Beretta, and Ruger in federal court in Boston for their roles in effectively facilitating the arming of marauding gangs. Mexico's lead lawyer, Jonathan Lowy, president of Global Action on Gun Violence, calls the lawsuit "historic" and says it could pull back the curtain on gun manufacturers the way lawsuits against Big Tobacco exposed unethical business practices and public harm. "Mexico has done what the US failed to do: bring an effective lawsuit that could change the way guns are sold in this country and trafficked to others," Lowy writes in an op-ed for *Newsweek*.

Matthew Soerens, vice president of advocacy and policy at World Relief and national coordinator for the Evangelical Immigration Table, which promotes a biblical view of immigration policy, says evangelicals in Honduras are utterly baffled by US evangelicals' embrace of firearms. In a blog post on the *Christianity Today* website, Soerens captures two Honduran pastors' incredulity that any Christian would carry a gun. "I do not believe that believers in Christ should carry weapons. Bearing arms is contrary to the gospel message," evangelical minister Miguel Álvarez told Soerens. "There is no theological or biblical reason that justifies the use of weapons."

Another pastor, Luis Luna, described to Soerens his shock at the notion that believers would champion gun ownership: "He reflected on his astonishment at witnessing an American missionary insisting to a local congregation in a violence-marred community that they had a responsibility to arm themselves. 'My God, no!' replied the shocked Honduran Christians, using the Lord's name not in vain but in intercession." American Christians' love for guns "will always be beyond my understanding," Luna said.

Like Luna, Latino evangelical Jorge Angulo stakes out an unambiguous anti-gun position. "You cannot support weapons of death and follow Jesus," he says, challenging a blog post provocatively titled: "Why Christians Are Ordered to Have Guns." "The Gospels, the writings of Paul, and the other letters reject violence against the government and others. The Sermon on the Mount clearly calls for nonviolence. Gun ownership in America is idol worship."

Within the larger context of Latin American Christians' rejection of gun ownership, Brazil presents something of a conundrum. While the Catholic church's centuries of influence is clearly declining, and Pentecostal Christianity—and secularism—are supplanting it, many evangelicals found themselves drawn to charismatic right-wing former President Jair Bolsonaro. He's out of office now and, like Trump, was hit with criminal indictments. But at the peak of Bolsonaro's popularity, evangelical pastors and churches who backed him and his campaign to loosen firearms restrictions often made "finger gun" gestures to show their support. A popular Bolsonaro campaign slogan was "Beef, Bibles, and Bullets."

For a time in the late 2010s, Brazil even saw the startling rise of the "Soldiers of Jesus": extremist evangelical Christians armed with guns who demonized—and terrorized—the country's Indigenous minorities for religious practices, such as Vodou, rooted in African influences that they perceived as pagan. But then Bolsonaro faced a backlash from some of the very evangelicals who'd helped propel him to power. Rejecting what they decried as the "Bolsonarization" of churches, more progressive Pentecostals broke ranks and helped sweep former president Luiz Inácio Lula da Silva back into office in 2022.

"In the past few years, we have seen the rise of an evangelicalism linked to the ideas of violence, hatred, guns—basically to the extreme right," Wesley Teixeira, a self-described left-wing evangelical and Lula supporter, tells the *North American Congress on Latin America*, an online reporting initiative focused on the Americas. Brazil's evangelicals who embrace gun culture diverge from their US counterparts in an important way, however: They're just as attuned as everyone else to concerns about environmental degradation and climate change, unlike American evangelicals, many of whom ignore it or deny it outright.

Ecuador, too, has taken a more US-centric approach, easing access to guns amid a spike in violence. Right-wing former President Guillermo Lasso signed a decree allowing civilians to own and carry guns legally as a defense against soaring murder rates, approving the measure with rhetoric echoing America's discredited "good guy with a gun" myth we examined earlier. Evangelical churches have been caught up in the Ecuadorean crime wave—early in 2024, an evangelical businessman was killed outside a church—but they're responding with prayers, not pistols. "We promote love, respect, justice, peace and the resolution of all conflicts through dialogue because violence is never the way," the Latin Evangelical Alliance says.

In Argentina, when fiery far-right President Javier Milei, widely seen as a Trump protégé, pushed the right to freely bear firearms, one of the South American nation's largest evangelical organizations pressed back hard. The Argentine Federation of Evangelical Churches published an open letter explicitly rejecting Milei's electoral platform, including "any project that promotes the right to freely bear firearms." Churches are called by God, the letter said, "to make an unavoidable commitment in favor of a society that guarantees social justice, defense of human rights, and the preservation of creation."

Closer to home, there is Mexico, where the ranks of evangelicals have surged by nearly 50 percent over the last decade, and where millions of guns are mostly in the hands of the military, police, and criminal enterprises. Evangelicals, especially in the south of the country, endure vicious persecution by gun-toting gangs. In the first five months of 2024 alone, the persecution-monitoring group Open Doors identified fifty-seven instances of violence against Mexican

Christians, ranging "from intimidation and extortion to direct attacks on houses of worship and their leaders."

The website of International Christian Concern, which assists persecuted churches around the world, describes how one evangelical pastor was arrested and imprisoned, his church burned, and his personal property confiscated. At one point, he was literally run out of town at gunpoint. It says evangelicals are frequently targeted by drug cartels because they disapprove of drug use and refuse to pay bribes. Other pastors have been shot. Yet most refuse to take up arms themselves.

Even the comparatively few Mexican evangelicals who have a gun are reluctant to use it. In an article for *The Christian Century*, Lynda Kristen Barrow, an assistant professor of political science at Coe College in Cedar Rapids, Iowa, describes the plight of an evangelical pastor in Oaxaca, a state known for its almost fanatical devotion to Catholicism and its hostility toward Pentecostals and charismatics. "Like many Protestants in the Mexican countryside, this pastor has suffered persecution," Barrow writes. "When his life and ranch were seriously threatened, he responded by placing a gun and a Bible side by side, saying he chose the latter."

Violence with and without guns has gotten so bad in the region that more than one hundred evangelical churches have closed their doors to protect the safety of pastors and believers, *El Sol de México* reports. Yet these evangelicals are neither arming themselves nor responding in kind. Nor, for that matter, are most Catholics: Mexico's Roman Catholic Church suspended a controversial priest who'd urged his parishioners to carry firearms for self-protection. Father Alfredo Gallegos, better known simply as Padre Pistolas, says he's carried a gun at times to ward off menacing cartel members. (In a sermon, he didn't pull any punches: "The cartel gunmen come, they take the livestock, they screw your wife and daughter, and you do nothing. Well, get yourself a gun; the government can go to hell. We have to defend our lives.")

The Reverend Meghan Brown, associate pastor of Georgetown Presbyterian Church in Washington, DC, has lived in both Mexico and Canada, and she believes our neighbors both to the north and the south do a vastly better job of containing and combating gun violence than we do in the United States. Brown's young children never had to endure frightening active shooter drills at school when they lived in those countries. Now they do.

"Canada is an incredibly safe country," Brown tells me in an interview. "Their [Canadians'] minds are boggled by the United States. They just don't understand how we could accept and embrace the life we do—not just with gun violence but with health care and things like that."

Canada's gun laws are significantly stricter than those in the US, but Canadians are allowed to own firearms for hunting after passing a safety course as a prerequisite to securing a license. The country, however, has taken steps to freeze handgun sales for most people, ban new sales of assault weapons, and keep firearms out of the hands of domestic abusers. Still, the porous 5,525-mile border with the United States hasn't stopped smugglers from illegally importing thousands of American guns. Police in Toronto say firearms smuggled in from the United States account for 90 percent of all gun crimes.

Although Mexico is a much more violent country, Reverend Brown says, "as a mother, I felt like I could control the circumstances in which myself and my children might encounter violence. I felt like we were much safer in Mexico than we were in the US, just because of the randomness" of gun violence here. "I didn't want to come back to the States, actually, because of that," Brown adds.

Georgetown Presbyterian, whose congregation includes several FBI and Secret Service agents, recently reviewed its own security protocols after an active shooter scare before a Sunday morning service. A man pushed past an unarmed security volunteer, became violent, and began yelling about taking shots. His threats prompted the choir to briefly take cover in the attic. He turned out to be unarmed, but it was "kind of a wakeup call," Brown says.

Hardening the church, however, isn't the answer, she says. "How do we allow people to just come and be at church? You know, in a way that they can transcend those worries?" Reverend Brown admits that these are not easy questions. "The church really thinks deeply theologically and wrestles with their faith in real ways. We want it to be a place of sanctuary. How do we continue to hold each other in our belonging to each other and in our belonging to God?"

Progressive believers like Brown and many in her congregation, while acknowledging that the fear of being harmed at church is real, are largely rejecting the gun culture. Evangelicals are not. Why, I ask her, does she think that's the case?

"I think it ties into our national identity and the myths of our origin story," she says. "It's like we still want to be on the frontier. We still think of ourselves as charting a course across this wild and unruly country. This idea of 'Manifest Destiny' is still so strong. It's about recognizing what our idols are: nationalism, violence, racism, colonialism."

If that's true—and it surely is—I ask: Can the United States, with all of that entrenched toxic Christian nationalist DNA, ever hope to rid itself of gun violence as Australia and the UK have done?

Brown doesn't hesitate: Yes, she says. But there's a catch. It could happen only "if we are able to reclaim a true Christian identity—a true and deep identity in Jesus, that stands in opposition to Christian nationalism and individualism, which I think is one of our greatest values as Americans." Individualistic freedom, Brown adds, "says I can do whatever I want. It may harm you, but I chose it and I'm free to do it." A higher and better way, she says, would be a more communal mindset, one in which we're more concerned with what is good for the whole.

"The idea of belonging to each other and belonging to God is powerful and transformative," she adds.

◆ ◆ ◆

Pacifism and nonviolence are articles of faith not only among many Latino evangelicals. They're also commonly held by believers in western and central Europe, where evangelicalism is on the rise and where I lived and worked for nearly two decades—first as an evangelical missionary in the 1980s and later as a journalist during the 1990s and 2000s.

The European Union's gun homicide rate is twenty-two times less than in the United States. That is a testament to the continent's notoriously strict firearms policies. When I lived in Belgium in the mid-eighties and in France a decade later, both countries were bloodied by Islamist terrorism. Yet not one of the hundreds of believers I interacted with weekly owned a weapon, let alone carried one into church services.

In fact, the only evangelical Christian I ever met in Europe who had a gun was René, a Belgian cop—and even he left it locked up at home on Sundays. No one I knew at evangelical churches I attended in Paris, Amsterdam, and Vienna showed up at services packing a pistol. Doing so would have never occurred to them.

Sure, US gun rights advocates argue, but these countries still endure acts of violence. No question about that. Mass killings in Europe, however, generally involve knives, not guns. And as horrible as knife attacks are, one simply cannot murder people in rapid succession and in the same kinds of numbers with a knife the way one can with a gun.

Having largely vanquished gun violence, authorities and lawmakers in the UK are free to react swiftly to contain attacks perpetrated by other means. After three women were killed by an assailant wielding a crossbow in Hertfordshire, England, and another man armed with one broke into Windsor Castle in an attempt to kill the queen, government ministers moved quickly to tighten restrictions on those weapons.

After back-to-back mass shootings at schools in 2007 and 2008, Finland toughened its firearms laws, raising the age limit for handguns to twenty, requiring applicants to pass an aptitude test, and ordering doctors to alert authorities to patients they think shouldn't have a gun. That angered many in the Nordic nation that has an entrenched tradition of hunting and one of Europe's highest rates of gun ownership. But it worked. Although a young boy fatally shot a twelve-year-old student and wounded two others at a Finnish school in 2024, such incidents remain extremely rare.

Serbia, another country awash in guns, also took decisive action after back-to-back mass shootings in May 2023, including one at a school where a young student killed eight others and a security guard. President Aleksandar Vucic vowed "an almost total disarmament," and citizens responded by turning in tens of thousands of unregistered firearms. The Balkan country also imposed a two-year moratorium on new gun permits, and it conducted a sweeping review of all existing permits to keep weapons out of the hands of minors, as well as those with criminal records or established mental illness.

The Czech Republic—which had some of Europe's most permissive gun laws, a deep love of firearms, and a tradition of gun manufacturing—tightened restrictions early in 2024 after a gunman fatally shot fourteen people at Charles University in central Prague. It was the former communist country's worst-ever mass shooting. Those restrictions on guns represent a massive shift in a nation that prides itself on gunmakers such as Ceská Zbrojovka, or CZ. But lawmakers decided enough was enough. Neighboring Germany, too, tightened its already strict gun laws after a teenager went on a shooting rampage in 2009 that killed fifteen people.

Asia is home to some of the world's most restrictive gun laws. Indonesia and Taiwan have virtually no civilian gun ownership of any kind. Japan, a nation of 125 million, sees only about fifty gun homicides a year. The Philippines, by contrast, has a glut of guns and citizens carrying them. Although its firearms homicide rate is one of the continent's highest and guns regularly factor into crime and political violence, it has very few mass shootings. That makes it an imperfect exception, even though pro–Second Amendment types frequently hold up the Philippines as an example of a safe society despite its preponderance of pistols.

In Africa, gun laws can be strict on paper but not always in practice. Nigeria, for instance, tightly controls civilian access, but its massive illegal market in illicit firearms has led to some of the world's worst firearms violence. Guns also flow freely in Sudan, riven by civil strife, and in South Africa, where the murder rate is at a twenty-year high and mass shootings are becoming more frequent.

Still, as in Latin America and Europe and Asia, many African Christians are reluctant to arm themselves. Hassan John, an Anglican priest in Nigeria's mainly Muslim north, tells the faith website *Unbelievable* he can't bring himself to get a gun—even after seeing people hacked to death on the streets. "At some point, I had wanted to get a gun to defend my church," he says. Yet he resisted that impulse, and he remains convinced he made the right decision. And just as in the United States, guns are often viewed differently by members of mainline denominations and evangelicals. Steve Dangana, a leader of the Pentecostal Fellowship of Nigeria, tells *Christianity Today* he believes there's "nothing sinful or inappropriate about owning guns or other weapons as long as it is for self-defense or other nonviolent use."

Then there's Australia and New Zealand. Down Under, like Dunblane, offers a roadmap to reason.

♦ ♦ ♦

## IN GUNS WE TRUST

In the battle against gun violence, resolve and determination are high-caliber weapons. At least that's been the experience of Australians and New Zealanders. When the horrors of a single gun massacre visited their shores, they summoned their collective courage and acted swiftly and decisively. Both nations faced obstacles, but they were determined not to see a repeat of their national tragedies.

Australia went first, and it remains a prime example of how single-mindedness and purposeful action are not merely aspirational; they save lives.

In 1996, a lone gunman calmly ate lunch at a café in the tourist city of Port Arthur, then pulled a semiautomatic rifle from his duffel bag and embarked on an hours-long killing spree that left thirty-five people dead and nearly two dozen others wounded. A mere two weeks later, lawmakers waded into a fierce debate over guns. It was combative and uncomfortable. But by the time they were done, both semiautomatics and pump-action shotguns were banned; the types of handguns civilians could own were restricted and a twenty-eight-day waiting period was imposed on purchases; nearly 650,000 firearms were surrendered nationwide via mandatory gun buybacks; and a new federal firearms registry was created.

As of early 2025, Australia has endured exactly *one* mass shooting since then. And that was a domestic tragedy, perpetrated not by a deranged stranger firing indiscriminately but by a grandfather with a grudge who killed family members and then himself.

Jenny Harland, a Christian I met at an anti–gun violence conference in New Mexico, was living in Australia in 1996 when the Port Arthur massacre—which occurred just six weeks after the shooting in Dunblane, Scotland—stunned the world. Less than a month after the slaughter, then–Prime Minister John Howard—a self-described social conservative in a nation with a robust gun culture and a fierce independent streak, like the United States—teamed up with lawmakers to craft the National Firearms Agreement.

"It was very unpopular to ban assault weapons. A lot of them [lawmakers] lost their seats," Harland recalls. Howard donned a bulletproof vest when he made the announcement, and he was later hanged in effigy. "But they did it. They said, 'I don't care. This is the right thing to do.'"

Today, back in the United States, Harland has ample reason to miss what she calls "Australian safety." Not long ago, she and her husband were driving on the interstate not far from their home in Santa Fe, New Mexico. She was dozing in the passenger seat when a bullet randomly struck the side of their car. Had the projectile not hit a thin piece of metal trim along the passenger-side window, state police said, it would have killed or maimed her.

It is true that while Australia has virtually eradicated gun violence, violence still occurs. A man fatally stabbed six people at a crowded shopping mall in Sydney in 2024 and was subdued only after a police officer with a gun shot and killed him. Still, the effectiveness of the nation's actions in the immediate aftermath of Port Arthur is undeniable, expressed in everything it has *not* had to endure: more national mourning and mass funerals.

"We could never do that here," you'll hear some pro-gun—and even anti-gun—Americans say; "Guns are just too entrenched in our culture." Yet Australia's many cultural similarities with the United States challenge such assumptions. In a blog post, Andrew Wilson, a teaching pastor at King's Church London, ticks off the obvious:

> Australia seems to me to share a number of cultural traits with the USA which European countries, including mine, do not—low population density, dangerous animals, a legacy of hunting, a Wild West, a popular culture of rugged masculinity—as well as a tragic recent history of mass shootings, and (interestingly) high popular support for tightening firearm restrictions. . . .
>
> Christians should oppose the use of deadly weapons on principle, because we are committed to the way of Jesus, the way of

the cross, the practice of nonviolence. Followers of Jesus should oppose the use of AR-15s or machine guns in self-defense for the same reason that we should oppose land mines, drone strikes, capital punishment, and abortion: Christians should never kill people. . . . Christians conquer not by killing but by dying: by the blood of the Lamb, the word of our testimony, and not loving our lives, even to death.

Australia's closest neighbor has proven that its approach can work elsewhere, too. When a white supremacist slaughtered fifty-one worshipers at a pair of mosques in Christchurch, New Zealand, in 2019, that country turned to its neighbor's playbook. Less than a week after the massacre, then–Prime Minister Jacinda Ardern announced a near-total ban on automatic and semiautomatic firearms. The government bought back peoples' guns and launched a registry to keep close tabs on sales.

New Zealand has not had a mass shooting since. Some New Zealanders, however, worry about how long that respite will last. Gun violence has been creeping up since Ardern left office and the country's government tilted more to the right, and it's been loosening some of the laws tightened after the Christchurch slaughter. It's no coincidence that New Zealand began reversing course on its restrictive gun laws after Christopher Luxon, a white evangelical, took over as prime minister late in 2023 and put a former gun lobbyist in charge of easing restrictions on firearms.

♦ ♦ ♦

Back in Dunblane, Scotland, a river known locally as the Allan Water gurgles cheerfully past a Gothic cathedral, and migrating salmon make splashy rises. A middle-aged woman in a checkered kerchief, cycling across one of the bridges that span the river, pedals slowly to take in the postcard-perfect view while reaching out to steady the groceries wobbling in her bike basket. Here, it's difficult to imagine the violent scene that took place at the primary school. As with any tragedy of such horrendous scale, though, there are hidden scars.

The Reverend Duncan Strathdee, pastor of Dunblane Christian Fellowship, ministers to the town's walking wounded. He is the last of the clergy who were present in 1996 to do so; the others have retired, moved away, or passed away. Strathdee rarely discusses the massacre and its aftermath, but he has agreed to sit down with me because rising gun violence worldwide has left him saddened. Each mass shooting in the United States is a trigger, traumatizing not only those who lost children here but the pastor, who remains in close touch with the families.

Strathdee's church is unabashedly evangelical, even charismatic, captured in the vision statement on its website: "In 1984, God said that Dunblane was like a basin and as water runs down the side of a basin and fills it up, the Holy Spirit would fill Dunblane. His presence would be so great it would impact the surrounding areas. In 1986, God confirmed this by saying the Holy Spirit would flow through Dunblane like a river and the effect would be felt across the nations. People would be drawn to the miracles and swept into the amazing things that were happening."

What, then, of 1996, Dunblane's annus horribilis? I ask him. How did that fit into the fellowship's prophecy?

Strathdee nods quietly. He still believes the prophecy of a spiritual awakening is being realized in Dunblane. For weeks on Sundays after the shooting, every church was packed, and he says hundreds have come to faith at his little church alone. The community, too, has changed: All these years later, its residents still place a lit candle in their windows every March 13. "It isn't much, but it's a recognition that we've not forgotten," he says.

Among the youngsters at the school on that fateful day was Andy Murray, who would become a tennis superstar, a Wimbledon winner, and an Olympic gold medalist. He was eight years old at the time and was walking to the gymnasium when gunfire began erupting inside. A teacher hustled Murray and other students into the headmaster's office, where they hid until the shooting ended and police arrived.

Dunblane is a small and intimate community, and Murray wrote in his autobiography about how he realized later to his horror that in the period leading up to the shooting, his mother had given the gunman lifts to the train station—and that he'd been sitting in the backseat. In a retrospective published after Murray retired from international tennis after the 2024 Paris Olympics, the British online newspaper *The Independent* praised him for "the impact Murray made on Dunblane, allowing a town scarred by tragedy to embrace the chance to be defined by something else."

*Independent* tennis writer Jamie Braidwood, another son of Dunblane, writes: "That may be Murray's greatest achievement of all. Even though, collectively, Dunblane has recovered, its past will always be there. Within my small class at primary school were children whose families had lost siblings or cousins a decade before. In the memorial services at school to mark the anniversary, I remember the quiet, the reflection, but also the resilience in the face of unspeakable tragedy. In Dunblane, there are families and parents who live with what happened every day. The rest of the town does too, but life, as it does, continues."

It would be false to suggest that effecting change after Dunblane proved easy for anti–gun violence activists. Nothing about getting gun restrictions enacted in the aftermath of the massacre was easy. As in Australia, firearms foes in the UK had to go up against those within an entrenched gun culture, who pushed back hard on disarmament. At one point, the late Prince Philip, husband to Queen Elizabeth II—who had laid a wreath at the school—told the BBC that banning guns was as pointless as banning cricket bats: Both can be misused by people intent on evil.

Evangelist Franklin Graham tweeted something similarly tone-deaf two days after the 2022 school shooting in Uvalde, Texas: "Contrary to what some want America to believe, it isn't the guns. You can put all the guns in a pile in Central Park & not a single gun will kill anyone. It takes a human being to plan & execute such brutality."

Emma Fowle, a Briton writing for the website *Premier Christianity*, acknowledges some "half-truths" in Graham's deflection, but challenges the logic of such thinking as "a gross over-simplification": "He is correct that a gun cannot fire itself (which is why we ought to be careful whom we let buy one). And yes, as Christians, we pray for a day when such evil will not exist, and recognize that God alone can bring that day about," she writes. "The UK consumes much of the same media as the US, and many here own guns for shooting and hunting (members of my own family included). Yet, since the 1996 massacre in Dunblane, where seventeen people died, there have been no school shootings here."

Britain has not completely eradicated gun violence. Although there have been no school shootings since Dunblane, there have been a few mass shootings, albeit far fewer than in the United States. There's also been an uptick in armed robberies and other crimes using so-called junk guns: non-firing firearms and realistic-looking imitation handguns that fire BBs or function essentially as glorified air pistols. Even so, statistics show that classic gun crimes, especially those involving traditional handguns, have declined substantially. In Scotland itself, handgun offenses fell by nearly 80 percent in the five years after Dunblane, according to data from Britain's Home Office.

You'd think the UK's example might persuade white American evangelicals of the virtues of commonsense gun restrictions, but so far, it hasn't. They're dug in, and most simply shrug off the progress across the pond. I ask Reverend Phil Guin, the Alabama pastor we met in chapter 4, what he thinks about the relative lack of mass shootings in countries that have imposed bans on handguns.

"What do I think about it? Well, that's their business—that's what I think about it," he bristles. "If you want to change the Constitution of the United States and eliminate the Second Amendment, then that can be done eventually. Of course, statistically, mass shootings are still fairly rare. But they're problematic. Oftentimes they're related to improper storage of weapons or allowing someone to have one who shouldn't. It's part and parcel of the cultural decline in our country. I understand why some Christians fall on one side of the issue and other Christians fall on the other. I have no problem with that, but respect my opinion as well, just as I respect yours."

Such ambivalence rings hollow in Dunblane, whose 9,300 residents have spent three decades reliving a nightmare. The Right Reverend Dr. Martin Fair of the General Assembly of the Church of Scotland calls the massacre "one of the darkest days in Scotland's modern history." Until that day, he says, "such atrocities happened elsewhere." On the twenty-fifth anniversary of the slaughter, in 2021, Fair led the townsfolk in prayer to *Lord Jesus Christ, yourself once a child, vulnerable and at risk.*

Monsignor Basil O'Sullivan, a Catholic priest in town who that day rushed to tend to the dead and wounded, tried to bring some measure of comfort to their families in the aftermath. He says it devastated him personally. "The whole town went into trauma, everyone went into trauma, including myself I suppose I had a kind of nervous breakdown," he told a reporter. "I didn't eat, sleep, I was drained. I was weak, physically, spiritually, and mentally. You just couldn't eat, you couldn't sleep. But the Lord keeps going." The Reverend Bryan Owen was an Episcopal priest whose young son was trapped in the school but survived. He and his wife, a chaplain at the local infirmary where the young dead were identified, were shattered. A letter to the editor of the Scottish newspaper *The Herald* captures his anguish: "The events in Dunblane subsequently led to a complete breakdown in my health and my attempted suicide a few years later even though by then we had moved away." The couple's church overseers, he recalls, offered no counseling or support.

Mick North, the widower whose daughter, Sophie, was shot that day, moved out of Dunblane the year after the shooting. "I was finding some things in the town difficult," he tells me. He'd lost his wife, Barbara, to cancer two years earlier, and Sophie "had become good company."

On the morning of the massacre, Sophie had helped her dad scrape the frost off their car before he dropped her off at school. A few hours later, North was supervising students in his biochemistry lab at Stirling University when the first fuzzy reports came in about a disturbance in Dunblane. He rushed to the school, only to wait for hours with other parents for word on the fate of their children. Eventually, two police officers and a social worker took him aside and told him Sophie had been shot in the head and chest. His "bright, inquisitive, intelligent" little girl was gone.

A few days later, he issued a statement that would launch Britain's gun control campaign: "For the sake of Sophie and her classmates and her teacher, no more guns and worship of guns."

North shakes his head now as he remembers those days and still seems baffled by what ensued. "That's all I said. But it made the national news because I'd been the first one to say anything." Shortly thereafter, a petition demanding restrictions on handguns began circulating. It was known as the Snowdrop Campaign, named for the only flower in bloom in Scotland at the time of the shooting, and more than 750,000 people signed on. Nine years earlier, a mass shooting that claimed sixteen lives in Hungerford, England, had led to a ban on semiautomatic weapons and restricted sales of some types of shotguns. Within weeks of Dunblane, the grassroots momentum behind even more comprehensive gun reform was unstoppable.

For just a moment as I listen to his story, I feel hope in small things, like a grieving father's simple request of a country. For just a moment, as so often happens, the words of Jesus console me. *Truly I tell you, unless a grain of wheat falls to the ground and dies, it remains by itself. But if it dies, it produces much fruit.* That's John 12:24, and in it, I glimpse something of Sophie's life, and of her father's words—and of redemption.

"Why can't we do this in America?" I ask North, as a bartender brings two coffees to our corner table. He ticks off a few reasons. Unlike in the United States, where gun control organizations frequently squabble over priorities and tactics, the UK's gun opponents presented a largely united front. That's not to say they didn't endure fierce opposition and even death threats; they did. And in the United States, he notes, the NRA's influence extends to some Democrats, who accept campaign contributions from the group. "If they're funding both sides, it's going to be difficult to get anything done," he tells me.

North, however, brushes off the notion that America's culture of independence and its affinity for guns somehow makes it a special case. "Australia and Canada have the same sort of frontier mentality, and they've managed to take action," he notes.

North says he finds America's endless cycle of back-to-back mass shootings both distressing and exhausting. The Sandy Hook school shooting was particularly traumatizing for him. What would you say to Americans? I ask.

"I think I have to wave the white flag. I honestly wouldn't know what to say," North responds. "I don't have an answer. I used to say, 'Look at what we did—you can do it, too.' But there's so much fear. Are Americans more fearful of other Americans than Brits are of other Brits? I would imagine the answer is yes."

◆ ◆ ◆

On the day that the primary school became a killing field, Duncan Strathdee was a head teacher at a school in Edinburgh and pastoring part-time in Dunblane, where he'd been born and raised. His wife,

Janet, had phoned him to say something had happened and helicopters were overhead. When news reports made clear the scope of the tragedy, he drove back to Dunblane and headed to the school, which had been cordoned off.

Strathdee, whom we met earlier in the chapter, has since mourned the countless mass shootings in the United States, and has struggled to understand the gun culture that makes such tragedies not only possible but commonplace. "It's like a cowboy and Indian thing, isn't it?" he tells me. "In America, the openness to the gun culture just blows my mind. It doesn't make sense. Here, what happened shocked people across the nation. We're talking about five- and six-year-old children. This had never happened before, and it didn't matter where you lived—it impacted you. People were sending money and teddy bears to Dunblane from all over the world to help the families, because it was just so horrendous. Even the guys in the jails wanted guns banned; some had used a gun themselves, but they were quite adamant that we needed to do something about it. In America, for people who've got guns, I think that unless [violence] comes to their door, with their child, they just don't get it."

I ask Strathdee the same question I'd posed to North: If you could address Americans, what would you tell them? Strathdee is as evangelical as they come. But his response is one you'll seldom hear from a fellow evangelical in the United States:

> We shouldn't need to be people who carry guns. We can't do this. We're living in the mid-2020s. We're not living in those days when people carried a sword. It breaks my heart every time there's another mass shooting [in the United States]. It takes me right back to what was a very dark time.
>
> One of the Ten Commandments is, "You shall not kill." If you're carrying a handgun to defend yourself, what are you going to do with it? You're going to kill somebody, right? That's why we get these things still happening. If you know there's a potential

for it to happen, why don't you just remove guns from the equation? That's what we've done here: We've removed it from the equation. And now we have a tremendous sense of victory that something good did come out of this, that hopefully will prevent it from happening again.

What would Jesus be doing? He would not be taking an AK-47 to church. I'd love to speak to those people and be able to unload everything I've experienced as a Christian through this situation, and then hear them justify their position.

Dunblane, he says, is nowhere near the point where it can put the shooting behind it because of its many survivors. "They've still got a long way to go in their lives. It's not going to go away for them for a long time. It's never far from mind."

Strathdee's own sister, Anne Beaton, was a nurse and among the first inside the gymnasium after the massacre. A devout Christian herself, Anne never talks about it, he says. Few do. "It's almost like there's a group of us who were there, who were involved, and it's an unwritten thing. We actually don't have to say anything. We're knit together."

I meet Anne two days later, while attending worship services at her brother's church. Duncan has told her about the book I'm writing, and he introduces us before the service. Before I can ask her about the carnage, an undeniable sadness in her soulful brown eyes warns me not to go there. "It must have left an indelible mark," I murmur instead.

"Yes, but God has helped over the years so that I can bear it," she responds.

Rising from my seat with the others to sing together in the compact church across from Dunblane's downtown rail station, I relish the collective effervescence of worship and a familiar but elusive sense of belonging. It feels like a homecoming—a return to a place I've never been, but one for which I've longed. I'm in the warm embrace of an evangelical faith community where no one is carrying a gun, I think. Just to be sure, after the song is over, I lean over and ask the pastor's wife, Janet: "No one's carrying a gun here, right?" She shoots me a quizzical look, arches her eyebrows, and shakes her head: "Absolutely no one."

At the end of the service, Strathdee invites me up on the platform to greet the congregation and explain why I'm visiting. I describe the book I'm writing, and that part of my research includes contrasting the dearth of guns here and in other parts of the world with the glut in my country. I tell the congregation about the relief I feel today, to be able to worship in a church free of firearms.

Then, in a gesture I find indescribably poignant—especially after receiving scorn from numerous US evangelicals when they heard the concept of this book—the pastor puts his arm around me. He asks his flock to pray to the Lord for me and the project, and then he leads out in a prayer. "That it would be something that will hit your target," he asks God. "That it would speak to the church, to those who advocate the carrying of guns."

I walk back to my seat as parishioners smile, nod, and give me the thumbs-up sign. As the pastor closes out the service with a final prayer, I bow my head and close my eyes. How is it, I wonder, that these Christians in a town traumatized by a shooting that occurred three distant decades ago are still so self-aware about the harm that guns can do to mind, body, and soul? How can their white evangelical counterparts in the United States be so dismissive of the human wreckage that is a daily consequence of our gun culture? On the train to the airport, oblivious to the castle-studded Scottish scenery whizzing past, I'm still turning these questions over in my mind.

It will take another journey to answer them—a trip to a dry and desolate corner of my own country, where I'm about to meet a vastly different breed of Christians: believers who are determined to reshape the narrative around God and guns in America.

# 9 | SWORDS INTO PLOWSHARES

Hammers rise and fall, striking red-hot steel and sending loud rhythmic thuds echoing across northern New Mexico's high desert. Sparks fly, acrid smoke fills the air, and a charm of hummingbirds scatters.

Clad in safety goggles and thick leather gloves, Scotty Utz stands at the propane-fired portable forge, heating up the barrel of an AR-15 to two thousand degrees Fahrenheit. As he flattens the metal, it slowly takes the shape of a garden spade. Blow by blow, the business end of the semiautomatic rifle is being transformed from a lethal weapon into a life-giving tool. This is more than a repurposing; it is a rebirth.

The power and poetry of the moment isn't lost on Utz. A Quaker and a former gun enthusiast himself, he's fulfilling a prophecy that the Hebrew prophet Isaiah penned millennia ago: *"They will beat their swords into plowshares and their spears into pruning hooks. Nation will not take up sword against nation, nor will they train for war anymore"* (Isaiah 2:4).

The first gun Utz ever destroyed was the first firearm he'd ever bought: a shotgun he had purchased from a fellow seminarian. "The more I read and thought about Jesus, the more I embraced the idea that loving your neighbor doesn't include shooting them, even if they're breaking into your house," he tells me. "There's so much hope in this work. We're actually doing something tangible. When we're cutting up a gun, it's making a real difference."

Utz is a leader of RAWtools, a group formed after the 2012 Sandy Hook school shooting to get guns off the street, dismantle them, and turn them into art, jewelry, and garden tools. In cities like Philadelphia, the organization has collected some serious firepower: not only assault rifles but grenade launchers, Uzis, and other weapons of war.

Utz works with Michael Martin, a Mennonite pastor-turned-professional blacksmith who founded RAWtools (RAW is *war* spelled backward.) Evangelical social activist Shane Claiborne threw his support behind the movement early out of a sense of anguish over the bloodshed staining his Philly neighborhood. "My weariness grew one mass shooting at a time," Claiborne laments in the introduction to his 2019 book, *Beating Guns: Hope for People Who Are Weary of Violence*. The project has inspired a spinoff known as Guns to Gardens Network that enables people to help others in their communities disable their guns. There's even an international counterpart, Forging for Peace, launched by a blacksmith in Germany who was upset that Russian bombs had destroyed a friend's workshop in Ukraine. He is now cutting up tank parts and making sculptures of doves and other emblems of peace.

Utz and I are at Ghost Ranch, a storied twenty-one-thousand-acre retreat center in the arid hills of Abiquiu, north of Santa Fe, New Mexico. Georgia O'Keeffe once lived and painted at the ranch, and American icons like Charles Lindbergh, John Wayne, and the Rockefellers rode horses in valleys and canyons laden with dinosaur fossils. The landscape is dotted with cacti, sagebrush, and squat adobe houses and creased by dried-up riverbeds.

I've joined six dozen leading US peace activists and gun violence reduction advocates at a conference organized by the Presbyterian Peace Fellowship. Many of the participants have known one another for years, but this is the first time they've gathered in person, and there's a palpable sense of excitement and anticipation. Organizers of the inaugural James Atwood Institute for Congregational Courage, as it's called, hope they'll look back at this as a historic turning point in a long and heartbreaking quest to rid the nation of needless gun deaths.

Northern New Mexico is a fitting backdrop. On the highway winding north out of Santa Fe, I'd followed a motorcyclist wearing a pro–Second Amendment T-shirt that mockingly read: *1776: Sure you're taking away my guns.* On the other side of the flat-topped mesa lies Los Alamos, where the first atomic bomb was tested in the desert in 1945 as part of the Manhattan Project. United Nations disarmament treaties have eased the nightmarish menace of global nuclear annihilation—barely—though not before the bomb was used to obliterate the Japanese cities of Hiroshima and Nagasaki and kill more than two hundred thousand unsuspecting civilians.

If the international community could find a way to contain the threat posed by the biggest "gun" of all, I think, surely, we can fix our firearms problem.

♦ ♦ ♦

In a society in which guns carry sirenic and totemic power, and in which even believers are arming themselves with Berettas and Brownings, efforts by dissidents and reformers to get America's firearms fetish under control are nothing short of countercultural. And sometimes they can be deliciously subversive.

Years ago, Seattle nun Sister Judy Byron took a vow of poverty, but these days, she's been buying stock in gunmakers Sturm, Ruger & Co. and Smith & Wesson, as well as gun retailer Dick's Sporting Goods. This is not for her own personal enrichment but in the name of social justice. The shares that Sister Judy and her fellow activist nuns are acquiring are far from a controlling interest, but they're enough to give them a seat at the table as concerned shareholders of these companies. Now they can pose probing questions about how the gun companies are run. In most cases, an investment of just $2,000 is enough to put forward shareholder resolutions that challenge how manufacturers market their weapons—especially where children are concerned—and press for more safety features on firearms. "The moral case for action grows more urgent each day," Sister Judy says on the website for her consortium, the Northwest Coalition for Responsible Investment.

Shareholder activism itself is nothing new—for decades, religious groups have bought shares in automakers, oil and gas companies, and Big Tobacco in attempts to force change. But targeting gun companies from within is a relatively recent tactic.

Not that it's always an effective one. After Sister Judy and her coalition of activist investors demanded that Ruger review the safety of its weapons, CEO Christopher Killoy said on an earnings call that the gunmaker would resist any move "to force us to change our business, which is lawful and constitutionally protected . . . to adopt misguided principles created by groups who do not own guns, know nothing about our business, and frankly would rather see us out of business." Gun owners have been even more uncharitable, ridiculing the nuns in profane social media posts and questioning the very concept of gun safety. (Snarky variations of "guns are *supposed* to be dangerous" dominate firearms forums frequented by NRA members and other Second Amendment defenders.)

When the nuns met with more such corporate resistance, they went a step further. They filed an unusual shareholder lawsuit against Smith & Wesson to substantially change the way the publicly traded company markets its AR-15 rifles. The suit, filed in state court in Nevada, said Smith & Wesson was exposing shareholders to liability because of how they promote and sell AR-15s—which, as we've seen, have become the weapon of choice in mass shootings. The nuns cited competitor Remington's $73 million settlement with the families of nine of the victims of the Sandy Hook school shooting. The plaintiffs included Sister Judy's order, the Adrian Dominican Sisters in Adrian, Michigan; the Sisters of Bon Secours USA, based in Marriottsville,

Maryland; the Sisters of St. Francis of Philadelphia, based in Aston, Pennsylvania; and the Sisters of the Holy Names of Jesus & Mary, US-Ontario Province, based in Marylhurst, Oregon.

Specifically, the lawsuit cited Smith & Wesson's AR-15 ads that mimic video games played from the perspective of an active shooter that are wildly popular among young men. Such marketing, the suit alleged, "played a significant role in contributing to many of the most heinous gun crimes in United States history." It said the company made more than $695 million in revenue from sales of AR-15s between 2012 and 2021. Significantly, large socially conscious investors, including BlackRock and Vanguard, joined with the nuns in their safety campaign. A judge eventually tossed out the lawsuit. But in a separate action, the sisters did manage to persuade Dick's Sporting Goods to stop selling assault rifles and to raise the minimum age to twenty-one for all firearms purchases.

An affiliated organization, the Interfaith Center on Corporate Responsibility—a global coalition of more than three hundred faith-based institutional investors—has also joined the fight. One of its chief goals is to stop the manufacture and sale to civilians of military-style semiautomatic assault rifles, as well as a ban on high-capacity magazines and a federally mandated universal background check for anyone looking to buy guns or ammunition. In 2024, the center's focus included Walmart, whose stores have reported hundreds of instances of gun violence, including well over one hundred deaths involving both customers and employees. Using its stock holdings as leverage, the center asked fellow shareholders to pressure the retail giant, a major seller of firearms, to review its workplace safety guidelines.

Success, though, comes incrementally, if at all, to shareholder activists and their proposals, which are usually nonbinding. After Smith & Wesson's then-CEO Ed Schultz agreed in 2000 to develop more gun safety mechanisms in exchange for the dropping of lawsuits against the company, gun wholesalers and retailers alike boycotted the firearms behemoth. Schultz was pushed out, and his enhanced safety plan was scrapped altogether.

"We'll continue to attempt to engage with the gun manufacturers," Sister Judy, who's been a nun since 1960, tells the National Catholic Reporter's *Global Sisters Report*. "We aren't saying, 'No guns,' or, 'Take people's guns away.' We want safe guns. You do wonder what the future of the gun manufacturers will be. Is this generation coming up going to be buying guns? . . . It just seems like we could be at a tipping point."

The Reverend Barry Randolph agrees. The longtime pastor of Detroit's Church of the Messiah, where young Black men under thirty account for an astonishing 60 percent of his congregation, launched a campaign called Silence the Violence. The effort has virtually eradicated gun violence in Randolph's neighborhood by working hard to provide everyone with jobs, affordable housing, free internet, and other daily needs. "Violence, especially gun violence, is virtually nonexistent in this area because we provide people with the things they need," he says.

In an interview with the PBS show *American Black Journal*, Randolph ticks off the numerous ways his church is offering poor Detroiters an alternative to using guns to get what they need, all as part of Silence the Violence:

> You can come to Church on the Messiah and you can rent an apartment or townhouse. You can come get free internet. You can come for workforce development training. You can come to find a job in our employment office. You can come and be part of our business incubation center. You can come be part of a marching band which will help you be able to get into school. You can come use our solar-powered charging station. You can come to our doctor's office and you can come to church on Sunday. You can come for all of the different things that you may need to improve your quality of life and those of the people who

are around you. It's all about being church. It's all about being about the community and making a difference. And one of the reasons why we're so successful with young people is because we take the activism of what it is that we believe and take it out to the community and neighborhood and make it happen. And it's all tangible. You can see, touch, feel, use it, and be a part of it. That's what Silence the Violence is all about: resources to be able to build our community so that it is a safe place. We can eradicate gun violence.

The New Mexico conference mentioned earlier in this chapter was named in honor of the late Jim Atwood, whose own gun violence activism began in 1975 after a member of his Virginia congregation was murdered with a $20 handgun. In 2000, Atwood organized the inaugural Million Moms March on Washington, DC, where he carried a sign that read: *Where is the church?* It has taken a couple of decades, but nationwide, there seems to be an awakening around guns, and it is starting with faith communities.

Lay It Down is a separate campaign aimed at persuading American Christians to surrender one million guns. "Our most vulnerable are suffering, and thoughtful Christians now sit at a crossroads," the group says. Its members have coalesced around a meditation that's become a mantra:

Because of our faith, we trust God for safety.
Because of our faith, we stand in solidarity with each other.
Because of our faith, we tell the truth about our past.
Because of our faith, we can build a better future.
Because of our faith, we can lay anything down.

There's also Faithful America, an online nonprofit community calling on Christians to resist Trump and his administration's "Christofascism." In a petition to the US Senate demanding action on guns, it says: "Loving our neighbors means no longer allowing angry, violent individuals to use weapons of war against our families, friends, and communities," and quotes Cardinal Blase Cupich of the Chicago archdiocese: "The right to bear arms does not eclipse the right to life, or the right of all Americans to go about their lives free of the fear that they might be shredded by bullets at any moment."

Incredibly, that's still a minority opinion. Gun owners' attachment to their guns runs deep. People involved in groups like RAWtools that organize urban gun surrender events tell me they've seen supervising police officers and sheriff's deputies close to tears when firearms are neutered by having their barrels cut off. (This strikes me as suspiciously Freudian.)

Groups like RAWtools also get their share of pushback from the pro-gun crowd. "Last week, someone wrote on a blog: 'Couldn't somebody kill someone with one of your garden tools?' And I was like, that would be tragic," Utz says. "But nobody's going into a school with garden tools."

He pauses. "You'll hear people say, 'You can stone somebody with a rock, and we don't outlaw rocks,'" he adds. "When someone comes to me with that sort of stuff, I listen to them and look for space to ask: 'Why do you feel like you need a gun?' Usually, it comes down to fear and being scared of something. That's how the machine makes its money. It pays for them to stoke the fear. They're literally making a killing."

At a panel discussion on the grounds of Ghost Ranch, Utz and others involved in the Guns to Gardens movement reaffirm their determination to make a difference. For Harry Eberts, who pastors a Presbyterian church in Santa Fe and serves as copresident of New Mexicans to Prevent Gun Violence, there's no time to waste. He's still shaken and a little numb when I speak with him: Just a week earlier, one of his parishioners, an eighty-three-year-old, was fatally shot by a carjacker outside a Best Buy store.

He also admits to having a hard time holding on to hope. "Even if we have 250 guns surrendered at an event, we all know full well how many guns were made that day," he says. In case you're curious, the National Shooting Sports Foundation estimates around 13.5 million firearms are produced annually in the United States alone. That's roughly 37,000 guns a day.

Jeff Wild, a retired Lutheran pastor who volunteers with Guns to Gardens in Wisconsin, once helped a woman destroy the .357-caliber handgun that her father had used to kill himself the previous year. "If the church continues to condone violence, we're screwed," he says. "We have to be able to take the position where I'm willing to give up my weapon for the sake of my neighbor."

Miranda Viscoli, the other copresident of New Mexicans to Prevent Gun Violence, tells of weeping mothers bringing her the guns their teenagers have used in suicides. Mike Martin, RAWtools's national executive director, says such experiences move him deeply. "For me, it's all about the survivors," he says, blinking back tears.

In New Mexico, to refurbish guns into garden implements as RAWtools is doing, you need to get permission. You need a court order to be able to legally destroy a firearm, and an expert must certify that the gun doesn't have historic value. "We take better care of our firearms than our people," Viscoli says, her eyes flashing with anger.

Viscoli is deeply invested in the fight. Her group has organized nineteen buyback events that have taken more than three thousand guns off the streets. Some 40 percent of those guns have been semiautomatics. I decide to drive down to Albuquerque to observe the group's twentieth firearms surrender firsthand. I hop into my rental car filled with hope. These buybacks seem like a promising way to get a lot of guns off the streets.

But after spending a little time there, and getting a closer look, my optimism fades.

◆ ◆ ◆

## IN GUNS WE TRUST

On a searingly hot Saturday morning, a long line of vehicles stretches across a parking lot and around the corner from Albuquerque Police Department headquarters. As each pulls up in front of a blue police tent, volunteers record the number and type of guns being turned in, and an officer carefully checks to ensure they're unloaded. Other officers run the guns' serial numbers through a federal database to see if any were reported lost or stolen or were used in a crime; those will be returned to their rightful owners or bagged as evidence.

For a man in his sixties with a long, white ZZ Top–style beard and a flatbed pickup, it's a good payday: $1,550 in exchange for a small arsenal of eight firearms. He has just turned in an assault rifle, three long guns, three semiautomatic handguns, and two pistols. A volunteer peels off crisp $50 banknotes from a stack on a table. Assault rifles fetch $250; semiautomatics, $200; and pistols and long guns, $100. I take a few steps in the man's direction to speak with him, but a cop in body armor stops me; it's a confidential surrender, the officer tells me sternly, and I'm not allowed to engage with the gun owners, assurances of journalistic anonymity notwithstanding.

A shower of white-hot sparks then fills the air, forcing me to beat a hasty retreat, as the bearded man's guns and most of the 200-plus others surrendered on this day are cut into unrecognizable pieces on a chop saw. Within a week, they'll be refashioned into garden tools, completing their dramatic transformation from instruments of death to implements of life. Dozens of gun owners are still lined up in idling vehicles when the cash runs out; they pull out of the lot, disappointed.

Do these buybacks work? Evidence of their effectiveness is thin, says the RAND Corporation, a centrist think tank. "Although it is possible that gun buybacks have prevented incidents of firearm-related harm, it is very unlikely that such small reductions in the number of guns available would lead to measurable decreases in firearm crime, injuries, or deaths," it concludes in a recent report. Maybe so, but as we've seen, suicides—not homicides—account for most gun deaths, and experts say a key contributing factor to suicide is the easy availability of guns. More than half of all suicide deaths involve firearms, according to CDC data.

Crimestoppers is among the community groups on hand to observe the Albuquerque buyback, and I ask one member how taking two hundred old guns out of circulation will make a difference when there are hundreds of millions of guns out there. "We have to keep trying," she says with a shrug.

That means looking for ways to get creative. Taking a page from the nuns' playbook, RAWtools's Utz recently got a federal firearms license so people can ship him guns through the mail, and he can buy weapons that police have confiscated. It's the only way to make sure the guns, or workable parts of them, don't resurface on a lucrative black market, especially in the eleven states where law enforcement isn't allowed to destroy firearms and must either store or sell them.

Indeed, a *New York Times* investigation in 2023 showed that guns collected by police in buybacks and amnesty programs often are dismantled and the parts sold off, sometimes even as kits, in what has become known as the "blue market." Many end up in the hands of criminals who reassemble them into weapons that are untraceable because they no longer bear the original serial numbers.

"It's easier to get a gun in America than it is to get rid of a gun," Shane Claiborne writes in an op-ed for *The Philadelphia Inquirer*. "This should be unthinkable—can you imagine if police sold the heroin seized in a drug bust? But alas, I fear that too many of the gun buybacks that we organize around the country become 'gun sellbacks' by police."

Undeterred, RAWtools is working apace to destroy and repurpose as many guns as it can. In Philadelphia, Claiborne says, a particular outreach has proven especially popular: "Groceries for Guns," which doles out a $250 food credit for each donated firearm. The personal stories behind these surrendered guns are compelling, according to Claiborne:

> One family I met had just moved to Philadelphia, and had a family member who thought they needed an assault rifle, so he bought one and had it delivered to their house. It was literally dropped off on the porch, and they had no idea it was coming. They Googled "How to get rid of a gun" and it pulled up us at RAWtools. I made them a piece of art for their kid's room from the AR-15. . . .
>
> A man in Philadelphia lost his wife to suicide and called RAWtools Philly, hoping that we could destroy the gun she used. I contacted the detective involved in the case, who listened intently and asked good questions. He seemed very interested in the reasonable request of this grieving widower. The detective ran it through the ranks, and eventually brought the firearm into the shop, where we destroyed it. Once he got here, the gun was gone in about five minutes. . . .
>
> Every time we turn a gun into a garden tool, we are declaring that all things can be made new. Metal that has been crafted to kill can be reimagined and repurposed. And what is true of metal is also true of policies.

In a particularly poignant instance, the Naval Criminal Investigative Service—the same *NCIS* of television drama series fame—shipped Utz a gun that a nineteen-year-old serviceman had used to take his own life. The veteran's parents and siblings flew out to Colorado for what Utz described as a "rite of transformation," in which the weapon was turned into a tool. "It was kind of a tough hour, but a really beautiful and important hour," he recalls, adding that he's now exploring how RAWtools might serve Gold Star families.

There are dozens of like-minded dissident faith groups springing up nationwide. Jim Curry, a retired Episcopal bishop in Connecticut, traded his robe and pulpit for a portable forge and anvil. Curry, who founded Bishops United Against Gun Violence and helped launch a RAWtools-inspired group called Swords to Plowshares, systematically dismantles guns under the watchful eyes of police officers so they can never again be used to maim or kill. "You have to try new ideas because the old ideas don't work," he tells the online newsmagazine *Rural Intelligence*. On its website, the group says its process "allows us to use creativity to make something inspiring and symbolic out of a weapon of death."

Groups devoted to prayer and advocacy are also flourishing. Among them is Heeding God's Call to End Gun Violence, a group that Cindy Scheetz, a Mennonite in Pennsylvania, says she felt compelled to join out of a sense of helplessness over endless mass shootings at schools. "In our mourning and horror, we say something needs to be done, and then life goes on and nothing happens. I believe strongly in the power of prayer, but I also believe that action is a form of prayer," she writes. "God wants us to do what we can. I can't do everything, but with God's help, I can do something."

Angela Ferrell-Zabala, executive director of Moms Demand Action, one of the nation's largest gun control advocacy organizations, is also a woman of faith whose activism is rooted in her conviction that the fight for stronger gun laws is God's work. "You can't be comfortable until you are actually exercising your faith, which means that I am looking out for my community," she tells *Sojourners* magazine.

RAWtools's Mike Martin sees "an unbelievable opportunity" for faith groups to take the lead in gun violence initiatives, starting with safe storage, which he views as a public health priority akin to needle exchanges for drug addicts. "What if we gave up our guns for Lent for forty days and find a safe place to store them? And then reflect afterward and say, 'Maybe I don't need this gun anymore,'" he suggests.

Pastors, too, need to address the gun crisis from the pulpit, Martin insists. Few, he laments, have the courage to do so for fear of alienating their congregations. That's the focus of the Ghost Ranch gathering: to muster the "congregational courage" required to take on guns head-on. Martin has given all of this deep thought. He lives and labors in Colorado Springs, for decades a mecca of white evangelicalism—and now Christian nationalism—where numerous fundamentalist organizations are headquartered. (Think Focus on the Family, The Navigators, the International Bible Society, the Association of Christian Schools International, Every Home for Christ, Young Life, and Compassion International.) The fifteen largest alone wield not just political but economic power, generating an estimated $2 billion in annual revenue. "I work in the belly of the beast," he tells me.

At the New Mexico conference, participants huddle to talk about the fraught subject of church security. But as the Reverend Rosalind Hughes, an Episcopal priest from Ohio, notes, securing a house of worship against a would-be attacker by locking the doors and deploying armed guards doesn't necessarily line up with the basic mission of a church. Hughes points to the biblical accounts of Jesus's betrayal, where Peter pulls a sword to defend Christ and slices off the ear of one of the men who'd come to arrest the Lord. In Matthew's retelling, Jesus orders Peter to put down his sword, then reaches out to heal the man's severed ear. "If we go down the road of swords and barricades and enmity, who will heal the servant's ear? Are we just buying into that fortress mentality?" she asks. "Don't trade our faith values for an illusion of security or locked doors. We don't accept that that's the way we're supposed to live."

"We have Christians who seem to think of a God who blesses guns; who see Jesus as a sort of Rambo," says Father John Dear, a Roman Catholic nonviolence activist and Nobel Peace Prize nominee who's been arrested for his activism more than seventy-five times.

Rather than glorifying guns, he says, believers should look to Gandhi and Martin Luther King Jr. as examples.

Nonviolence goes beyond working for commonsense restrictions on guns, Dear insists. It extends to disavowing capital punishment. "There's no cause for which we ever again support the taking of a single human life. We don't kill people who kill people to show people we don't kill people. Stop the killing—that's what it means to be people of universal love," he pleads, pacing back and forth as the Ghost Ranch attendees all nod. "*Put down the swords*—these are some of the last words of Jesus to the church." Peter, he says, "is willing to kill for Jesus, but he's not ready to die unarmed for Jesus."

"We're told guns make us safer," he adds. "If that were true, we'd be the safest place on the planet."

♦ ♦ ♦

Too many of us see guns as the ultimate antidote to violence and fear. Can we ever rewire our minds? Yes, Father Dear says—but it will take what he calls "active nonviolence," and it will begin with each of us. What he says next makes me squirm in my seat.

When you are self-critical and too hard on yourself, he says—when you beat yourself up for past mistakes—that is violence against yourself. When you are being aggressive behind the wheel and tailgating people, flashing your lights in impatience, that is violence against them. All of this is violence, and before we can rid our societies of gun violence, we'll have to purge ourselves of its seeds in ourselves. "There's nothing passive about it," Dear says. "It's an active way of life. It's the spiritual path to the God of peace and a new future. . . . Be compassionate to yourself and make peace with yourself. When you want to put yourself down or hate yourself, take a deep breath. It feels good not to be full of anger and hatred."

As noble and aspirational as all of this is, it's essential if people of goodwill can ever hope to persuade gun owners at large to reconsider their positions, Dear insists—especially NRA members and others "who feel that guns give them power, that guns give them security, their guns protect them, their guns are their birthright, their guns are attached to their bodies, that they trust their guns, that guns give them their identity."

"What we're trying to do as church people [is] to help one another realize that we're not sons and daughters of America or guns or the NRA or bombs or any political party," he says. "We don't trust in our bank accounts or in a Glock 19. We are the sons and daughters of the beloved God of peace. We have to teach people who they are. The minute I forget I'm a human being and the beloved of God, I don't know who *you* are and I dehumanize you. And then I can shoot you."

John Dear's brother lived next door to Sandy Hook Elementary School, and after the 2012 massacre there, Dear telephoned his sibling to check on him. A priest at the local Catholic church who presided over many of the slain children's funerals turned out to have a side hustle selling guns—an enterprise he'd even advertised on the back of the parish bulletin. In the wake of that news, Dear's brother, reeling from that hypocrisy, abruptly stopped going to church.

"God raises Jesus from the dead and he comes back as nonviolent as ever, and he says: *Peace be with you.* What you and I are trying to do is wake up and say '*no*,'" rejecting violence in all its forms, "and welcome his gift of resurrection peace and spread it as far as we can." Dear pauses, wondering aloud about the nature and meaning of resurrection, before concluding: "Resurrection is having nothing to do with death." Then he quotes the poet Edna St. Vincent Millay: *I shall die, but that is all I shall do for Death; I am not on his payroll.*

Just as fear stokes gun sales, it also prompts some gun violence activists to give up for fear of failure; fear of ridicule; fear of retribution. But fear, Dear says, is a luxury we cannot afford. "We don't have time for fear, or anxiety, or worries, or sitting back and doing nothing, despairing," he says. "That's what the culture of gun violence wants you to think: *There's nothing you can do. Just give up.* Jesus says: *Arise.* But people can no longer imagine this country without mass shootings. We're blinded by our own violence, and so we have no vision."

Father Dear likens the campaign against gun violence to the early fight nearly two centuries ago to abolish slavery, when abolitionists such as Frederick Douglass and William Lloyd Garrison advocated the immediate emancipation of all slaves long before Lincoln's presidential proclamation—outraging landowners who said: *You can't do that. We've always had slaves.* "Here at Ghost Ranch, we are announcing the abolition of gun violence," the priest bellows to applause. "A new world is coming; a new future of nonviolence."

Amid the euphoria, though, I look around and realize that nearly all the gun control advocates who've trekked into the New Mexican foothills to turn their local efforts into a nationwide movement are in their sixties and seventies. Just a couple of twentysomethings are among us. "Where are the young people?" I ask one of the conference organizers. She suggests it's trickier for millennials and Gen Zers to turn out for a midweek conference in a far-flung locale.

That makes sense—although it seems important, to me, that young Christians be involved in this work as well. But I also realize I may be asking the wrong question. A more compelling one might be: Where are the evangelicals? There are none here among this gathering, made up mostly of progressive Christians from mainline denominations and a few Catholics and Unitarians.

In John 14:6, Jesus says: "*I am the way, the truth, and the life. No one comes to the Father except through me.*" But it's as if white evangelicals in the United States these days are saying: "We are the way, the truth, and the life. No one comes to the Father except through us."

Father Dear is uncharacteristically subdued when I ask him about white evangelicals and guns. "How do you reach them?" I ask him over lunch in the ranch cafeteria, and he initially responds with a thousand-yard stare. But the question quickly rouses him.

"I try different things, because Jesus tried different things," he tells me. "I try to persuade them that guns are too dangerous—that we're supposed to be living nonviolent lives. But if that doesn't work, I just say: 'You're not following Jesus.' I've told thousands of people that, and they usually want to kill me. And then they hear what I said: It's all fine, but please, don't fool yourself that you're following Jesus and you're claiming to be a fundamentalist taking Jesus at his word. You're not taking Jesus at his word. You're following the Book of Chronicles or somebody else. You have nothing to do with Jesus. Jesus is saying, *Love your enemies. Offer no violent resistance to one that is evil. Put down the sword.* Those are the last words of Jesus to the church. He's totally nonviolent."

Worked up now, Dear adds: "If you want to follow this guy, you have to do what he says, whether you like it or not. It doesn't matter what you think. You're supposed to be doing what the guy says, and you're not. You are not a follower of Jesus—you're a follower of the Second Amendment. It's all mixed up in some crazy false theology. I tell people that a lot, and it shocks them. Maybe that's what you have to do. But you may not be able to tell people that often. They simply cannot hear it."

Dear thinks the faith community, with its endorsement of violence and war and its misplaced trust in nation-states over the divine, needs to hit the reset button. "I think we're starting all over with Christianity. . . . The culture of violence wants us shooting each other. No! The days of killing are over."

Unless it's killing with kindness, like a young friend of mine in Texas is determined to do.

♦ ♦ ♦

Rene Sanchez is trying to change the narrative around God and guns, one gently challenging conversation at a time.

I first met Sanchez a decade ago when we attended the same dynamic urban church in Providence, Rhode Island. He and his family now live in San Antonio in his native Texas, where gun culture is inseparable from society, open carry of handguns is commonplace, and firearms bleed into faith.

Now in his mid-thirties, with young children of his own, Sanchez was rattled when a gunman slaughtered nineteen children and two adults in 2022 at Robb Elementary School in Uvalde, just a ninety-minute drive from his home. Texas's deadliest-ever school shooting literally brought him to his knees. "I did what everyone said they were doing and I prayed. I just prayed, harder than I'd ever prayed before," he tells me. "I felt horrible, heartbroken, frustrated—all the things. Like, how can this still be a thing that we are dealing with?"

Even today, the anguish is fresh. As we talk, Sanchez wonders aloud what he'd do if he got an active shooter alert from his daughter's school: "I'm dropping absolutely everything. I'm driving as fast as I possibly can to the school, and I'm doing everything I possibly can to get into that school and save my daughter. Right? Like, I . . . I . . . " He chokes up and his voice trails off. The scenario is hypothetical, but only barely, and it has brought him to tears.

Three days after the massacre in Uvalde, the NRA went ahead with its annual convention in Houston. It was the group's first national gathering in three years because of the COVID-19 pandemic. Sanchez couldn't shake the feeling that he needed to be there. He's not a gun owner, though his uncle, a "self-proclaimed redneck" who claims to own two hundred guns, had taught him how to shoot a rifle at a tree as a child. And two of his best friends—a cop and an evangelical worship leader—both hunt and embrace gun culture. "They're kind of unique, to my perspective, because they're some of the best people I know, just solid dudes. They can wholeheartedly say that Jesus Christ is their Lord and Savior, and they don't flinch at that and [they] also own guns." It bugs Sanchez, who now attends a Mennonite church whose teachings are firmly rooted in nonviolence, but he loves his friends.

Sanchez wasn't sure what he was supposed to do at the NRA convention—only that he felt called to be there. "I just went, with what I truly feel was an open mind and an open heart to understand," he tells me.

You need to be an NRA member to get into their convention, so Sanchez joined, despite his wife's misgivings. I did, too, out of pure journalistic curiosity, as I began writing this book. I wanted to see how the NRA communicates to its members, and I found out—fast.

Overnight, my email inbox and my mailbox were flooded with fearmongering propaganda: *Gun-banners have made it crystal clear—they won't rest until your Second Amendment freedoms have been wiped from the face of the earth forever. . . . Ultimately, they'll try to use the brute force of the federal government to BAN and CONFISCATE your guns—and haul you off to prison if you refuse to comply. . . . You and I are in the fight of our lives. Victory means going on the offensive—and defeating the forces that have aligned against our freedom.* As we talk about the promotional material we now receive from the NRA, Sanchez and I share a chagrined laugh: These, we agree, are not shiny happy people holding hands.

Inside the vast convention center in downtown Houston, dozens of vendors hawked the same type of AR-15 military-style rifle that had been used to butcher Uvalde's children earlier that week. Outside, more than a thousand protesters chanted and waved signs that read: *Their blood is on your hands*. Bewildered, and decidedly out of his element, Sanchez wandered the hall dressed in his favorite Jesus shirt: a tee from the Seattle Christian rock band Kings Kaleidoscope. Suddenly, he became aware of what was, for him, an entirely new sensation:

> I was surprised at myself, and I'm just gonna keep it honest, about how empowered I felt. I, too, could buy all these guns if I had the money. I'd walk up to this high-caliber weapon, a sniper rifle or something crazy, and I'm like: "I could buy this right

now? I mean, I could walk out of here with this right now?" And the guy would say: "Yes, and you can even customize it." It was insane. But I thought, I guess I kind of get it now, and I was a little surprised that I felt that internally.

Everybody was kind of ready for war—war with each other. Do I really want to be the one who kills somebody? Do I? Do you understand the hypocrisy of: I'm here to protect life, so I'm going to use this weapon that destroys it?

Stepping outside to get some air and clear his head, Sanchez saw an NRA member red in the face from screaming at the gun control activists assembled across the street. It took him back to a boisterous Black Lives Matter protest a few years earlier, on the steps of the Rhode Island Statehouse, where he saw demonstrators offer an enraged counter-protester a bottle of water. For Sanchez, it was a poignant, teachable moment that left a deep impression, and he decided to take the same peaceable approach with the angry NRA guy.

So, he walked up to him, took the man out for a coffee, and they talked. Neither persuaded the other to come around to his way of thinking about guns, but they listened to one another. Before they parted, they recited the Lord's Prayer together.

This is how Sanchez has decided to approach the rancorous divide over guns: by dialoguing with gun owners rather than demonizing them. Today, when he meets NRA members, he engages with them, extending compassion and a listening ear. "This stuff is going to keep happening because the kingdom of God isn't here yet," he says, adding: "I've had some really interesting conversations with my two best friends. They know exactly where I am with guns. Where I've landed with them is: *It's your choice. We each have a choice. But do you fully understand the extent of the choice you're making? Are you truly ready to kill someone even if they hurt you?*"

Part of what motivates him to keep having these conversations, he tells me, is the possibility—however remote it might seem—that one day he might miraculously encounter a mass shooter in the making and alter the would-be gunman's dark trajectory. "Maybe I'll have a chance to meet this potential criminal and talk to them before any of that happens, and God changes their heart," he says. So he keeps on talking, even when the other person isn't listening.

Sanchez is a Democrat, and one of his politically conservative cousins—a man who founded a church and posts frequently on social media about his firearms—confronted him about the party's abortion rights platform "and how they're killing babies." Sanchez pushed back: *All you do is share about your guns, which are also killing babies.* "And he goes: *I'll pray for you. You just don't understand.*"

"People say Jesus would have owned a gun. No! Jesus died because he didn't want this kind of power. He had a different kind of power," Sanchez says. And then, channeling Father Dear and more forcefully calling out evangelicals, he adds: "You're building *your* kingdom. You're not building God's kingdom. That's your choice. You can do it; just own it. Don't call it this other thing."

I walk away from my conversation with Sanchez feeling refreshed and upbeat. If more Christians like him would decide to hold respectful conversations with other believers about guns, to encourage them to think about what Jesus calls us to, what might happen?

Then I make the mistake of refreshing my social media feeds and surface a provocative video by the white evangelical country artist Mary Kutter, who's promoting a recently released single. In the New Testament, the church is called the Bride of Christ, but the first few twangy lines of the Nashville star's song are a stark reminder of modern evangelicalism's extramarital affair with guns. She sings about the Bible that sits on her nightstand, right above the pistol nestled in her drawer. All she'll be is "a smoking gun," she warbles, "if they show up at my door."

The lyrics are unclear who the "they" is who might show up at her door. In any case, the Jesus described in the Bible on that table, who calls his followers to love their enemies, would surely suggest not shooting them.

As those once-popular rubber bracelets asked, WWJD? *What Would Jesus Do?* It's a question I've been asking myself daily since I began this deep dive into what place, if any, guns have in the gospel.

# 10 | NO GUNS IN HEAVEN

The Reverend Abigail Henrich—pastor, wife, suburban dog mom—is an unconventional warrior in the battle for reasonable gun restrictions.

Henrich spent her childhood in a farm town in upstate New York, where neighbors hunted and modeled responsible gun use while she ran an orphanage of dolls. Her first car was a 1931 Model A roadster, complete with an *ahoogah* horn; in fact, that very automobile is parked in her Massachusetts driveway now. She holds a master's in divinity from Princeton Theological Seminary, and casually uses words like *shibboleth*, which means a long-held but now-outmoded belief. But she's fiery, she suffers fools badly, and she's the first to admit she's a minister with a mouth—especially when she's calling out hypocrisy within the body of Christ.

On the morning of my visit, Henrich, who looks like she could be the elder sister of the actress Emma Stone, is wearing a bright blue T-shirt that reads: *I love Jesus but I cuss a little*. And when our conversation at her dining room table moves to America's gun crisis, the founder of Christians United Against Gun Violence doesn't mince words.

"My big theological statement on guns," she tells me, "is fuck them."

Henrich, who grew up Methodist and now pastors two progressive Boston-area churches—Grace Community Church and Stratford Street United Church—is among a small but spirited group of

Christians who are challenging the white evangelical embrace of gun culture head-on. "There are many grassroots Christians doing this work," she says. But it's exhausting.

"Love is a complicated world that has no road signs," she tells me. "It's constantly ambiguous. It means I need to love the gun owner, and that's really hard work. Whereas they get to just hate the snowflake I am and say I'm not a Christian."

♦ ♦ ♦

Henrich's story is instructive. The work of changing hearts and minds to achieve gun reform is frustrating and hard. In an era in which so many believers have been bewitched by the MAGA movement, trying to win friends and influence people in white evangelical spaces can feel like laboring in vain in the graveyard of good works.

We're meeting at her home in Walpole, Massachusetts, about twenty-five miles southwest of Boston, a community that, to its chagrin, was long best known for its forbidding maximum-security prison ringed with razor wire and sniper nests perched atop cement towers. I grew up next door in Foxborough, and I have deep personal ties to this quaint New England town. Less than a mile from the Henrich homestead is a middle school operating out of what once was a vibrant evangelical church—Christian Life Center, the now defunct Assemblies of God congregation where I made my first confession of faith in 1981. A few doors down is the chiropractor's office on Turner's Pond, named for two-time Olympic figure skater Roger Turner, where my late brother, Brian, rented an upstairs apartment for two decades. And in the center of town is a storefront that once housed the newsroom of *The Walpole Times*, the award-winning weekly newspaper where I made my start in journalism.

"We say the uncomfortable, difficult stuff," Henrich is telling me, describing her churches' approach to guns and other social issues. She has a stream-of-consciousness way of speaking, peppered with plenty of good-natured profanity. I ask her what she means, and she elaborates: "What are we going to do with the gospel that tells us we have to sell all we have and give it to the poor? We do so much poverty work, but we're all still rich. What do we do with that? How do we live in that space?" She pauses and adds: "We get comfortable with being uncomfortable."

Henrich founded Christians United Against Gun Violence in 2022 after yet another US school shooting. There have been so many such massacres, she acknowledges, she can't even remember exactly which one. "Nobody's doing anything about this, and Christians have to stand up and do something," she says. Yet the campaign has sputtered. "We put together all this liturgy, we put together all this activism, we created this website, and fifteen churches signed up—that's it. It just fizzled out."

Henrich ticks off the reasons why: Ministers like her are slammed and overstretched, juggling pulpit ministry, pastoral care, and a myriad of other responsibilities. And like anyone else, they are conflict averse. Even so, she's pushing ahead with gun activism, helped and inspired by linking arms with the Presbyterian Peace Fellowship, the nonviolence group that organized the New Mexico gun gathering. She's currently organizing gun buybacks, offering Target gift cards to people who turn in their AR-15s, semiautomatics, rifles, and shotguns, which are then cut up on the spot.

It's work that comes naturally to Henrich, partly because of her brash, animated personality and partly because she went to seminary with Shane Claiborne, who cofounded RAWtools Philadelphia, the initiative we examined in the preceding chapter, and Scotty Utz. She and her allies bought high-performance saws capable of slicing through reinforced steel; raised $10,000 to buy back the guns; and found a parking lot whose owners were willing to work with her to ensure the seamless and safe transfer of the weapons.

After her first few gun surrenders were a success, Henrich called the Boston Police Department, hoping they'd be interested in partnering with her. Their response? "Fucking crickets," she says.

"I'm like, 'We'll destroy them for you, however you want to do it. We'll meet you where you keep all these guns. We'll let you run the whole show. If you don't want us doing it, I get it. We'll teach you. I'll buy you the saws. I'll raise all the money.' Like, this is the easiest thing in the universe. 'Partner with me. Don't partner with me. Make me your silent partner. I will buy you the guns. I will train you. I will get people to train your police officers, or let us do it. We'll do it. Like, this is a win for you guys.'"

Why does she think they've been so unreceptive? "Fear and bureaucracy," Henrich answers. Then I ask her a more pointed follow-up question, one that's been nagging at me: Why is her organization called Christians United Against Gun Violence? After all, if there's one thing American believers aren't united against, it's guns.

"Because we were making a statement," she responds. "We got some pushback from people who asked, 'Why are we saying this is *Christian*?' I was the originator, and I would not move on that. It's Christian because someone in the Christian church has to stand against this. You'll hear people say: 'There's no such thing as progressive Christians.' Really? We're the people who led child labor laws. We were union organizers. There are lots of Christian leaders who are adamantly opposed to gun violence. Now, I didn't say *all* Christians are against gun violence, but I wanted to make it clear that there are groups of Christians who *are* united against it." Underscoring that conviction, the group's website unequivocally declares: "Some of the loudest voices preventing gun safety in our country are Christians. We cannot serve God and guns."

Henrich invokes the story of slain civil rights leader Martin Luther King Jr.'s own crisis of conscience involving a weapon. It's January 30, 1956, a month into a bus boycott staged by Black people protesting racial segregation in Montgomery, Alabama, and King is deep into his leadership of the increasingly acrimonious civil rights movement when his house is bombed. King is away on the evening of the bombing, speaking at a large meeting, but his wife, Coretta, their seven-week-old daughter, Yolanda, and a neighbor are inside. The explosion heavily damages the front porch, but thankfully, no one is injured. King rushes home and finds a crowd of three hundred angry supporters, some carrying knives and guns, gathered outside the house, along with Montgomery's mayor and police commissioner, who plead for calm and pledge to investigate. King tells the crowd: "If you have weapons, take them home. If you do not have them, please do not seek them. We cannot solve this problem through violence. We must meet violence with nonviolence."

What they don't know is that inside his house, King himself has several handguns within easy reach for self-protection. It's early in his ascendance to the national stage, and King has been getting daily death threats. A visiting journalist, William Worthy, says he once went to plop down in an armchair in King's living room, and nearly sat on a loaded pistol. Two weeks after his house is bombed, King even applies for a concealed carry permit; local police, quick to discriminate against African Americans, deny his application. Meanwhile, friends who have noticed the firearms strewn around King's household beg him to get rid of them.

King's crisis of conscience around guns culminates in a late-night debate with fellow civil rights activist Bayard Rustin. As Rustin argues with King about how he's compromising the nonviolent resistance movement by keeping firearms in his house, King stares hard at the handgun on his kitchen table. By the next morning, he has concluded that guns are not the path to peace.

But as the sixtieth anniversary of MLK's 1968 assassination approaches, Henrich acknowledges that even her own extended family, much less the nation, doesn't see eye to eye on guns. She has a "gun-loving brother" whom, she estimates, owns about one hundred and fifty guns. He bought his family body armor when the pandemic hit. "I don't have any conversations with him," says Henrich. She has also had to argue her position with her father, using the evolution of automobile safety as an example: "We figured out cars harmed people, so we got seat belts. And then we got shoulder belts and airbags." Why would we place more safety regulations around cars than guns? She's flabbergasted at white evangelicals' refusal to accept what she insists is a scripturally unambiguous stance on guns.

Just look at Jesus, she finds herself pleading: "Everything the Prince of Peace says about violence, about how we respond to violence—how, when somebody brings out a sword, he says, 'No, don't do that'—is turn the other cheek. But once again, these people are more concerned about unborn babies than they are about living children. I would put the American flag, Donald Trump, and guns as a shibboleth of evangelical American Christianity that has absolutely nothing to do with the gospel. And yet guns have just become so interwoven."

Her comments, which encapsulate the very book I'm writing, stop me in my tracks. In an instant, sitting at Henrich's dining room table, I am transported back to Alabama and Rocky Mount Methodist Church's parish pistol range; back to rural Indiana and FosTecH's glib justification of its killing machines, proudly made in America by evangelicals, all for the glory of God. My pulse quickens, my temples throb, and my throat goes dry. I find myself overwhelmed by an all-too-familiar mix of rage and disbelief and helplessness at the cognitive dissonance of excremental NRA talking points masquerading as New Testament theology.

How, I ask Henrich in a fog of incredulity, do you get through to people? *Can* you get through to people? What can you possibly say that will persuade them to reconsider their position?

She pauses, gathers her thoughts, and answers with a pronouncement reminiscent of Father John Dear's epitaph for contemporary far-right evangelicalism:

> I think the evangelical church is killing itself. It's becoming absolutely irrelevant. And what makes me sad is people think that means the Christian church is dying. Let me rephrase: I think the Christian church *is* dying. I don't think the gospel is. And as a committed Jesus follower, I think one of the best things that could happen for the gospel is for the church to die, because then we will get the gospel back.
>
> We've watched in Christian history this happen multiple times. The church dies and reforms in new ways. I think the evangelical church is nailing its coffin shut with predominantly these issues: abortion, LGBTQ [rights], and guns.
>
> And so I think the evangelical church is going to kill itself.

♦ ♦ ♦

If there's a solution to the gun conundrum, Henrich is convinced that women will find it. "Because they're the caregivers. Their niece is gay, and they love their niece. They support abortion, because they don't want their daughter to be trapped. And they don't want gun violence. On the street, Moms Demand Action is one of the biggest anti-gun organizations in the country."

Indeed, women are taking the fight to pro-gun Americans of all religious and political backgrounds. Consider Tennessee's Covenant Moms, the group launched by mothers of children who were attending The Covenant School, a private Christian academy in Nashville, when a mass shooter walked inside and slaughtered three youngsters and three staff members in 2023. These mostly white evangelical moms were lifelong conservatives and staunch Second Amendment supporters. But after a gunman targeted their own vulnerable children, they made it their mission to press for tighter restrictions on firearms. Tennessee, where the GOP enjoys a legislative supermajority, is one of the reddest states in the United States, but that hasn't stopped the Covenant Moms from lobbying hard for change. "Be brave and show up" is how group cofounder Becky Bailey Hansen sums up the approach by the moms, who were included among *USA Today's* 2024 Women of the Year.

"When moms get their minds made up about something, there is no stopping us," another founding member, Mary Joyce, tells the independent nonprofit news organization *The 19th*. "You saw that happen with drunk driving. Well, we are here for gun safety and we're not going anywhere."

Elaborating, she says:

> As the degrees of separation of gun violence get smaller, more and more people are just waiting for their turn, for it to be them next. That shifts the narrative from, "This is my freedom and my right to own a firearm," to, "Man, I am living in fear every day that I might be killed or that my child might be killed." Where do my rights end and someone else's rights begin?
>
> Nothing is scarier to me than what our children experienced, what my daughter saw, what she heard. She was shot at over and over and over again by a big weapon in her classroom. Glass was breaking everywhere, smoke filling up the room. She had trouble breathing. They had trouble seeing. Kids were crying. Her friends got hit by glass and were bleeding. Three of her friends were murdered in seconds outside of their classroom door. She lost hearing. She was terrified and confused. So I think about that image, and there is nothing scarier than that.

The key, Henrich says, is to persuade evangelicals not to look away every time a mass shooter armed with an AR-15 turns a classroom of giggling second-graders into a blood-spattered crime scene. "While they turn the other way, they're actually turning their back to the gospel," Henrich says. "It is a simpler and easier route for Christians to turn our backs to the complications of a changing culture; to get more entrenched into our shibboleths; to get angrier and more fearful."

◆ ◆ ◆

Before we part, Henrich tells me—almost as an afterthought—something astonishing. Earlier in her life and career, she had a job at a mental hospital where she worked with America's first mass shooter: Howard Unruh, a schizophrenic who fatally shot thirteen people on September 6, 1949, during what became known as the "Walk of Death" through his neighborhood in Camden, New Jersey. The case of Unruh, she contends, epitomizes the nation's poor job in treating mental illness. "I knew him as an old man, and he was afraid of his own shadow," she recalls. "He's such a classic example of somebody who, once he got treatment, wouldn't hurt anybody. He was very gentle and sweet."

Could the dark trajectory of Unruh's life, and the tragedy he perpetrated, have been altered with more situational awareness on the part of those who knew him, and through a more intentional societal effort to destigmatize, identify, and treat mental illness? That's the idea driving the "whole of government" approach that President Joe Biden took in his final year in office. Biden signed an executive order creating a task force to track and investigate emerging firearms threats, and several federal agencies and departments announced expanded plans for safe gun storage, community violence intervention, and gun suicides involving military veterans.

The CDC, meanwhile, has outlined an enhanced effort to gather better data on gun deaths and injuries, many of which go unreported. Biden called the steps part of an orchestrated campaign "to drive and coordinate the government in a nationwide effort to reduce gun violence in America."

The CDC succeeded in helping us tame the COVID-19 pandemic, and former director Rochelle Walensky thinks it should take a more prominent harm-reduction role on guns. Walensky tells CNN it's "pedal to the metal time" to throw all the nation's vast public health resources at the crisis. Unfortunately, Trump's reelection and the veering to the right of the American electorate will mean slamming the brakes on gun safety measures rather than hitting the accelerator.

Walensky is an infectious diseases expert by training, but she isn't any more immune than the rest of us to gun violence: In 2012, she was teaching at Massachusetts General Hospital when one of her residents lost a young member of her extended family in the mass shooting at Sandy Hook Elementary School. It's the CDC's job to understand "the scope of the problem," she says, and it has nothing to do with taking away people's guns. "Let's agree we don't want people to die. Let's just agree there. What can we do to stop people from dying? And what can we do to stop people from being injured?"

As we've seen, it's a problem that's easier to frame than to fix. Federal funding for the CDC to merely study gun violence is perennially in danger of being stripped from the agency's budget by congressional Republicans like Rep. Robert Aderholt, an evangelical from Alabama and a longtime member of the powerful House Appropriations Committee.

He's not the only white evangelical standing in the way of commonsense reforms—not by a long shot. "'God, guns and Trump' is an omnipresent bumper sticker here, the new trinity," Susan Stubson, a dissident member of the Wyoming Republican Party, writes in a guest essay for *The New York Times*. "The evangelical church has proved to be a supplicating audience for the Christian nationalist roadshow."

◆ ◆ ◆

## NO GUNS IN HEAVEN

At its essence, gun violence is a public health crisis, not merely a crime problem, and we need to treat it as such. Vivek Murthy, the US surgeon general under Biden, has called for precisely this approach. In mid-2024, after yet another spate of mass shootings, he issued an advisory—one of his office's most compelling ways to alert the public to an urgent health crisis. It was the first-ever surgeon general report on gun violence. It has taken this long despite a damning statistic: More than *half* of all US adults say they or a family member have experienced one or more forms of gun violence—being threatened with a gun, witnessing a shooting firsthand, being shot, or losing a loved one.

Murthy's unprecedented public health advisory on gun violence is more than just talk. It marks a turning point, at least conceptually, in how we approach the scourge. It was surgeon general reports on the dangers of tobacco in the 1960s and '70s that eventually helped slash cigarette smoking rates by well over half, ultimately saving millions of lives.

In an interview with my colleagues at *Axios*, where I work as an editor, Murthy expressed the frustration and anger so many of us feel with every avoidable mass-casualty event. "For too long, this issue has been mired in polarization and politics, but our goal, my goal, is to take this issue out of the realm of politics and put it into the realm of public health, which is where it belongs," he said.

Murthy ticks off a list of action items, none of which should strike a thinking person as unreasonable. They include more funding for research and risk-reduction strategies, such as community violence intervention programs; teaching people how to securely store their firearms to keep them out of children's hands; and tightening safe storage laws to punish gun owners who don't. In a country where guns kill more kids than car crashes, inaction—like failure—is not an option.

Before Trump's reelection, Murthy also urged Congress to enact universal background checks and a ban on assault weapons. Those admittedly are trickier, especially among lawmakers so divided that they very nearly didn't confirm Murthy as surgeon general because of his stance on guns. But easier said than done isn't the same as undoable. As Murthy says: "I think we have to now look at this as a kids' issue, and if we understand it in that sense, my hope is that we can come together to protect our children, to protect the mental health and well-being of the country. And ultimately, I think that's within our hands to do."

The American novelist and poet Wendell Berry argues the same thing in a cover story for *The Christian Century*. "Sooner or later," he writes, "we will have to ask how we can so disvalue the lives of other people's children without, by the same willingness, disvaluing the lives of our own."

◆ ◆ ◆

Do twenty-first-century Christians really believe Christ would holster a Glock beneath his tunic or conceal an AR-15 within the folds of his robe? Too many may answer yes. But I can't buy that. Not my Jesus in any of his incarnations, past, present, or future. Certainly not as the gentle Lamb of God, but not even as the roaring Lion of Judah. The Messiah has no use for a machine gun.

I'll be the first to confess that taking this deep dive into white evangelicals' defiant support for the right to bear arms at any cost, despite a staggering body count and cost to society, has shaken my own faith to its core. As an evangelical worship leader, I used to jump around onstage like Jagger—not performatively but passionately—and Sunday was the best day of the week. Now, my Stratocaster electric and Taylor acoustic decorate a wall of my study and gather dust. Like the tangled clusters of media credentials and marathon medals hanging next to the fireplace, my guitars are mute reminders of another life.

*The joy of the Lord is your strength*, the prophet Nehemiah exhorts in the Old Testament, and that's still true. But the heady exhilaration

I felt as a new convert has long since evaporated. The bright-eyed, bubbly, idealistic me—the me my wife fell in love with while we were doing missionary work together in Belgium—is gone. On my darkest and most cynical days—when my faith, like that of the doubting disciple, Thomas, falters—that's me in the corner, losing my religion.

Even so, I cling to Christ, for I know no other way. The initial bliss of belief in something larger than life itself has been replaced by a blessed assurance, like a marriage that began as a love affair with sparks and passion and has settled into something more quotidian but comfortable and dependable. She's my rock, but Jesus is my Gibraltar. Christianity is a religion of hope, and even as I deconstruct my faith, I'm committed to reconstructing it.

Like so many of us, I yearn for the day we'll finally realize the answer to escalating gun violence isn't more guns. As Winston Churchill famously said, at the height of World War II: "Americans will eventually do the right thing, but only after they have tried everything else."

We know what to do. We're just not doing it. The answers are within our grasp. Declare a truce in the culture wars and make the preponderance of guns our common enemy. Treat gun violence as the public health epidemic that it has become. Turn "our heartache into action," as Katherine Hoops, a researcher at Johns Hopkins' Center for Gun Violence Solutions, says.

If Republicans and evangelicals view the Second Amendment as breathed by God, what about the preamble to the entire Constitution: *We the People . . .?* Following their own logic, if the citizenry—*We*—decides it wants to make a collective dent in gun violence, shouldn't it be God's will to respect the people's desire and make that happen? Isn't that how self-determination in a representative democracy is supposed to work?

Guns represent an opportunity for the Christian faith community, which has lost integrity and credibility in many people's eyes, to burnish its battered reputation simply by doing the right thing and leading by example. With apologies to blockbuster romance novelist Colleen Hoover, it starts with us. Or as a former pastor of mine used to say: This is family business.

Pastors need to muster the courage to take on the gun issue from the pulpit. I can tell you from deep personal experience that white evangelical ministers hate doing that. They'll tell you they don't want to touch politics; they just preach the gospel. But there are times when one bleeds into the other, and our highest calling as believers is to speak truth to power. This is an area where white Christians can learn from our brothers and sisters of color, who have no such qualms. In the mid-1990s, when gun violence surged among young people in Boston, most white pastors stood back silently while Black ministers tackled the problem head-on, both in their sermons in church and in their community activism on the streets. Youth homicides declined by more than 60 percent in two years, in what has been called "the Boston miracle." A nonprofit group powered largely by Black clergy and churches, Faith in Indiana, is trying to replicate that success in Indianapolis. "Over the years, we built lots and lots of relationships with everyday people, and started to build some serious power," Rosie Bryant, who is working to advance similar efforts nationwide, tells *The Chronicle of Philanthropy*.

Bishop William Barber II exemplifies what it means to speak truth to power, and he's become one of my heroes. Bishop Barber is a professor at Yale Divinity School and co-led the relaunch of the Poor People's Campaign that Dr. Martin Luther King began. Barber makes connections between different issues—such as inequality, racism, militarism, religious nationalism, and environmental decay—that many white Christians seem unable to do. Demonstrating the interlocking nature of injustice, he calls Christians to moral action led by people most affected by injustice.

"As extreme as our gun problem is in this nation, ten times as many people are dying from poverty as are dying from gun violence," he writes in an op-ed for *The Tennessean* newspaper. "This is not a tragic result of things beyond our control. It is policy murder. Extremists in statehouses across the country are manufacturing death in our name." What if more evangelical pastors followed the lead of people like Bishop Barber, who has decided to speak out no matter the cost?

My wife and I are still wincing from an experience in the mid-2010s at the large, mostly white Massachusetts church where I served as a worship leader. Muslim families were fleeing Syria in large numbers and seeking refuge in the United States, much as many Americans' white European ancestors had done.

My wife is an art teacher, and her teen students had created striking pencil and acrylic portraits of Syrian refugees, using news photographs from AP as reference. Would our church allow her to display her students' drawings and paintings done in solidarity with these downtrodden souls, she asked? No, said the pastor—it would be divisive.

We were demoralized. Angry. And confused: Joseph and Mary fled Israel for Egypt to escape persecution when Jesus was a baby. Didn't that make him a refugee? I can't imagine what the pastor's response would have been had we approached him with what we *really* wanted to do: organize a team of folks to visit some of these beautiful Muslim families being held in detention centers while the government evaluated their asylum applications.

Shutting down grassroots compassion shouldn't be the default stance in white evangelical churches. Pastors, if your people feel called to stand with the oppressed in practical ways—whether that's fellow human beings escaping war and famine or fellow Americans moved by the scourge of gun violence—empower them, for the love of God. And breathe a prayer of thanks that your congregation includes some—whether because of you or despite you—who give a damn.

◆ ◆ ◆

Believers and nonbelievers alike also need to resist the impulse to demonize conservative Christians for their militant position on guns. Doing so might make us feel better—I'll be the first to confess I have infinite patience with atheists and agnostics and nearly none with pro-gun evangelicals—but it's counterproductive. Caricaturing them won't change hearts and minds, much less lead to meaningful reforms. Only thoughtful engagement can accomplish that. So let's talk to each other, even if it makes us squirm. And even more importantly, as RAWtools founder Mike Martin pleads, let's listen.

Martin recalls overseeing a gun surrender event in Bend, Oregon, which is in the conservative east of the state, when a belligerent gun owner angrily confronted him about dismantling firearms. "His point of view was that we'd need these guns to protect ourselves in the next dispensation, when God comes back and we have to kill all the nonbelievers or at least protect ourselves from them," he tells me, paraphrasing some highly controversial evangelical theology. "Everybody's hairs went up."

But then something shifted. After listening carefully to the man, Martin told him about a mother who'd turned in the gun her son had used to take his own life. "A switch flipped," he recounts, describing how the man's resistance melted away: "He went from 100 to nothing."

Benjamin Cremer, a pastor who abandoned the extreme fundamentalism in which he was raised in Idaho and who now helps people fleeing toxic faith, had a parallel experience. Cremer says he carried a concealed Glock .45 for years and enjoyed shooting assault rifles at the firing range. It wasn't until seminary that he reevaluated his evangelical gun ideology. In a ministry newsletter, he describes that transformation:

> Guns were treated as a symbol of pride and independence. The way the 2nd Amendment was presented in my social circles, I understood it to be on the same level of sacredness as my Christian faith and patriotism.

In my church, it was also made clear to me that faithful Christian patriots would play a pivotal role in defending the cause of Christ during the tribulation period of the End Times, and gun training was part of what we needed to do in order to be prepared. I thought about this often as I learned how to reload ammunition in my garage as a kid. The gun was not only presented as a symbol of my patriotism but also my faith. . . .

As I studied church history and scripture more closely than I ever had before, the symbolism around guns began to change for me. . . . The narratives of patriotism, Christianity, and especially masculinity just didn't seem to fit what I was learning about Jesus. . . . I would eventually let my concealed weapons license expire and would part ways with my Glock.

Today, Cremer is far from confrontational in his approach to the pro-gun evangelicals with whom he once identified. He is determined, he writes, "to encourage a more thoughtful dialogue around dismantling and reimagining the narratives around guns in cultures like ours." And Cremer is particularly interested in reaching white men. An analysis by The Violence Project, a nonprofit, nonpartisan research center at Hamline University in St. Paul, Minnesota, finds that 98 percent of all mass shootings dating back to 1966 have been committed by men. "I cannot help but think of my experience growing up with guns every time the shooter is someone just like me," Cremer says. "Dismantling and reforming these narratives in our churches wherever necessary with the life and teachings of Jesus is an incredibly powerful way for us to do even more to prevent further gun violence."

Here's some wise advice from Blair Braverman, the agnostic dogsledder in rural Wisconsin we met briefly in chapter 5:

> Instead of mocking rural Americans for owning twice as many guns as their urban counterparts, for thinking guns make them safer, ask why they're really afraid. . . .

In three years of living here, I've never seen a police car within 20 miles of my home, and when I called the sheriff last fall over a threatening trespasser, it took him three hours to show up. Because wanting the ability to physically defend yourself feels pretty darn visceral when you live out of screaming range from your nearest neighbor.

No number of mass shootings will convince my neighbors that guns should be banned, because the greater the tragedy, the greater their desire for the means to protect themselves. Theirs is an argument of values, not statistics. But listening to them, taking their concerns seriously, understanding the needs that guns meet for them and prioritizing those needs in policy? Now we're talking.

Deep empathy with gun owners isn't a distraction from gun control. It's a prerequisite for implementing it successfully.

Treating individual gun owners with respect and giving them space to reconsider their position doesn't mean staying silent, of course—no more than pacifism equates to passivity. If you're troubled by the endless cycle of mass shootings, there's a lot you can do, starting by insisting that the firearms industry stops marketing weapons to children.

We all need to ratchet up pressure on Congress, which should have expanded mandatory background checks beyond gun sales conducted by licensed dealers and imposed waiting periods decades ago. No one who isn't a police officer or an active-duty member of the military needs an assault rifle, and if you agree, write or call your congressional representatives and demand they take a stand. While you're at it, press them to pass a national safe storage law; it's a no-brainer that will prevent distraught teens from using a parent's gun at school and stop the needless deaths of young children who find a firearm in the home and play with it. Ask your federal lawmakers to change immunity laws so gun manufacturers are no longer shielded from civil liability and public accountability. And demand that they lift their long-standing ban on federal funding for firearm injury prevention research. For how can we fight the scourge unless, and until, we fully understand the myriad factors that are driving it?

If federal reforms—far and away the best solution—still elude us, we can lobby our state legislatures to end those liability protections, and close loopholes that let domestic abusers and other violent offenders buy guns. We can ask our state lawmakers to outlaw bump stocks and high-capacity magazines that turn semiautomatic rifles into machine guns. States must crack down on so-called untraceable ghost guns to ensure DIY weapons and parts can't be sold without serial numbers and background checks.

Consider joining, or donating to, one of the gun reform organizations that are holding lawmakers, the gun industry, and the NRA and other pro-gun groups to account. Giffords Law Center to Prevent Gun Violence, Everytown for Gun Safety, Moms Demand Action, Christians United Against Gun Violence, and the Prevention Institute are all great places to start. Or write a letter to your local news outlet to let your community know you're committed to stopping the seemingly endless cycle of shootings, injuries, and deaths.

And we should all, regardless of our politics, push back, hard, at fatalism about our gun crisis. After yet another massacre at a school in 2024, JD Vance glibly called such shootings "a fact of life," shrugging off an act of unspeakable madness with the same flippant language we use to describe death and taxes.

Before every social movement that transformed the world, people said it was impossible. Our gun crisis is no different. As Alan Noble, the editor-in-chief of *Christ and Pop Culture*, says: "Conservative evangelical politics must reflect a desire for the good of all people."

◆ ◆ ◆

Meanwhile, hope supplants despair with every defiant plea for reason and every attempt at change.

If you're feeling helpless in the face of the NRA's billions of dollars and white evangelicalism's *'Til death do us part* refusal to divorce itself from the gun culture, consider Fred Martin, who works with RAWtools in Colorado. Martin says he'll never tire of "taking something that destroys life and turning it into something that sustains life" and helps establish the kingdom of heaven right here on Earth. "We're not going to wait for Jesus to come back and fix everything. We're going to start now and make it look like his kingdom here," he says.

There's also Bobby Watson, a young man I met who works with Texas Impact, an interfaith coalition intent on enacting sensible gun reforms in what is arguably America's most firearms-friendly state. Watson, who's in his mid-twenties, acknowledges he's trying to effect change in a decidedly adversarial pro–Second Amendment environment. "But Texas is also having a ton of momentum right now—a really large, wide-reaching coalition. We've got teachers, medical professionals, state and community leaders, and a lot of parents, so this is getting traction in the greater culture," he tells me. At the same time, gun reform advocates face a huge challenge in a state where MAGA extremism, and the star power of far-right icons such as Republican Gov. Greg Abbott, have resulted in the mainstreaming of hardline pro-gun positions that once were fringe. "Our extreme polarization allows for extremist positions to dominate the Legislature," he says.

Texas gun culture flourishes, despite clear evidence linking it directly to murder and mayhem. Over the past decade, domestic violence homicides—most of them involving guns—have nearly doubled, according to a recent report by the Texas Council on Family Violence. And those deaths represent just a fraction of the lives that have been shattered. Survivors often suffer life-altering wounds and PTSD. They include Mariah Gardner, whose ex-husband shot her multiple times five months after their divorce in 2023 and stabbed their two children, fatally injuring her eleven-month-old daughter. Gardner and her older daughter lived—barely. "Because we survived, we weren't captured in the data," she tells the NPR affiliate in North Texas, adding: "Imagine how many lives have been broken, how many lives have been destroyed, but they didn't die."

Watson, who is Gen Z, personifies his generation's unique stake in the gun violence fight. School shootings are all they've known. The oldest Gen Zers were just two years old when fifteen people were killed in the mass shooting at Columbine High School in 1999; the youngest were born in 2012, when twenty-six perished in the Sandy Hook massacre. "We are the school shooter drills generation," he says. So he plugs away in Texas, of all places, determined to change minds one policymaker at a time.

It's tempting to dismiss what an individual like Martin or Watson can achieve as minimal, if not futile. But Joash Thomas, the social justice activist we met in chapter 5, makes a convincing case for the power of one. In an essay published on Substack, Thomas invokes the example of Telemachus, an early Christian monk. Telemachus despised the violence of gladiatorial games, where enslaved people were forced to fight each other to the death to entertain bloodthirsty crowds. Playing peacemaker, he jumped into the ring, screaming, "No more! In the name of Jesus, no more!" Telemachus was then stoned to death by angry spectators. "It seemed like Telemachus died a meaningless death trying to be a peacemaker," Thomas writes. "But that was the last gladiator fight ever. And a few years later, the Roman Emperor banned gladiator fights."

In these pages, we've met a number of modern-day Telemachuses: leaders, activists, and clergy who are taking daring and creative action to write a more hopeful ending to the gun crisis. There is Reverend Rob Schenck, who has paid dearly, personally and professionally, for breaking with his fellow evangelicals on guns and abortion. There are Shane Claiborne, Mike Martin, and Scotty Utz at RAWtools, literally bringing the heat and getting guns off the streets one at a time. There is former New Zealand premier Jacinda Ardern, who reined in rampant gun ownership from the top down within a week of her country's worst mass shooting. There is Mick North, who did the same thing in Scotland from the grassroots up, defying death threats and channeling his grief over the loss of his daughter into action. There is Vivek Murthy, who as surgeon general in a nation divided over guns took a clear stand against unfettered access to firearms; and Bishop Barber, who is still doing so. There are Tennessee's Covenant Moms; New Mexico's intrepid anti-guns activist, Miranda Viscoli; and Seattle's Sister Judy Byron and her fellow stock-buying nuns. There is my young Texas friend, Rene Sanchez, never one to shy away from a gentle but persuasive argument with an NRA member. All these people, and untold thousands of others, are dreaming of—and working for—a safer world in the spirit and tradition of Telemachus.

Lately, I've been thinking about another Telemachus as well. Twenty-seven-year-old Telemachus Orfanos of Thousand Oaks, California, survived America's worst-ever mass shooting, the 2018 massacre in Las Vegas . . . only to die six weeks later in another mass shooting, less than ten minutes from his home. His grieving mother told reporters: "My son was in Las Vegas with one of his friends and he came home. He didn't come home last night. And I don't want prayers, I don't want thoughts, I want gun control and I hope to God nobody else sends me more prayers. I want gun control. No. More. Guns."

Pro-gun Republicans and white evangelicals who blame gun violence on spiritual apostasy want the Old Testament's Ten Commandments (*Thou shalt not kill, steal, covet, commit adultery*, etc.) posted in public schools, courthouses, and government buildings. Doing so is a flagrant violation of the constitutional separation of church and state—a bedrock doctrine that evangelicals increasingly reject. Yet I find it interesting that no one ever suggests publicly displaying the words of Jesus recorded in the New Testament books of Matthew and Luke and known as the beatitudes—a series of blessings that lift up the under-resourced and downcast.

## NO GUNS IN HEAVEN

I'm certainly not advocating for scripture of any kind, from any religion, to be displayed in that way. It's as inappropriate as the American flags so many evangelical churches have placed on their altars. I'm just saying that it's interesting what Christians choose to foreground. Why do so many white evangelicals unite around the posting of the Ten Commandments and not the words of the Savior himself? Here they are, for the record:

> Blessed are the poor in spirit, for theirs is the kingdom of heaven.
> Blessed are those who mourn, for they will be comforted.
> Blessed are the meek, for they will inherit the Earth.
> Blessed are those who hunger and thirst for righteousness, for they will be satisfied.
> Blessed are the merciful, for they will be shown mercy.
> Blessed are the pure in heart, for they will see God.
> Blessed are the peacemakers, for they will be called children of God.
> Blessed are those who are persecuted because of righteousness, for theirs is the kingdom of heaven.
> Blessed are you when people insult you, persecute you and falsely say all kinds of evil against you because of me. Rejoice and be glad, because great is your reward in heaven, for in the same way they persecuted the prophets who were before you.

"For some reason, the most vocal Christians among us never mention the beatitudes," *Slaughterhouse-Five* novelist Kurt Vonnegut once observed. "But, often with tears in their eyes, they demand that the Ten Commandments be posted in public buildings. . . . *Blessed are the merciful* in a courtroom? *Blessed are the peacemakers* in the Pentagon? Give me a break."

I'm a journalist, not a theologian, but I encourage gun-loving Christians to spend some time in the Gospels (the first four books of the New Testament: Matthew, Mark, Luke, and John.) Learn about, or reacquaint yourself with, the unfiltered life of Jesus. Then consider your stance on firearms through the divine lens of what he said and did. Without fail, whenever I do that myself, the bewilderingly blurred line between God and guns comes into sharp focus.

Where is Christ in an America where there are more guns than citizens? Where is Christ in a nation bloodied by more mass shootings than there are days of the year? Where is Christ in a country in which white evangelicals not only own far more guns than anyone else but run many of the weapons manufacturing companies? Where is Christ in a republic where a plurality of people views guns as their No. 1 public health menace? Some of us who profess to follow the Son of God have clearly lost our way.

*But the world is a dangerous place, and I need my guns*, some may say. Do you really? As Martin Luther King Jr. observed, Christ himself lived his entire earthly life under oppression and the threat of violence. At every turn, Jesus encountered real enemies in real time, so there's nothing abstract about his command: *Love your enemies*. Again, what would Jesus do? To all those Ten Commandments people out there, a reminder that the first one warns: *You shall have no other gods before me*.

How is a carbon-steel Glock any different from a golden calf?

◆ ◆ ◆

Evangelicals love the Bible-ending book of Revelation, scripture's epic and enigmatic final flourish about the end of time. Their obsession has even fueled an entire industry of books, movies, and websites within a niche corner of eschatology, which is the study of last things. There are many ways to imagine doomsday, and exploring the perspective that dominates in much of white evangelicalism, dispensational premillennialism, is another book for another time.

Revelation was written by John, who is said to have had prophetic visions while exiled on the Greek island of Patmos. The book is heavily symbolic, deeply mysterious, and slightly disturbing. It tells of mythical beasts, including a dragon with ten horns and seven heads, and creatures with multiple wings covered in eyes. It describes the triumphant return of Christ and his victory in the Battle of Armageddon, a final showdown pitting Satan and human governments against God and his angels.

As a new convert, I was taught that Revelation was written as a comfort to the persecuted church, whose early members were burned alive, crucified upside-down, and sawed in two. "I've read the back of the book and we win!" my first pastor used to thunder from the pulpit. But to be honest, the book has always freaked me out. That, along with an introvert's lifelong reluctance to publicly share my faith, made me a lousy evangelical.

Many evangelicals, however, revel in Revelation because they project themselves into the story. They see themselves as armed Christian soldiers, marching behind a weaponized Jesus and fighting on God's side to vanquish evil once and for all and to help usher in a new heaven and a new Earth.

Before any of that happens, though, there's a passage in Revelation in which God praises believers for their hard work and perseverance but cautions that he has one thing against them: *"You have forsaken the love you had at first"* (Revelation 2:4). Love is a golden thread running through all of scripture, from the Hebrew Bible where Deuteronomy 6:5 commands, *"Love the Lord your God with all your heart and with all your soul and with all your strength,"* to Jesus in Matthew 22:38–39 invoking that verse as the greatest commandment while offering a runner-up: *"Love your neighbor as yourself."* Sadly, many white evangelicals' love has grown as cold as the barrel of an AR-15. For how can one love his neighbor while carrying on his hip the means, and in his heart the willingness, to dispatch that person into eternity?

You may not believe in an afterlife, but if you do, I can say with certainty that there won't be any guns in heaven.

How can I be so sure? Revelation. Its last chapter says this: *"Look! God's dwelling place is now among the people, and he will dwell with them. They will be his people, and God himself will be with them and be their God. He will wipe every tear from their eyes. There will be no more death or mourning or crying or pain, for the old order of things has passed away"* (Rev. 21:3–4). I think of the tears of survivors of gun violence, of those who have lost loved ones to guns, of those who are longing for a world in which such violence is a bad dream. Introduce just one small-caliber handgun chambered with a single round into heaven, and it will immediately cease to be paradise.

But heaven can wait. I'm far more interested in the here and now. So, apparently, is Jesus. *"Your kingdom come, your will be done, on Earth as it is in heaven,"* he famously said in the Lord's Prayer (Matt 6:10). How would it feel to live in a nation that didn't have guns in half of its homes? What would it look like for *"the old order of things,"* rather than our children, to pass away?

In my own vision of the future, of a country that has finally broken free of its fealty to firearms, I reimagine the evening described in the preface of this book—the evening that John, my bass player, brought his 9mm semiautomatic to worship practice. In the renewal of all things, in the redeemed version of this story, there is no gun. There are no bullets. There is no holster. There is no fear. The objects of the highest caliber and capacity are Christian charity and compassion.

In this future we could build together, if somehow we could summon the collective will to do so, there is no yellow crime scene tape. There are no plastic numbers marking the locations of spent shell casings, no chalk outlines of human beings on the pavement. There is only love.

# ACKNOWLEDGMENTS

This is as much a book about faith as it is about guns, so I must begin by thanking those who placed their faith in me.

My deepest gratitude once more to my agents, Rick Richter and Caroline Marsiglia at Aevitas Creative Management, who saw the merit in this project from my first slapdash email. You helped me both broaden my scope and sharpen my focus (it turns out that those things are not mutually exclusive.) Thank you both.

Special thanks to my supremely talented editor, Valerie Weaver-Zercher, and the irrepressibly enthusiastic team at Broadleaf Books for seeing the urgency of this project and getting it across the finish line in what felt like record time. Valerie, your insights and suggestions made this a far, far better read than anything I could have done by myself in a hundred attempts. Collaborating with you has been an absolute joy!

Thanks as well to those who read the manuscript early and offered both affirmation and invaluable feedback; especially my dear friends, Brian Murphy and Anwar Georges-Abeyie. We are all stunted in our ability to perceive certain things; thank you for gently pointing out my errors and shortcomings and helping me fix them.

I'll be forever grateful to the activists, pastors, scholars, thinkers, and writers who consented to be interviewed on such a prickly subject: Anne Beaton, Reverend Meghan Brown, Tim Carey,

## ACKNOWLEDGMENTS

Nobel Peace Prize nominee Father John Dear, Harry Eberts, Jenny Harland, Reverend Abigail Henrich, Michael Martin, Mick North, Rene Sanchez, Reverend Rob Schenck, Reverend Duncan Strathdee, Janet Strathdee, Scotty Utz, Miranda Viscoli, Bobby Watson, and German Zárate. Special thanks to Reverend Phil Guin at Rocky Mount Methodist Church in Alabama, as well as Charlotte Powell and John Wortham, for your transparency; and to Mark, David, Paul, and Todd Foster at FosTecH in Indiana, along with Randy Gilbert, for your candor in answering my more probing questions. My gratitude to the Presbyterian Peace Fellowship, especially Christa Galvin, Rita Niblack, Jan Orr-Harter, and Margery Rossi, for accommodating me at the last minute in New Mexico and connecting me to so many remarkable human beings who care deeply about our gun crisis.

As ever, my wife, Terry DeYonker Kole, offered encouragement and helpful feedback throughout. Our children, Nicholas and E., and their partners were faithful sounding boards and cheerleaders. I cherish you all more than mere words could ever convey.

Finally, I want to thank the evangelical community for introducing me to the person of Jesus. We've certainly had our differences, but I'll always cherish the friendship and fellowship you extended to me, particularly in moments of personal struggle. I pray you've read these pages with the same grace I earnestly sought as I wrote them.

# NOTES

## CHAPTER 1: THE GOSPEL OF GUNS

8 ***there are far more guns than Americans:*** Kara Fox, Krystina Shveda, Natalie Croker, and Marco Chacon, "How US Gun Culture Stacks Up with the World," *CNN*, February 15, 2024, https://www.cnn.com/2021/11/26/world/us-gun-culture-world-comparison-intl-cmd/index.html.

9 ***more gun dealers than McDonald's restaurants:*** Leanna Garfield, "There Are 50,000 More Gun Shops than McDonald's in the US," *Business Insider*, October 6, 2017, https://www.businessinsider.com/gun-dealers-stores-mcdonalds-las-vegas-shooting-2017-10.

9 ***more mass shootings than there are days in the year:*** "Past Summary Ledgers," Gun Violence Archive, accessed January 7, 2025, https://www.gunviolencearchive.org/past-tolls.

9 ***Firearms are now the leading cause of accidental death among young children and teenagers:*** Roni Caryn Rabin, "Gun Deaths Rising Sharply Among Children, Study Finds," *New York Times*, October 6, 2023, https://www.nytimes.com/2023/10/05/health/gun-deaths-children.html.

9 ***Firearms deaths in some states now rival those in far-flung conflict zones:*** Evan D. Gumas, Munira Z. Gunja, and Reginald D. Williams II, "Comparing Deaths from Gun Violence in the US with Other Countries," Commonwealth Fund, October 30, 2024, https://www.commonwealthfund.org/publications/2024/oct/comparing-deaths-gun-violence-us-other-countries?check_logged_in=1.

9 ***Suicides are also rising in the United States:*** CDC Newsroom, "Provisional Suicide Deaths in the United States, 2022," Centers for Disease

# NOTES

Control and Prevention, August 10, 2023, https://www.cdc.gov/media/releases/2023/s0810-US-Suicide-Deaths-2022.html.

9 ***access to a gun also increases the chances that a domestic dispute will turn deadly:*** Elizabeth Tobin-Tyler, "Intimate Partner Violence, Firearm Injuries and Homicides: A Health Justice Approach to Two Intersecting Public Health Crises," National Institutes of Health, Spring 2023, https://doi.org/10.1017/jme.2023.41.

10 ***there are still, by some estimates, 24 million AR-15 military-style assault rifles alone in circulation:*** Jennifer Mascia and Chip Brownlee, "How Many Guns Are Circulating in the U.S.?," *The Trace*, August 28, 2023, https://www.thetrace.org/2023/03/guns-america-data-atf-total/.

10 ***little indication that the number of firearms overall will significantly diminish:*** Kim Parker, Juliana Menasce Horowitz, Ruth Igielnik, J. Baxter Oliphant, and Anna Brown, "The Demographics of Gun Ownership," Pew Research Center, June 22, 2017, https://www.pewresearch.org/social-trends/2017/06/22/the-demographics-of-gun-ownership/.

10 ***Forty-one percent of white conservative Christians own a gun:*** Kate Shellnutt, "Packing in the Pews: The Connection Between God and Guns," *Christianity Today*, November 8, 2017, https://www.christianitytoday.com/2017/11/god-gun-control-white-evangelicals-texas-church-shooting/.

10 ***65 percent of white evangelicals "own and carry guns":*** Gina Zurlo, X, May 12, 2021, https://x.com/gina_zurlo/status/1392524520599195648?s=51&t=QZVE1dz2F3WICzqs-sh3Zw.

11 ***widely read op-ed for The Washington Post:*** Rob Schenck, "I'm an Evangelical Preacher: You Can't Be Pro-Life and Pro-Gun," *Washington Post*, December 28, 2015, https://www.washingtonpost.com/posteverything/wp/2015/12/28/im-evangelical-you-cant-be-pro-life-and-pro-gun/.

11 ***what is an evangelical?:*** "What is an Evangelical?," National Association of Evangelicals, accessed January 7, 2025, https://www.nae.org/what-is-an-evangelical/.

12 ***Culling from numerous firearms studies:*** Kim Parker et al., "The Demographics of Gun Ownership," Pew Research Center, June 22, 2017, https://www.pewresearch.org/social-trends/2017/06/22/the-demographics-of-gun-ownership/.

12 ***"Guns should be used in a God-glorifying and moderate way":*** T. S. Weaver, "A Christian Perspective on Guns," *Surrendered and Free*, June 18, 2022,

# NOTES

https://surrenderedandfree.org/2022/06/18/a-christian-perspective-on-guns/.

14 ***recently fined for illegal lobbying:*** Kayla Dwyer, "Indiana Gunmaker That Offered GOP Lawmakers Discounted Rifles Is Fined After Investigation," *Indianapolis Star*, November 30, 2023, https://shorturl.at/IUkd8.

14 ***Spike's Tactical markets a Christian "Crusader" assault rifle:*** Staff report, "US Arms Maker Markets Christian Assault Rifle Called 'The Crusader,'" *Tico Times*, September 15, 2015, https://ticotimes.net/2015/09/15/us-arms-maker-markets-christian-assault-rifle-called-the-crusader.

15 ***the company has posted this prayer prominently on its website:*** "About CMMG," CMMG, accessed January 7, 2025, https://cmmg.com/about.

16 ***asked adherents of all the major religions if they supported gun control measures:*** Diana Orces, "The Gun Ownership Bubble," Public Religion Research Institute, June 10, 2022, https://www.prri.org/spotlight/the-gun-ownership-bubble-gun-owners-are-more-likely-to-have-other-gun-owners-as-close-friends/.

17 ***"nones" already comprise 28 percent of the population:*** "Religious 'Nones' in America: Who They Are and What They Believe," Pew Research Center, January 24, 2024, https://www.pewresearch.org/religion/2024/01/24/religious-nones-in-america-who-they-are-and-what-they-believe/.

18 ***Trump touted himself as "the most pro-gun, pro–Second Amendment president":*** Jonathan Allen, "Trump Says Mass Shootings Are Not 'a Gun Problem' as 2024 GOP Hopefuls Pledge Loyalty to the NRA," *NBCNews.com*, April 14, 2023, https://www.nbcnews.com/politics/donald-trump/trump-says-mass-shootings-arent-gun-problem-nra-convention-rcna79775.

18 ***full-page ad featuring a Thompson submachine gun:*** Rosie Gray, "Donald Trump Jr. Ventures Into the Lifestyle Space—and Brings the Culture War with Him," *Politico*, February 16, 2024, https://www.politico.com/news/magazine/2024/02/16/donald-trump-jr-lifestyle-influencer-magazine-00131445.

18 ***Neil Gorsuch criticized the bump stocks ban:*** Damon Root, "Another Trump-Appointed Judge Benchslaps the Trump Administration for Rewriting Federal Gun Laws," *Reason*, April 1, 2020, https://reason.com/2020/04/01/another-trump-appointed-judge-benchslaps-the-trump-administration-for-rewriting-federal-gun-laws/.

# NOTES

18 ***Trump asked his advisers why he couldn't take action on banning assault rifles:*** Michael D. Shear, "Trump Stuns Lawmakers with Seeming Embrace of Comprehensive Gun Control," *New York Times*, February 28, 2018, https://www.nytimes.com/2018/02/28/us/politics/trump-gun-control.html.

19 ***uniquely religious brand of nationalism traces back at least to the late Reverend Jerry Falwell's Moral Majority:*** For more on the origins of Christian nationalism, see Matthew D. Taylor's excellent book, *The Violent Take it by Force: The Christian Movement That is Threatening Our Democracy* (Broadleaf Books, 2024).

19 ***South Carolina's fundamentalist Bob Jones University:*** Cindy Landrum, "A Brief History of the World's Most Unusual University," *Greenville Journal*, April 12, 2017, https://greenvillejournal.com/news/brief-history-worlds-unusual-university-2/.

19 ***Falwell framed the dispute as one of religious freedom, not racism:*** Randall Balmer, "The Real Origins of the Religious Right," *Politico*, May 27, 2014, https://www.politico.com/magazine/story/2014/05/religious-right-real-origins-107133/.

20 ***Fox News and the far right falsely portrayed her as transgender:*** Li Zhou, "The Far Right is Using the Lakewood Church Shooting for Anti-Trans Attacks," *Vox*, February 13, 2024, https://www.vox.com/politics/2024/2/13/24072287/lakewood-church-shooting-anti-trans-messaging.

20 ***"a complex relationship that may be impossible to disentangle":*** Jessica Dawson, "Shall Not Be Infringed: How the NRA Used Religious Language to Transform the Meaning of the Second Amendment," *Nature*, July 2, 2019, https://www.nature.com/articles/s41599-019-0276-z.

21 ***three in ten white evangelicals agreed with the statement:*** "Threats to American Democracy Ahead of an Unprecedented Presidential Election," *Public Religion Research Institute*, October 25, 2023, https://www.prri.org/research/threats-to-american-democracy-ahead-of-an-unprecedented-presidential-election/.

22 ***mental health problems "the root cause":*** Kelly Garrity, "Texas Gov. Abbott Calls for Addressing Mental Health Issues in Wake of Texas Mass Shooting," *Politico*, May 7, 2023, https://www.politico.com/news/2023/05/07/texas-governor-abbott-mass-shooting-00095685.

22 ***mental illness plays a negligible role in mass shootings:*** Michelle Berglass et al., "Mental Illness and Gun Violence in the United States, Australia, and United Kingdom: Clinical and Public Health Challenges,"

# NOTES

*American Journal of Medicine* 137, no. 4, (2023): 295–297, https://www.amjmed.com/article/S0002-9343(23)00738-6/fulltext.

23 ***a devout Southern Baptist who opposes universal background checks:*** Dave Lawler, "Speaker Johnson on Shootings: 'Problem is the Human Heart, Not Guns,'" *Axios*, October 27, 2023, https://www.axios.com/2023/10/27/speaker-mike-johnson-gun-control-gay-marriage.

23 ***"paranoid fantasy undergirds much of religious conservatives' opposition":*** Neil J. Young, "Why Do Evangelicals Oppose Gun Control?," *The Week*, August 11, 2019, https://theweek.com/articles/857806/why-evangelicals-oppose-gun-control.

24 ***They believed God wanted them to do this:*** Peter Manseau, "Some Capitol Rioters Believed They Answered God's Call, Not Just Trump's," *Washington Post*, February 11, 2021, https://www.washingtonpost.com/outlook/2021/02/11/christian-religion-insurrection-capitol-trump/.

24 ***Gun purchases soared to an all-time high of 22.5 million at the peak of the pandemic:*** Jennifer Mascia and Chip Brownlee, "How Many Guns Are Circulating in the U.S.?," *The Trace*, March 6, 2023, https://www.thetrace.org/2023/03/guns-america-data-atf-total/.

24 ***half were women, a fifth were Black, and another fifth were Latino:*** Matthew Miller, Wilson Zhang, and Deborah Azrael, "Firearm Purchasing During the COVID-19 Pandemic: Results From the 2021 National Firearms Survey," *Annals of Internal Medicine*, 175, no. 2 (2021): 219–225, https://doi.org/10.7326/m21-3423.

24 ***surge of LGTBQ+ people buying guns for personal protection:*** Zoe Greenberg, "The Queer People Who Are Buying Guns to Prepare for Trump's America," *The Philadelphia Inquirer*, January 5, 2025, https://www.inquirer.com/identity/guns-trump-lgbt-philadelphia-20250105.html.

25 ***Public Religion Research Institute's most recent American Values Atlas:*** Russell Contreras, "Survey: 55% of Latino Protestants Support Christian Nationalism," *Axios*, February 29, 2024, https://www.axios.com/2024/02/29/christian-nationalism-latino-hispanic-protestant-evangelical.

25 ***"Talibanistic," he calls it:*** Benjamin Wallace-Wells, "How Trump Captured Iowa's Religious Right," *New Yorker*, January 7, 2024, https://www.newyorker.com/news/the-political-scene/how-trump-captured-iowas-religious-right.

25 ***landmark 2018 study:*** Andrew L. Whitehead, Landon Schnabel, and Samuel L. Perry, "Gun Control in the Crosshairs: Christian

# NOTES

Nationalism and Opposition to Stricter Gun Laws," *Socius* 4 (2018), https://doi.org/10.1177/2378023118790189.

25 ***says Perry, of the University of Oklahoma:*** Samuel L. Perry, "School Shootings Confirm That Guns Are the Religion of the Right," *Time*, May 25, 2022, https://time.com/6181342/school-shootings-christian-right-guns/.

25 ***Second Amendment as far and away the most sacred constitutional right:*** Joshua Davis, Samuel Perry, and Joshua B. Grubbs, "Liberty for Us, Limits for Them: Christian Nationalism and Americans' Views on Citizen's Rights," *SocArXiv* (February 27, 2021), https://osf.io/preprints/socarxiv/b3zgc.

26 ***"Gun ownership is a more important right than voting":*** Matt Walsh, *X*, March 23, 2021, https://x.com/MattWalshBlog/status/1374475403075588103.

26 ***the most religious and the most armed of all the wealthiest Western nations:*** Dalia Fahmy, "Americans Are Far More Religious than Adults in Other Wealthy Nations," Pew Research Center, July 31, 2018, https://www.pewresearch.org/short-reads/2018/07/31/americans-are-far-more-religious-than-adults-in-other-wealthy-nations/.

26 ***new report warning that the threat of armed insurrection is rising:*** "Defending Democracy: Addressing the Dangers of Armed Insurrection," Johns Hopkins Bloomberg School of Public Health, December 2023, https://efsgv.org/press/insurrection-report/.

27 ***"God has not given us a spirit of fear":*** "Everytown Announces New Initiative With Interfaith Leaders and Organizations to Mobilize People of Faith Around Gun Safety in 2020," *Everytown for Gun Safety*, accessed January 7, 2025, https://www.everytown.org/press/everytown-announces-new-initiative-with-interfaith-leaders-and-organizations-to-mobilize-people-of-faith-around-gun-safety-in-2020/.

27 ***practically impossible to build the bipartisan support needed to enact even the simplest gun reforms:*** Jeff Brumley, "Christian Nationalism Links Gun Rights and 'Christian Nation' Ideals in Dangerous Mix, Tyler and Hollman Say," *Baptist News Global*, June 27, 2022, https://shorturl.at/WScx4.

28 ***"We believe in a God who would rather die than kill . . .":*** Shane Claiborne and Michael Martin, *Beating Guns: Hope for People Who Are Weary of Violence* (Brazos Press, 2019), 176.

# NOTES

29 **"open carry celebration":** Katharine Q. Seelye, "Pastor Urges His Flock to Bring Guns to Church," *New York Times,* June 25, 2009, https://www.nytimes.com/2009/06/26/us/26guns.html.

29 ***Benjamin Boyd offers startlingly blunt advice to religious Americans:*** Benjamin Boyd, "Take Your Guns to Church: The Second Amendment and Church Autonomy," *Liberty University Law Review* 8, no. 3 (2014), https://digitalcommons.liberty.edu/lu_law_review/vol8/iss3/7/.

## CHAPTER 2: HOW GUNS BECAME GOOD

35 **"the earliest case of murder in the hominin fossil record":** Rachel Nuwer, "Investigating the Case of the Earliest Known Murder Victim," *Smithsonian Magazine,* May 27, 2015, https://www.smithsonianmag.com/science-nature/investigating-case-earliest-known-murder-victim-180955409/.

35 ***forensic analysis of the skeletal remains of Shanidar-3:*** "What Does it Mean to be Human?," National Museum of National History, https://humanorigins.si.edu/exhibit/exploring-human-origins-what-does-it-mean-be-human.

38 ***early Anabaptist confession:*** Schleitheim Confession: https://www.anabaptistwiki.org/mediawiki/index.php/Schleitheim_Confession_(source)#We_have_been_united_as_follows_concerning_the_sword.

39 ***an account deeply embedded in Quaker mythology:*** Paul Buckley, "Time to Lay Down William Penn's Sword," *Friends Journal,* December 1, 2003, https://www.friendsjournal.org/2003142/.

39 **conflicted about when violence is justified:** "About Our Bold Legacy," *Moody Bible Institute,* accessed January 7, 2025, https://www.moody.edu/about/our-bold-legacy/d-l-moody/.

40 ***few American Christians rejected military service:*** Ted Grimsrud, "Pacifism in America: The Roots of War Resistance," *ThinkingPacifism.net,* May 31, 2019, https://thinkingpacifism.net/2019/05/31/pacifism-in-america-part-one-the-roots-of-war-resistance/.

41 **"Jesus' teaching and example of nonviolence as normative for Christians":** Ronald J. Sider, "Pacifism in Church History," *Mennonite World Review,* January 9, 2020, https://anabaptistworld.org/pacifism-in-church-history/.

## NOTES

41 ***Pentecostals "are uncompromisingly opposed to war":*** "Pentecostal Saints Opposed to War," *Weekly Evangel*, June 19, 1915, https://pcpj.org/pentecostal-pacifism/.

42 ***"under God, we want to do right":*** "Resolution On Violence, Disregard For Law," Southern Baptist Convention, June 1, 1968, https://www.sbc.net/resource-library/resolutions/resolution-on-violence-disregard-for-law/.

42 ***In a post on the faith blogging platform Patheos:*** Daniel K. Williams, "The Churches That Honor Guns," *Anxious Bench* (blog), April 25, 2023, https://www.patheos.com/blogs/anxiousbench/2023/04/the-churches-that-honor-guns/.

43 ***conservative evangelicals would be drawn to a nostalgic, rugged masculinity:*** Kristen Kobes du Mez, "John Wayne Will Save Your Ass," in *Jesus and John Wayne* (Liveright Publishing of W. W. Norton, 2020), 37.

44 ***some evangelicals had begun raising their sons as "future warriors":*** Kobes du Mez, "No More Christian Nice Guy," in *Jesus and John Wayne*, 178.

44 ***"The minute parsing of Bible verses about swords misses the forest for the trees":*** Christopher B. Hays, "Gun Culture and the End of American Christianity," *The Presbyterian Outlook*, May 26, 2023, https://presoutlook.org/2023/05/gun-culture-and-the-end-of-american-christianity/.

46 ***"I would like to have a couple of guys licensed to carry":*** Staff, "Arkansas Churches Face Decision: Guns or No Guns?," *Fort Smith Times Record*, May 5, 2013, https://www.swtimes.com/story/news/state/2013/05/05/arkansas-churches-face-decision-guns/26299821007/.

46 ***"It keeps us guarded and focused on fear . . .":*** Sarah Whites-Koditschek, "Arkansas' 'Enhanced Concealed Carry' Allows Guns In Churches, Bars, State Capitol," *NPR*, April 30, 2018, https://www.npr.org/2018/04/30/606990239/arkansas-requires-training-for-enhanced-concealed-carry-permit.

52 ***gun owners manage to successfully defend themselves in fewer than 1 percent of crimes:*** Samantha Raphelson, "How Often Do People Use Guns In Self-Defense?," *NPR*, April 13, 2018, https://www.npr.org/2018/04/13/602143823/how-often-do-people-use-guns-in-self-defense.

52 ***"Self-defense gun use is a rare event":*** David Hemenway and Sara J. Solnick, "The Epidemiology of Self-Defense Gun Use: Evidence From the National Crime Victimization Surveys 2007–2011," *Preventive Medicine* 19 (October 2015), 22–27, https://doi.org/10.1016/j.ypmed.2015.03.029.

# NOTES

54 ***simulations that can be incredibly stressful and traumatic for young children and their families:*** Erin Doherty, "School Gun Violence Torments America's Youngest Generation," *Axios*, May 20, 2023, https://www.axios.com/2023/05/20/gun-violence-children-schools.

54 ***"Guns are like a wildfire that becomes more powerful the bigger it gets":*** Christopher B. Hays and C. L. Crouch, eds., *God and Guns: The Bible Against American Gun Culture* (Westminster John Knox Press, 2021), 69–70.

54 ***"Gun organizations are conventionally masculine in cultural style . . .":*** R. W. Connell, *Masculinities* (Routledge, 2021), 212.

55 ***"Too many Christians worship the gun instead of God":*** Hays and Crouch, *God and Guns*, 131–132.

## CHAPTER 3: A WELL-REGULATED MILITIA

57 ***"in defense of the Church":*** Raymond Alger, O.P., "The Third Order of Saint Dominic," *Dominicana* 17, no. 2 (June 1932).

58 ***"a ruffianly lot; mafia types in armor":*** Richard Weber, O.P., "History of the Dominican Laity Rule," date unspecified.

59 ***"For much of American history, gun rights did not extend to Black people":*** Adam Winkler, "Racist Gun Laws and the Second Amendment," *Harvard Law Review* 135, no. 8 (June 2022), https://harvardlawreview.org/forum/vol-135/racist-gun-laws-and-the-second-amendment/.

60 ***armed "as according to law":*** "The Militia and Minute Men of 1775," National Park Service, accessed January 8, 2025, https://www.nps.gov/mima/learn/historyculture/the-militia-and-minute-men-of-1775.htm.

61 ***"Where is the militia today?:*** "The Well-Regulated Militia," The Heritage Foundation, accessed January 8, 2025, https://www.heritage.org/the-essential-second-amendment/the-well-regulated-militia.

61 ***"Surely the authors of the Constitution had in mind a militia organized by and subject to the government":*** Walter C. Clemens Jr., "Forgotten Words: 'A Well Regulated Militia,'" *The Hill*, February 3, 2023, https://thehill.com/opinion/criminal-justice/3837733-forgotten-words-a-well-regulated-militia/.

61 ***"If the founders were alive today":*** Eliga Gould, "Why the Second Amendment Protects a 'Well-Regulated Militia' but Not a Private Citizen Militia," *The Conversation*, June 14, 2021, https://theconversation.com/why-the-second-amendment-protects-a-well-regulated-militia-but-not-a-private-citizen-militia-162489.

# NOTES

62 ***they joined others in laying siege to the Capitol:*** For more on evangelicals' involvement in the events of January 6, 2021, see Matthew D. Taylor's *The Violent Take It by Force: The Christian Movement That Is Threatening Our Democracy* (Broadleaf Books, 2024).

63 ***"There's a war going on between the truths of God and the lies of this world":*** Ryan J. Reilly, "Trump Supporter Charged with Firing a Gun During the Jan. 6 Capitol Attack," *NBC News*, March 8, 2024, https://www.nbcnews.com/politics/justice-department/trump-supporter-charged-firing-gun-jan-6-capitol-attack-rcna142538.

63 ***sixty-page report on evangelical complicity reads like a biblical lament:*** "Christian Nationalism and the January 6, 2021, Insurrection," Christians Against Christian Nationalism, February 9, 2022, https://www.christiansagainstchristiannationalism.org/jan6report.

64 ***the New Apostolic Reformation, a network of politically ambitious church leaders:*** For a deeper dive into the New Apostolic Reformation, see Taylor, *The Violent Take It by Force*.

64 ***Texas pastor Brandon Burden urged his congregation at Kingdom Life Church to keep their guns loaded:*** Madison Dapcevich, "Did Texas Pastor Say Keep Weapons 'Loaded' Before Inauguration?," *Snopes*, January 14, 2021, https://www.snopes.com/fact-check/texas-pastor-weapons-loaded/.

64 ***wake up to the culture wars or reckon with "bullets and bombs":*** Michelle Goldberg, "In Indiana, the MAGA Revolution Eats Its Own," *New York Times*, June 17, 2024, https://www.nytimes.com/2024/06/17/opinion/indiana-christian-nationalist-republican-party.html.

65 ***committed to overthrowing democracy completely "and replace it with this right here":*** Alex Woodward, "Far-Right Influencer Calls for 'End of Democracy' at CPAC as Republicans Downplay January 6," *The Independent*, February 23, 2024, https://www.the-independent.com/news/world/americas/us-politics/posobiec-democracy-cpac-january-6-b2501566.html.

68 ***"a relic of the 18th century":*** John Paul Stevens, "John Paul Stevens: Repeal the Second Amendment," *New York Times*, March 27, 2018, https://www.nytimes.com/2018/03/27/opinion/john-paul-stevens-repeal-second-amendment.html.

68 ***"The gun lobby has long peddled an extremist and dangerous view of the Second Amendment":*** "The Second Amendment," Gifford

# NOTES

Law Center, accessed January 8, 2025, https://giffords.org/lawcenter/gun-laws/second-amendment/.

70 ***Clarence Thomas's majority opinion included material copied from a brief written by the Firearms Policy Coalition:*** Dahlia Lithwick and Mark Joseph Stern, "The Group Helping the Supreme Court Rewrite America's Gun Laws Is Worse Than the NRA," *Slate*, June 15, 2024, https://slate.com/news-and-politics/2024/06/supreme-court-nra-gun-laws-bump-stocks.html.

70 ***according to a 2024 analysis by three law professors:*** Rebecca Brown, Lee Epstein, and Mitu Gulati, "God, Judges, and Trump," *USC Gould School of Law*, https://dx.doi.org/10.2139/ssrn.4873330.

70 ***"It's akin to the Christian right's abortion playbook, but for guns.":*** Will Van Sant, "Inside the Secret Multimillion-Dollar Operation to Dismantle America's Gun Laws," *The Trace/Mother Jones*, July 30, 2024, https://www.thetrace.org/2024/07/gun-rights-lawsuits-donors-trust-funding/.

71 ***a flawed argument you'll often hear from pro-gun religious fundamentalists:*** Michael W. Austin and Ron Gleason, "The Gun Control Debate: Two Christian Perspectives," *Christian Research Institute*, April 12, 2023, https://www.equip.org/articles/gun-control-debate-two-christian-perspectives/.

72 ***"it is not clear how an armed populace would prevent such tyranny":*** Michael W. Austin and Ron Gleason, "The Gun Control Debate: Two Christian Perspectives," *Christian Research Institute*, April 12, 2023, https://www.equip.org/articles/gun-control-debate-two-christian-perspectives/.

73 ***By 2024, just 20 percent agreed:*** Megan Brenan, "Majorities Still Back Stricter Gun Laws, Assault Weapons Ban: Support for a Ban on Handguns in the US Has Dropped to a Near-Record Low," *Gallup News*, November 18, 2024, https://news.gallup.com/poll/653489/majorities-back-stricter-gun-laws-assault-weapons-ban.aspx.

73 ***"They did not intend to create a Christian nation":*** Gregg Frazier, PhD, "The Faith of the Founding Fathers," The Master's University, https://www.masters.edu/master_tmu_news/the-faith-of-the-founding-fathers/.

74 ***if the framers had intended to include references to Christian doctrine, they'd have done so explicitly:*** Nicholas Rathod, "The Founding Fathers' Religious Wisdom," *AmericanProgress.org*, January 8, 2008, https://www.americanprogress.org/article/the-founding-fathers-religious-wisdom/.

# NOTES

74 ***"America's first freedom because it protects all the others":*** J. Kenneth Blackwell, "America's Two First Freedoms: A Biblical Christian Perspective on How the Second Amendment Secures First Amendment Rights," *Liberty University Law Review* 9, no. 2 (2015), https://digitalcommons.liberty.edu/lu_law_review/vol9/iss2/2/.

75 ***"those who want to be truly 'pro-life' need to do more than oppose abortion":*** Tony Campolo, "Commentary: If You're Truly 'Pro-Life,' You Should Be Anti-Gun," *Religion News Service*, June 11, 2024, https://www.sltrib.com/religion/2024/06/11/commentary-if-youre-truly-pro-life/.

75 ***"the oxymoron of being both anti-abortion and pro-gun":*** Earl Chappell, "The Oxymoron of Being Both Anti-Abortion and Pro-Gun," *Baptist News Global*, June 15, 2022, https://baptistnews.com/article/the-oxymoron-of-being-both-anti-abortion-and-pro-gun/.

75 ***". . . they express little willingness to advocate for changes that might reduce gun deaths":*** Dave Verhaagen, "Why Do White Evangelicals Oppose Gun Control Legislation?" *Evangelical Psychology*, August 8, 2023, https://www.evangelicalpsych.com/post/why-do-white-evangelicals-oppose-gun-control-legislation.

76 ***"Most of us are card-carrying members of the NRA,":*** Martin Pengelly, "Kari Lake's Vow to Defend Trump with Guns Threatens Democracy, Democrat Says," *The Guardian*, June 12, 2023, https://www.theguardian.com/us-news/2023/jun/12/kari-lake-trump-nra-threat-threatens-democracy-arizona-democrat-ruben-gallego.

76 ***the threat of more armed insurrection:*** Tim Carey, Kelly Roskam, and Joshua Horwitz, "Defending Democracy: Addressing the Dangers of Armed Insurrection," Johns Hopkins Bloomberg School of Public Health, December 2023, https://publichealth.jhu.edu/sites/default/files/2023-12/dec-2023-cgvs-defending-democracy.pdf.

77 ***direct link between owning a gun and the willingness to consider violence:*** Garen J. Wintemute, Andrew Crawford, and Sonia L. Robinson, "Firearm Ownership and Support for Political Violence in the United States," *JAMA Network Open* 7, no. 4 (2024), https://jamanetwork.com/journals/jamanetworkopen/fullarticle/2817319.

79 ***Montenegro launched a crackdown on illegal firearms:*** Predrag Milic, "Montenegro to Tackle Gun Control After Mass Killing Left 12 Dead," *Associated Press*, January 3, 2025, https://apnews.com/article/montenegro-shooting-weapons-ban-government-fdffebbf53d52b3a74c6026389e2bdb5.

# NOTES

79 ***"Americans' increasing reliance on guns even in the face of escalating horrors is unfathomable":*** Philip Alpers, "This is What Happened When 3 Nations that Experienced Mass Shootings Did Something About It," *CNN Opinion*, June 1, 2022, https://www.cnn.com/2022/06/01/opinions/australia-uk-new-zealand-mass-shootings-gun-laws-alpers/index.html.

80 ***more regulations on fireworks in America than firearms:*** Shane Claiborne, X, July 4, 2023, https://x.com/ShaneClaiborne/status/1676248250699972608.

81 ***"Guns are practically an element of worship in the church of white Christian nationalism":*** Samuel L. Perry, "School Shootings Confirm That Guns Are the Religion of the Right," *Time Ideas*, May 25, 2022, https://time.com/6181342/school-shootings-christian-right-guns/.

## CHAPTER 4: HOME ON THE RANGE

85 ***an evangelical megachurch in Florida, went viral a few years ago when it posted this menacing sign:*** "Tampa Church's Pro-Gun Sign Goes Viral, Warns of 'Deadly Force' Against Threats," *ABC Action News/Tampa Bay*, November 17, 2017, https://www.abcactionnews.com/news/region-tampa/tampa-churchs-pro-gun-sign-goes-viral-warns-of-deadly-force-against-threats.

85 ***"People have this idea that Christians have to turn the other cheek":*** Valerie Richardson, "Kentucky Pastor Drops Flock for His Glock," *Washington Times*, October 12, 2009, https://www.washingtontimes.com/news/2009/oct/12/ky-pastor-drops-flock-for-his-glock/.

86 ***Ada Bible Church shut down its own Rocky Mount–style gun range:*** Bob Brenzing and Erica Francis, "Church Closes Shooting Range After Neighbor Complaints," *FOX 17 News*, June 12, 2015, https://www.fox-17online.com/2015/06/12/church-closes-shooting-range-after-neighbor-complaints.

87 ***"I don't see anything un-Christian about shooting":*** Sheila M. Poole, "Bibles and Bullets: Church Holds Men's Group Meetings at Gun Range," *Atlanta Journal-Constitution*, December 14, 2017, https://www.ajc.com/lifestyles/bibles-and-bullets-church-holds-men-group-meetings-gun-range/tKiXBE0yap9fNQEInWYsAK/.

88 ***an opportunity to socialize while practicing their shooting skills:*** Kristy Deer, "Church Members Shoot for Fellowship," *Pendleton Times-Post*,

# NOTES

April 27, 2017, https://www.pendletontimespost.com/2017/04/27/local_church_members_enjoy_fellowship_while_firing_as_a_group/.

89 ***"what I've got in my back pocket right now":*** "University President to Students: Arm Yourselves," *CNN* via YouTube, December 5, 2015, https://www.youtube.com/watch?v=zHmwD2VElyE.

89 ***Stewart teaches his flock how to handle a firearm:*** Holly Bailey, "Carrying a Bible and a Gun, a Pastor Tends to an Unsettled New Orleans," *Washington Post*, May 12, 2023, https://www.washingtonpost.com/nation/2023/05/12/new-orleans-pastor-gun-violence-firearm-safety/.

90 ***"Violence is the ethos of our times":*** Walter Wink, *Engaging the Powers: Discernment and Resistance in a World of Domination* (Fortress Press, 1992), 13.

93 ***Dr. Brian H. Williams describes the damage an AR-15 can do:*** Brian H. Williams, *The Bodies Keep Coming: Dispatches from a Black Trauma Surgeon on Racism, Violence, and How We Heal* (Broadleaf Books, 2023), 208.

98 ***Such laws are objectively racist:*** Kami Chavis, "The Dangerous Expansion of Stand-Your-Ground Laws and Its Racial Implications," *Duke Center for Firearms Law*, January 18, 2022, https://firearmslaw.duke.edu/2022/01/the-dangerous-expansion-of-stand-your-ground-laws-and-its-racial-implications.

105 ***Dana Gould captures the inherent disconnect between patriotism and nationalism perfectly:*** Dana Gould, X, February 23, 2018. (Gould's X account has since been deleted.)

## CHAPTER 5: THE FEAR FACTOR

108 ***double the rate of firearms theft:*** Jay Szkola, Megan J. O'Toole, and Sarah Burd-Sharps, "Gun Thefts from Cars: The Largest Source of Stolen Guns," *Everytown for Gun Safety*, May 9, 2024, https://everytownresearch.org/report/gun-thefts-from-cars-the-largest-source-of-stolen-guns-2/.

108 ***"people tend to overestimate their chances of becoming victims":*** Neil Gross, "People Get Scared and Buy a Gun: Here's What Happens Next," *New York Times*, August 1, 2023, https://www.nytimes.com/2023/08/01/opinion/fear-crime-rates.html.

109 ***asked Americans if they thought life has become harder:*** "Religion in Public Life," Pew Research Center, October 27, 2022, accessed January 9, 2025, https://www.pewresearch.org/religion/2022/10/27/religion-in-public-life/.

# NOTES

109 ***asking people if they thought Christianity was under attack:*** Daniel A. Cox, "Why Most Evangelicals Say They Face 'A Lot' of Discrimination," *Survey Center on American Life*, September 7, 2023, https://www.americansurveycenter.org/newsletter/why-most-evangelicals-say-they-face-a-lot-of-discrimination/.

111 ***"paranoid fantasy undergirds much of religious conservatives' opposition to gun control":*** Eil J. Young, "Why Do Evangelicals Oppose Gun Control?," *The Week*, August 11, 2019, https://theweek.com/articles/857806/why-evangelicals-oppose-gun-control.

111 ***Alan Noble frames it more forcefully:*** Alan Noble, "The Evangelical Persecution Complex," *The Atlantic*, August 4, 2014, https://www.theatlantic.com/national/archive/2014/08/the-evangelical-persecution-complex/375506/.

112 ***lived within a mile of a mass shooting:*** Amy O'Kruk, Kenneth Uzquiano, and Anna Brand, "Americans Living Near Mass Shootings," *CNN*, August 30, 2023, accessed January 9, 2025, https://www.cnn.com/interactive/2023/08/us/americans-living-near-mass-shootings-statistics-dg/.

112 ***anxiety is "way out of proportion with the risk":*** Shirin Ali, "Why Are Mass Shootings on the Rise This Year?," *Slate*, May 15, 2023, https://slate.com/news-and-politics/2023/05/how-to-make-sense-of-the-recent-increase-in-mass-shootings.html.

112 ***"Mass shootings are very low probability but very high consequence events":*** "Scientists Use New Method to Calculate the Annual Probability of a Mass Shooting," Phys.org, August 22, 2023, https://phys.org/news/2023-08-scientists-method-annual-probability-mass.html#google_vignette.

113 ***What if we're afraid of the wrong things?:*** Anthony L. Fisher, "America's Tragedy Is Its Culture of Fear—Armed With Millions of Guns," *Daily Beast*, May 30, 2024, https://www.thedailybeast.com/americas-tragedy-is-its-culture-of-fearthat-happens-to-be-armed-with-millions-of-guns/.

114 ***"Fear is a powerful weapon":*** Matthew Teutsch, "The Violence of Fear in Evangelical Christianity," *Medium*, April 28, 2024, https://interminablerambling.com/2024/05/08/the-violence-of-fear-in-evangelical-christianity/.

114 ***keeps America from properly addressing gun violence:*** Chrissy Stroop, "Beyond 'Thoughts and Prayers': How the Christian Right's Politics of Providentialism Keeps America from Addressing Gun Violence," *Religion Dispatches*, August 7, 2019, https://religiondispatches.org/

# NOTES

beyond-thoughts-and-prayers-how-the-christian-rights-politics-of-providentialism-keeps-america-from-addressing-gun-violence/.

115 *"Christian nationalism on steroids":* David R. Brockman, "The New Apostolic Reformation Wants God's Government Back," *Texas Observer*, June 3, 2024, https://www.texasobserver.org/new-apostolic-reformation-texas-leaders/.

117 *"People have been panicking about the collapse of Christianity since the nation's founding":* Leslie Cohen, "Fear and Power: Christian Nationalism in America," *The Cairo Review of Global Affairs*, February 8, 2023, https://www.thecairoreview.com/essays/fear-and-power-christian-nationalism-in-america/.

118 *this head-scratcher on Facebook:* Franklin Graham, Facebook, April 25, 2014, https://www.facebook.com/FranklinGraham/posts/ive-been-asked-to-pray-at-the-opening-session-of-the-nra-annual-meeting-and-for-/701575996565251/.

119 *fear the 'collapse of society, as they know it':* Stowe Boyd, *Medium*, January 28, 2016, https://medium.com/@stoweboyd/paul-krugman-potemkin-ideologies-b21b32d4b974.

120 *"The fear kept me crippled with anxiety":* Emily Strohm, "Jinger Duggar Vuolo on Growing Up Under 'Cult-Like' Religious Beliefs: 'I Was Terrified of the Outside World,'" *People*, January 18, 2023, https://people.com/tv/jinger-duggar-vuolo-on-growing-up-following-cult-like-religious-beliefs/.

120 *being traumatized as a girl by the gospel of fear:* Sarah McCammon, "The Exvangelicals: Loving, Living, and Leaving the White Evangelical Church" (St. Martin's Press, 2024), 22–23.

121 *"fear porn":* Sarah Ford, "Fear Porn and the Religious Right," *Medium*, December 10, 2019, https://medium.com/@sarahford_9556/every-time-i-read-a-super-negative-take-on-america-that-makes-it-sounds-like-were-about-to-descend-cd726178695f.

122 *French ticks off a number of white evangelical beliefs:* David French, "Evangelicals Are Supporting Trump Out of Fear, Not Faith," *Time*, June 27, 2019, https://time.com/5615617/why-evangelicals-support-trump/.

122 *video urging us all to arm ourselves:* NRA, X, March 21, 2020, https://x.com/NRA/status/1241418470341980167.

122 *a stinging rebuke from Everytown for Gun Safety:* "Amidst Global Pandemic, the NRA Fear Mongers to Sell Guns," *Everytown for Gun Safety*,

# NOTES

March 23, 2020, https://www.everytown.org/press/amidst-global-pandemic-the-nra-fear-mongers-to-sell-guns/.

124 ***"an almost pathological preoccupation with fear and survival"***: Morwari Zafar, "Among Gun Rights Activists, Fears About Survival Reign," *Sapiens*, February 28, 2024, https://www.sapiens.org/culture/gun-rights-militias-political-extremism/.

125 ***"a shared culture of fear"***: Joseph M. Pierre, "The Psychology of Guns: Risk, Fear, and Motivated Reasoning," *Palgrave Communications* 5, no. 159 (2019), https://doi.org/10.1057/s41599-019-0373-z.

125 ***just as afraid as non-gun owners of being victimized:*** Benjamin Dowd-Arrow, Terrence D. Hill, and Amy M. Burdette, "Gun Ownership and Fear," *SSM Population Health* 8 (August 2019), https://doi.org/10.1016/j.ssmph.2019.100463.

126 ***owning a gun raises an individual's anxiety levels:*** "How Owning a Gun Raises Anxiety," *Association for Psychological Science*, October 27, 2023, https://www.psychologicalscience.org/observer/gun-ownership-anxiety.

126 ***"More guns in America means more gun victimizations":*** Allison Jordan, Chandler Hall, and Devin Hughes, "Debunking the 'Guns Make Us Safer' Myth," *Center for American Progress*, February 12, 2024, https://www.americanprogress.org/article/debunking-the-guns-make-us-safer-myth/.

127 ***What made her feel more secure?:*** Blair Braverman, "When I Was Scared, My Gun-Owning Neighbors Helped Me Feel Safe," *The Guardian*, September 22, 2016, https://www.theguardian.com/us-news/2016/sep/22/when-i-was-scared-my-gun-owning-neighbors-helped-me-feel-safe.

127 ***injustice of gun violence in America:*** Joash Thomas, "The Gospel and Gun Violence," *Jesus, Justice & Joash* (Substack), May 8, 2023, https://joashpthomas.substack.com/p/the-gospel-and-gun-violence.

128 ***it is a terror that still stalks her:*** Patti Davis, "How Gun Violence Changed My Father, Ronald Reagan, and Our Family," *New York Times*, July 5, 2022, https://www.nytimes.com/2022/07/05/opinion/guns-highland-park-ronald-reagan.html.

129 ***"most of America's gun culture is driven by Christians":*** Scott Baker, "America's Gun Culture is Driven by Christians," *Premier Christianity*, March 28, 2023, https://www.premierchristianity.com/opinion/americas-gun-culture-is-driven-by-christians-heres-how-to-stop-school-shootings/15230.article.

# NOTES

129 ***tired of the hypocrisy of evangelicals defending their stockpiling:*** John Pavlovitz, "Americans Who Love Guns More Than People," *JohnPavlovitz.com*, December 6, 2021, https://johnpavlovitz.com/2021/12/06/americans-who-love-guns-more-than-people/.

130 ***"our country continues to sacrifice human life to the gun idol":*** Ed Gaskin, "God, Guns, Mass Shootings and Evangelicals," *Ed Gaskin* (blog), *The Times of Israel*, September 8, 2023, https://blogs.timesofisrael.com/god-guns-mass-shootings-and-evangelicals/.

## CHAPTER 6: GUNMAKERS FOR GOD

144 ***a surge in fatal shootings excluding suicides:*** Chip Brownlee, "Permitless Carry Will Deter Shootings, Proponents Said: That's Not What's Happened.," *The Trace*, August 9, 2024, https://www.thetrace.org/2024/08/permitless-concealed-carry-gun-super-bowl/.

144 ***"a population the size of Florida":*** Matt Manda, "Since the 2020 Election, the Number of New Gun Owners Equals the Population of Florida," *NSSF*, June 5, 2024, https://www.nssf.org/articles/since-2020-election-new-gun-owners-equal-population-of-florida/.

145 ***even FosTecH, for all its earnestness, has run afoul of the law:*** Kayla Dwyer, "Indiana Gunmaker That Offered GOP Lawmakers Discounted Rifles is Fined After Investigation," *Indianapolis Star*, November 30, 2023, https://www.indystar.com/story/news/politics/2023/11/30/gunmaker-fostech-fined-after-offering-gop-lawmakers-discount-ar-15-style-rifles/71742654007/.

147 ***being shot by Jesus rifles:*** "U.S. Military Weapons Inscribed With Secret 'Jesus' Bible Codes," *ABC News*, January 15, 2010, , https://abcnews.go.com/Blotter/us-military-weapons-inscribed-secret-jesus-bible-codes/story?id=9575794.

147 ***Islamic terrorists won't be able to use their rifles:*** Ben Hooper, "Florida Gun Shop's Rifle Designed to Repel 'Muslim Terrorists,'" *UPI*, September 3, 2015, https://www.upi.com/Odd_News/2015/09/03/Florida-gun-shops-rifle-designed-to-repel-Muslim-terrorists/3181441309655/.

148 ***a rifle is "perhaps the least desirable" place to put a Bible verse:*** "US Assault Rifle Sports Christian Symbols to Prevent Middle East Shipments: Company," *Middle East Eye*, September 16, 2015, https://www.middleeasteye.net/news/us-assault-rifle-sports-christian-symbols-prevent-middle-east-shipments-company.

# NOTES

148 ***"Our country is being taken away from us":*** Tracey Eaton, "Gun store owner: Freedom is slipping away in the U.S.," *TraceyEaton.com*, August 19, 2021, https://traceyeaton.com/index.php/2021/08/19/rapture-guns/.

149 ***an illuminating expose on T.REX:*** Lila Hassan, "They Make Viral Gun Videos—With Hardline Christian Values," *Mother Jones*, March/April 2024, https://www.motherjones.com/politics/2024/03/t-rex-arms-hardline-christian-nationalism-lucas-botkin/.

151 ***now headquartered in Wyoming:*** "Rifle Maker CEO Builds on His Ministry Background," *Liberty Journal*, October 31, 2019, https://www.liberty.edu/journal/article/rifle-maker-ceo-builds-on-his-ministry-background/.

151 ***"has operated for decades with minimal oversight":*** "The Gun Industry in America," Center for American Progress, August 6, 2020, https://www.americanprogress.org/article/gun-industry-america/.

151 ***allegedly used a ghost gun and a 3D-printed silencer:*** "National Firearms Commerce and Trafficking Assessment (NFCTA): Protecting America from Trafficked Firearms—Volume Four," ATF, January 8, 2025, https://www.atf.gov/firearms/national-firearms-commerce-and-trafficking-assessment-nfcta-firearms-trafficking-volume-four.

152 ***Christmas ornaments and wreaths fashioned from spent shotgun shells:*** Jordan Liles, "Did Hobby Lobby Sell a 'Shotgun Shell Ornament' for Christmas in 2023?," Snopes, December 14, 2023, https://www.snopes.com/fact-check/hobby-lobby-shotgun-ornament/.

152 ***duplicitous "merchants of death":*** Philip Pullella, "Pope Says Weapons Manufacturers Can't Call Themselves Christian," *Reuters*, June 21, 2015, https://www.reuters.com/article/world/pope-says-weapons-manufacturers-cant-call-themselves-christian-idUSKBN0P10U2/.

153 ***marketing firearms to young people:*** Pooja Salhotra and Berenice Garcia, "Families of Uvalde Shooting Victims Suing Gun Manufacturer, Instagram, Video Game Company," *Texas Tribune*, May 24, 2024, https://www.texastribune.org/2024/05/24/uvalde-shooting-lawsuits-gunmaker-instagram-texas/.

154 ***begun exporting tens of millions of rapid-fire firearms worldwide:*** Michael Riley, David Kocieniewski, and Eric Fan, "How the US Drives Gun Exports and Fuels Violence Around the World," *Bloomberg*, July 24, 2023, https://www.bloomberg.com/graphics/2023-us-made-gun-exports-shootings-violence-sig-sauer/.

# NOTES

## CHAPTER 7: PISTOLS AND POLITICS

157 ***Boebert's viral remarks there underscored her tone deafness:*** Chloe Fomar, "Boebert: Jesus Didn't Have Enough AR-15s to 'Keep His Government from Killing Him,'" *The Hill*, June 17, 2022, https://thehill.com/homenews/house/3528049-boebert-jesus-didnt-have-enough-ar-15s-to-keep-his-government-from-killing-him/.

158 ***"a Christian who seems to know nothing about basic Christianity":*** Matt Lewis, "On Guns and Jesus, Lauren Boebert Is a Complete Ignoramus," *The Daily Beast*, June 17, 2022, https://www.thedailybeast.com/on-guns-and-jesus-lauren-boebert-is-a-complete-ignoramus/.

159 ***the effort has also been denounced by the ultraconservative Heritage Foundation:*** Amy Swearer, "Sorry, Gov. Newsom, but Citizens Want to Use Guns to Defend Themselves, Others," *The Daily Signal*, July 14, 2023, https://www.heritage.org/firearms/commentary/sorry-gov-newsom-citizens-want-use-guns-defend-themselves-others.

160 ***white evangelicals tend to be overwhelmingly Republican or libertarian:*** Dave Verhaagen, "Why Do White Evangelicals Oppose Gun Control Legislation?," *Evangelical Psychology*, August 8, 2023, https://www.evangelicalpsych.com/post/why-do-white-evangelicals-oppose-gun-control-legislation.

160 ***"Evangelicalism has become a political monoculture":*** Ryan Burge, "The Echo Chamber: On God and Guns in American Christianity," *Interfaith Voices*, June 11, 2022, https://interfaithradio.org/Story_Details/The_Echo_Chamber__On_God_and_Guns_in_American_Christianity.

161 ***"Gun ownership and Republican identity have become inseparable":*** Noah Berlatsky, "Trump and Republicans Don't Hate Gun Control Because of the NRA: They Just Love Guns," *NBCNews.com*, September 24, 2019, https://www.nbcnews.com/think/opinion/trump-republicans-don-t-hate-gun-control-because-nra-they-ncna1057841.

162 ***"the root cause of this rampant violence":*** Neil J. Young, "Why Do Evangelicals Oppose Gun Control?," *The Week*, August 11, 2019, https://theweek.com/articles/857806/why-evangelicals-oppose-gun-control.

162 ***half of all gun owners say most or all their friends also own guns:*** Diana Orcés, PhD, "The Gun Ownership Bubble: Gun Owners Are More Likely To Have Other Gun Owners As Close Friends," *PRRI*, June 10, 2022, https://www.prri.org/spotlight/the-gun-ownership-bubble-gun-owners-are-more-likely-to-have-other-gun-owners-as-close-friends/.

# NOTES

162 ***conservative extremists laced gun rights into their Christian nationalist and anti-government narrative:*** Lila Hassan, "As Midterms Loom, Right Wingers Are Revving Up the Faithful with Talk of Religion and Guns," *The Trace*, September 19, 2022, https://www.thetrace.org/2022/09/christian-nationalism-guns-election/.

163 ***politicians have been trying to out-MAGA one another:*** Michelle Goldberg, "In Indiana, the MAGA Revolution Eats Its Own," *New York Times*, June 17, 2024, https://www.nytimes.com/2024/06/17/opinion/indiana-christian-nationalist-republican-party.html.

163 ***people with "evil intent" needed to be put to death:*** Greg Sargent, "MAGA Gov Candidate's Ugly, Hateful Rant: 'Some Folks Need Killing!,'" *New Republic*, July 5, 2024, https://newrepublic.com/article/183443/mark-robinson-north-carolina-gov-candidate-hateful-rant-killing.

165 ***Republican senators have been displaying small white flags with a pine tree in the center:*** Steve Ahlquist, "The Pine Tree Flag is Popping up on the Desks of RI Senators: What Does it Mean?," *Steve Ahlquist* (Substack), June 13, 2024, https://steveahlquist.substack.com/p/the-pine-tree-flag-is-popping-up.

165 ***meaningless legislative diversions instead of practical actions:*** Andrew L. Whitehead, Landon Schnabel, and Samuel L. Perry, "Gun Control in the Crosshairs: Christian Nationalism and Opposition to Stricter Gun Laws," *Socius* 4 (2018), https://doi.org/10.1177/2378023118790189.

167 ***"If somebody breaks in my house, they're getting shot":*** Jess Bidgood, "Kamala Harris Tells Oprah if Somebody Breaks Into Her Home, 'They're Getting Shot,'" *New York Times*, September 20, 2024, https://www.nytimes.com/2024/09/20/us/politics/kamala-harris-gun-oprah.html.

169 ***Covenant Moms launched a campaign to enact some modest gun control measures:*** Frank Gluck, "'Be Brave and Show Up': Tennessee's Covenant Moms Are Among USA Today's Women of the Year," *The Tennessean*, March 5, 2024, https://www.tennessean.com/story/news/2024/02/29/usa-today-women-of-the-year-tennessee-covenant-moms/72160339007/.

171 ***"Fighting crime needs more than that":*** Ayah Galal, "City of Hartford Launches Office of Violence Prevention," *WFSB-TV*, April 1, 2024, https://www.wfsb.com/2024/04/01/city-hartford-launches-office-violence-prevention/.

175 ***central role that Christian conservatives often play in not only defending but expanding gun rights:*** Eleanor Klibanoff, "A Gun and

## NOTES

a Prayer: How the Far Right Took Control of Texas' Response to Mass Shootings," *The Texas Tribune*, May 29, 2022, https://www.texastribune.org/2022/05/29/texas-mass-shootings-self-defense-gun-ownership/.

175 ***only Christians should hold leadership positions:*** Jasper Scherer and Robert Downen, "Former Texas House Speaker Says GOP Megadonor Tim Dunn Told Him Only Christians Should Hold Leadership Positions," *Texas Tribune*, April 4, 2024, https://www.texastribune.org/2024/04/04/tim-dunn-joe-straus-christian-texas/.

178 ***Americans accustomed to daily gun violence have become numb to it:*** Alanna Durkin Richer, "Chief Enforcer of US Gun Laws Fears Americans May Become Numb to Violence with Each Mass Shooting," *Associated Press*, February 24, 2024, https://apnews.com/article/maine-shooting-victims-gun-violence-atf-dettelbach-12c3ed0f8d8826b6d13dd88bf185f4e9.

178 ***Burger denounced the amendment:*** Sarah Lynch Baldwin, "Repealing the Second Amendment—Is it Even Possible?" *CBS News*, March 28, 2018, https://www.cbsnews.com/news/repealing-the-second-amendment-is-it-even-possible/.

179 ***a way forward:*** Walter Shapiro, "Democrats Need to Start Talking About Repealing the Second Amendment," *The New Republic*, May 26, 2022, https://newrepublic.com/article/166628/democrats-repeal-second-amendment-guns.

179 ***"nothing should be written in stone":*** Paul Veliyathil, "Repeal the 2nd Amendment," *Medium*, March 28, 2023, https://paulflorida88.medium.com/repeal-the-2nd-amendment-bde5e0907129.

179 ***on a quest for commonsense policy responses:*** Bill Frist, "The Massive New Public Health Threat to Kids: What Policies Would You Consider To Address Gun Safety?," *Forbes*, May 3, 2023, https://www.forbes.com/sites/billfrist/2023/05/03/the-massive-new-public-health-threat-to-kids-what-policies-would-you-consider-to-address-gun-safety/.

180 ***"Evangelical used to denote people who claimed the high moral ground":*** Timothy Keller, "Can Evangelicalism Survive Donald Trump and Roy Moore?," *New Yorker*, December 19, 2017, https://www.newyorker.com/news/news-desk/can-evangelicalism-survive-donald-trump-and-roy-moore.

181 ***"The more guns we have, the more gun violence we have":*** Deanna Hollas, "From Despair to Hope: Mobilizing Your Church to End Gun Violence," *Presbyterian Outlook*, November 17, 2023, https://pres-outlook.org/2023/05/from-despair-to-hope-mobilizing-your-church-to-end-gun-violence/.

# NOTES

## CHAPTER 8: GUNS AND THE GLOBAL CHURCH

186 ***the brutality that Hondurans endure:*** Patrick Gothman, "I Was an American Missionary in Honduras: I Witnessed Firsthand the Violence They Endure," *America Magazine*, November 27, 2018, https://www.americamagazine.org/faith/2018/11/27/i-was-american-missionary-honduras-i-witnessed-firsthand-violence-they-endure.

187 ***American firearms are flowing illegally into the region:*** "The Iron River of Weapons to Mexico: Its Sources and Contents," Stop US Arms to Mexico, June 11, 2024, https://stopusarmstomexico.org/iron-river/.

187 ***$10 billion lawsuit against US gunmakers:*** Jonathan Lowy, "Mexico May Save Us From Our Own Crazy Gun Laws," *Newsweek*, February 9, 2024, https://www.newsweek.com/mexico-may-save-us-our-own-crazy-gun-laws-opinion-1868373.

187 ***shock at the notion that believers would champion gun ownership:*** Matthew Soerens, "This Love of Guns: It's Way Beyond Our Understanding," *Christianity Today*, June 8, 2022, https://www.christianitytoday.com/better-samaritan/2022/june/this-love-of-guns-its-way-beyond-our-understanding.html.

188 ***an unambiguous anti-gun position:*** C. Michael Patton, "Why Christians Are Ordered to Have Guns," *Parchment and Pen* (blog), 2016, https://credohouse.org/blog/christians-guns.

188 ***"we have seen the rise of an evangelicalism linked to the ideas of violence, hatred, guns":*** Constance Malleret, "Progressive Evangelicals Reject the Bolsonarization of Churches," *NACLA*, October 28, 2022, https://nacla.org/progressive-evangelicals-reject-bolsonarization-churches.

189 ***Brazil's evangelicals who embrace gun culture diverge from their US counterparts:*** Amy Erica Smith and Robin Globus Veldman, "Evangelical Environmentalists? Evidence from Brazil," *Journal for the Scientific Study of Religion* 59, no. 2 (2020), 341–340, https://doi.org/10.1111/jssr.12656.

189 ***evangelical organizations pressed back hard:*** Martina Jaureguy, "Latin American Ex-Presidents, Military Officers, and Evangelicals Weigh in on Milei," *Buenos Aires Herald*, November 13, 2023, https://buenosairesherald.com/politics/latin-american-ex-presidents-military-officers-and-evangelicals-weigh-in-on-milei.

189 ***fifty-seven instances of violence against Mexican Christians:*** "Following Jesus Under Drug Cartels in Mexico," *Open Doors*, May 28, 2024, https://www.opendoorsus.org/en-US/stories/following-Jesus-drug-cartels-Mexico/.

# NOTES

190 ***evangelicals are frequently targeted by drug cartels:*** Linda Burkle, PhD, "Persecution of Evangelical Protestants in Southern Mexico," *Persecution.org*, January 9, 2024, https://www.persecution.org/2024/01/09/persecution-of-evangelical-protestants-in-southern-mexico/.

190 ***the plight of an evangelical pastor in Oaxaca:*** Lynda Kristen Barrow, "Mission in Mexico: An Evangelical Surge," *Christian Century*, February 28, 2001, https://www.christiancentury.org/article/mission-mexico.

190 ***he's carried a gun at times to ward off menacing cartel members:*** Mark Stevenson, "Mexican Church Suspends Priest Who Advised Carrying Guns," *AP/National Catholic Reporter*, October 13, 2022, https://www.ncronline.org/news/mexican-church-suspends-priest-who-advised-carrying-guns.

195 ***he can't bring himself to get a gun:*** Hassan John, "Should Christians Ever Defend Themselves with Weapons?," Unbelievable, July 18, 2023, https://www.premierunbelievable.com/articles/should-christians-ever-defend-themselves-with-weapons/15930.article.

195 ***guns are often viewed differently:*** Morgan Lee, "Should Christians Own Guns for Self-Defense? A Global Snapshot," *Christianity Today*, October 10, 2022, https://www.christianitytoday.com/2022/10/guns-christians-self-defense-mass-shootings-protection/.

197 ***Australia's many cultural similarities with the United States challenge such assumptions:*** Andrew Wilson, "How Should Christians Think About Gun Control?," *Think Theology* (blog), May 5, 2022, https://thinktheology.co.uk/blog/article/how_should_christians_think_about_gun_control.

198 ***New Zealand began reversing course on its restrictive gun laws:*** Charlotte Graham McLay, "An Ex-Gun Lobbyist is Revising New Zealand's Gun Laws, Tightened After the 2019 Mosque Attack," *Associated Press*, June 21, 2024, https://apnews.com/article/new-zealand-gun-laws-mosque-shooting-0b535aab57fc47a4986e3ba53490d898.

200 ***"the impact Murray made on Dunblane":*** Jamie Braidwood, "Thank You Andy Murray, for What You Have Done for Dunblane," *The Independent*, August 1, 2024, https://www.the-independent.com/sport/tennis/andy-murray-dunblane-olympics-wimbledon-thank-you-b2588403.html.

201 ***Evangelist Franklin Graham tweeted something similarly tone-deaf:*** Franklin Graham, Twitter (now X), May 25, 2002, https://x.com/Franklin_Graham/status/1529519719031660552.

201 ***some "half-truths" in Graham's deflection:*** Emma Fowle, "Using the Bible to Sell Guns is Never OK," *Premier Christianity*, May 30, 2022,

# NOTES

https://www.premierchristianity.com/opinion/using-the-bible-to-sell-guns-is-never-ok/13159.article.

202 ***He says it devastated him personally:*** Donna Birrell, "'The Fragility of Life': Priest Who Comforted the Bereaved at Dunblane Reflects on 65 Years of Ministry," *Premier Christian News*, June 25, 2021, https://premierchristian.news/en/news/article/the-fragility-of-life-priest-who-comforted-the-bereaved-at-dunblane-reflects-on-65-years-of-ministry.

202 ***A letter to the editor of the Scottish newspaper The Herald captures his anguish:*** Reverend Bryan Owen, "Senior Clergy Guilty of Exercising Power Instead of Offering Compassion," *The Herald*, August 8, 2011, https://www.heraldscotland.com/opinion/13034364.senior-clergy-guilty-exercising-power-instead-offering-compassion/.

## CHAPTER 9: SWORDS INTO PLOWSHARES

210 *"My weariness grew one mass shooting at a time":* Shane Claiborne and Michael Martin, *Beating Guns: Hope for People Who Are Weary of Violence* (Baker, 2019).

212 ***the gunmaker would resist any move:*** Amy Whyte, "These Churches Buy Shares in Gun Companies. Their Goal: Confront Them," *Institutional Investor*, August 20, 2018, https://www.institutionalinvestor.com/article/2bsxl9hsu6x4eehp5h8u8/portfolio/these-churches-buy-shares-in-gun-companies-their-goal-confront-them.

212 ***an unusual shareholder lawsuit against Smith & Wesson:*** Cameron McWhirter and Zusha Elinson, "Activist Nuns, with Stake in Smith & Wesson, Sue Gun Maker Over AR-15 Rifles," *Wall Street Journal*, December 5, 2023, https://www.wsj.com/us-news/activist-nuns-with-stake-in-smith-wesson-sue-gun-maker-over-ar-15-rifles-40759544.

214 *"We'll continue to attempt to engage with the gun manufacturers":* Dan Stockman, "Q&A with Sr. Judy Byron on Forcing Sturm Ruger to Report on Gun Safety," *Global Sisters Report*, May 29, 2018, https://www.globalsistersreport.org/blog/ministry-qas/q-sr-judy-byron-forcing-sturm-ruger-report-gun-safety-54001.

214 ***offering poor Detroiters an alternative to using guns:*** David Beckford, "Silence the Violence March Advocates for Ending Gun Violence in Communities of Color," *Detroit PBS*, April 13, 2024, https://thenarrativematters.com/silence-the-violence-march-advocates-for-ending-gun-violence-in-communities-of-color/.

# NOTES

218 ***Do these buybacks work?:*** Amanda Charbonneau, "Gun Buyback Programs in the United States," RAND Corporation, January 10, 2023, https://www.rand.org/research/gun-policy/analysis/essays/gun-buyback-programs.html.

219 ***guns collected by police in buybacks and amnesty programs often are dismantled and the parts sold off:*** Mike McIntire, "The Guns Were Said to Be Destroyed. Instead, They Were Reborn," *New York Times*, December 10, 2023, https://www.nytimes.com/2023/12/10/us/guns-disposal-recycling.html.

219 ***"It's easier to get a gun in America than it is to get rid of a gun":*** Shane Claiborne, "I Turn Guns into Garden Tools: We Need More Options for Destroying Firearms," *Philadelphia Inquirer*, June 27, 2024, https://www.inquirer.com/opinion/commentary/gun-violence-police-how-destroy-decommission-firearms-20240627.html.

221 ***"I also believe that action is a form of prayer":*** Cindy Sheetz, "Thoughts and Prayers AND Action," *Mennonite Women USA*, June 18, 2024, https://www.mennonitewomenusa.org/post/thoughts-and-prayers-and-action.

221 ***the fight for stronger gun laws is God's work:*** Siobhan Neela-Stock, "The Stubborn Faith That Fuels a Leading Gun Safety Activist," *Sojourners*, December 18, 2023, https://sojo.net/articles/stubborn-faith-fuels-leading-gun-safety-activist.

## CHAPTER 10: NO GUNS IN HEAVEN

237 ***"We must meet violence with nonviolence:"*** "Dr. Martin Luther King Jr.'s Home Bombed in Montgomery, Alabama," *Equal Justice Initiative*, https://calendar.eji.org/racial-injustice/jan/30.

237 ***King himself has several handguns:*** Adam Winkler, "MLK and His Guns," *Huffington Post*, May 25, 2011, https://www.huffpost.com/entry/mlk-and-his-guns_b_810132.

237 ***King's crisis of conscience around guns:*** Mark Engler and Paul Engler, "When Martin Luther King Gave Up His Guns," *The Guardian*, January 20, 2014, https://www.theguardian.com/commentisfree/2014/jan/20/martin-luther-king-guns-pacifism.

240 ***hasn't stopped the Covenant Moms from lobbying hard for change:*** Frank Gluck, "'Be Brave and Show Up': Tennessee's Covenant Moms are Among USA Today's Women of the Year," *The Tennessean*,

# NOTES

February 29, 2024, https://www.tennessean.com/story/news/2024/02/29/usa-today-women-of-the-year-tennessee-covenant-moms/72160339007/.

240 *"we are here for gun safety and we're not going anywhere":* Jennifer Gerson, "After Their Children Survived a School Shooting, These 'Lifelong Republicans' Entered the Gun Conversation," *The 19th*, July 11, 2024, https://19thnews.org/2024/07/conservative-moms-gun-safety-covenant-school-shooting-nashville/.

242 *"What can we do to stop people from dying?":* Jordan Williams, "Walensky Says 'Now Is the Time' to Tackle Gun Violence: Report," *The Hill*, August 27, 2021, https://thehill.com/policy/healthcare/public-global-health/569818-walensky-says-now-is-the-time-to-tackle-gun-violence/.

242 *not the only white evangelical standing in the way of commonsense reforms:* Susan Stubson, "What Christian Nationalism Has Done to My State and My Faith Is a Sin," *New York Times*, May 21, 2023, https://www.nytimes.com/2023/05/21/opinion/wyoming-republicans-christian-nationalism.html.

243 *gun violence is a public health crisis:* Tina Reed, "Surgeon General Calls Guns a Public Health Threat in New Advisory," *Axios*, June 25, 2024, https://www.axios.com/2024/06/25/surgeon-general-gun-violence-advisory.

244 *"how we can so disvalue the lives of other people's children":* Wendell Berry, "Against Killing Children," *Christian Century*, October 3, 2024, https://www.christiancentury.org/features/against-killing-children.

246 *"the Boston miracle":* US Department of Justice, "Reducing Gun Violence: The Boston Gun Project's Operation Ceasefire," September 2001, https://www.ojp.gov/pdffiles1/nij/188741.pdf.

246 *Faith in Indiana is trying to replicate that success in Indianapolis:* Sono Motoyama, "Black Faith Groups Have Been Fighting Neighborhood Gun Violence for Decades: They're Finally Getting Support," *Chronicle of Philanthropy*, January 23, 2023, https://www.philanthropy.com/article/black-faith-groups-have-been-fighting-neighborhood-gun-violence-for-decades-they-finally-getting-support.

247 *Bishop William Barber II exemplifies what it means to speak truth to power:* Bishop William Barber II, "How to Turn Thoughts and Prayers into Action," *The Tennessean*, April 25, 2023, https://www.tennessean.com/story/opinion/contributors/2023/04/25/bishop-william-barber-how-to-turn-thoughts-and-prayers-into-action/70150402007/.

# NOTES

249 ***98 percent of all mass shootings dating back to 1966 have been committed by men:*** "Mass Shooters," The Violence Project, https://www.theviolenceproject.org/mass-shooter-database/.

250 ***some wise advice from Blair Braverman:*** Blair Braverman, "When I Was Scared, My Gun-Owning Neighbors Helped Me Feel Safe," *The Guardian*, September 22, 2016, https://www.theguardian.com/us-news/2016/sep/22/when-i-was-scared-my-gun-owning-neighbors-helped-me-feel-safe.

252 ***"Conservative evangelical politics":*** Alan Noble, "How Trump Happened: The Wages of Fear and the Brave Way Forward," *Christ and Pop Culture*, January 27, 2016, https://christandpopculture.com/how-trump-happened-evangelicals-fear-and-the-need-for-a-better-way/.

253 ***Survivors often suffer life-altering wounds and PTSD:*** Caroline Love, "Report: Texas Domestic Violence Homicides Have Almost Doubled in the Past 10 Years," *KERA News*, October 2, 2024, https://www.keranews.org/news/2024-10-02/texas-domestic-violence-homicides-have-almost-doubled-in-the-past-10-years.

253 ***a convincing case for the power of one:*** Joash Thomas, "The Beatitudes and Empire: A Recent Sermon," *Jesus, Justice & Joash* (Substack), October 9, 2024, https://substack.com/home/post/p-149991945.

254 ***only to die six weeks later in another mass shooting:*** "Man Who Survived Vegas Shooting Died in Thousand Oaks Massacre," CBSNews.com, November 9, 2018, https://www.cbsnews.com/news/california-mass-shooting-telemachus-orfanos-man-survived-vegas-shooting-died-in-thousand-oaks-borderline-bar-and-grill-massacre/.

256 ***"the most vocal Christians among us never mention the Beatitudes":*** Matt Stone, "Kurt Vonnegut on Christless Christianity," *Curious Christian* (blog), August 16, 2019, https://curiouschristian.blog/2019/08/16/kurt-vonnegut-on-christless-christianity/.